Using and Developing Measurement Instruments in Science Education

A Rasch Modeling Approach

A volume in
Science and Engineering Education Sources

Series Editor:
Calvin S. Kalman, *Concordia University*

Science and Engineering Education Sources

Calvin S. Kalman, Series Editor

Using and Developing Measurement Instruments in Science Education (2010)
by Xiufeng Liu

College Teaching and the Development of Reasoning (2009)
edited by Robert G. Fuller, Thomas C. Campbell,
Dewey I. Dykstra, Jr., and Scott M. Stevens

Using and Developing Measurement Instruments in Science Education

A Rasch Modeling Approach

by

Xiufeng Liu
State University of New York at Buffalo

Information Age Publishing, Inc.
Charlotte, North Carolina • www.infoagepub.com

Library of Congress Cataloging-in-Publication Data

Liu, Xiufeng, 1962-
  Using and developing measurement instruments in science education : a
Rasch modeling approach / by Xiufeng Liu.
      p. cm. — (Science and engineering education sources)
    Includes bibliographical references.
    ISBN 978-1-61735-003-0 (paperback) — ISBN 978-1-61735-004-7 (hardcover) —
ISBN 978-1-61735-005-4 (e-book)
    1. Science—Study and teaching. 2. Educational tests and measurements. 3.
Rasch models. I. Title.
    Q181.L747 2010
    507.1—dc22

                                                                2010006704

CONTENTS

LIST OF FIGURES

PREFACE

Xiufeng Liu

Since the beginning of the twenty-first century, the landscape of research methodology in science education has changed. While qualitative research methods remain popular among many science education researchers, more and more are turning to quantitative research methods, and the demand for measurement instruments is growing. For example, there are frequent postings on the NARST (National Association for Research in Science Teaching) listserv looking for measurement instruments for specific research questions. In fact, in her presidential address to the 2009 NARST annual conference, Charlene Czerniak identified measurement as one of top 10 grand challenges in science education research based on a survey of NARST members. Quantitative research using measurement instruments is gaining momentum.

No one can dispute the importance of measurement instruments in scientific research. Becoming familiar with standardized measurement instruments and developing new measurement instruments are integral to scientific inquiry and thus an essential component of graduate research training in natural sciences; this has not been the case in science education, regrettably. Few current doctoral programs in science education offer a course specifically on measurement instruments in science education. As a result, many science education researchers are not knowledge-

Using and Developing Measurement Instruments in Science Education:
A Rasch Modeling Approach, pp. ix–xi
Copyright © 2010 by Information Age Publishing
All rights of reproduction in any form reserved.

able in using and developing measurement instruments; often they find themselves to be at a loss. There is a need to improve the status of using and developing measurement instruments in science education. Unfortunately, there is currently not a single book devoted to measurement instruments in science education. This book, *Using and Developing Measurement Instruments in Science Education*, should fill this void. It intends to be a comprehensive and introductory measurement book in science education.

This book is for anyone who is interested in knowing what measurement instruments are available and how to develop measurement instruments for science education research. For example, science education researchers may use this book as a reference for locating measurement instruments when designing a research study. This book can be a main text for a course related to measurement in science education or science education research methods at the doctoral level. Although the book contains some statistics, no prerequisites in mathematics beyond the high school level are assumed.

This book contains seven chapters. Chapter 1 provides an overview of the historical evolution of measurement instruments in science education, validity and reliability of measurement, and current standards of measurement; it also reviews fundamental skills in writing questions for developing measurement instruments. Chapter 2 introduces approaches to developing measurement instruments; the focus is on Rasch modeling to develop measurement instruments. Rasch modeling applies a statistical model to raw data (no matter if they are nominal or ordinal) to produce measures of item difficulties and student abilities; as an outcome of the measurement revolution since the 1960s it is considered to be one of best approaches currently available for developing measurement instruments. Although applications of Rasch modeling in testing industries (e.g., the Educational Testing Services) and large-scale international assessments (e.g., the Trend in International Mathematics and Science Study) are routine, its application in science education is still preliminary. A focus on Rasch modeling in this book intends to change this situation by promoting a broader application in science education research.

Based on the conceptual framework and technical skills developed in chapters 1 and 2, the subsequent chapters introduce measurement instruments published in refereed science education research journals over the last few decades related to common domains of measurement, and describe step-by-step procedures for developing measurement instruments. Specifically, chapter 3 focuses on using and developing instruments for measuring conceptual understanding; chapter 4 focuses on using and developing instruments for measuring affective variables; chapter 5 focuses on using and developing instruments for measuring science inquiry; chapter 6 focuses on using and developing instruments for measuring science learning progression; finally chapter 7 focuses on using and developing instruments for measuring science learning environments. Chapters 3 through 7 are independent from each other; they can be completed in any order.

It is my hope that this book will serve as a starting point for science education researchers to use and develop measurement instruments for science education research. Although measurement is a highly technical and well-developed field, this book emphasizes the applied side of measurement theories and techniques. This book is fully grounded in science education research literature. All the instruments are from refereed science education research journals; all the examples are specifically related to science education research problems. Readers should be able to develop a sound understanding of measurement theories and approaches, particularly Rasch modeling, in using and developing measurement instruments for science education research.

ACKNOWLEDGMENTS

This book would not be possible without the support of many individuals. First and foremost, I thank my family (my wife, son and daughter) for their unconditional support and love over the years. Dr. William Boone of Miami University (Ohio) has been inspirational in my pursuit of scientific measurement in science education; I thank you, Bill, for your shared passion in Rasch measurement and collaboration over the years.

I thank master's and doctoral students at the University at Buffalo, the State University of New York, for their interests in science assessment. This book is a result of courses related to science assessment, science education research designs, and measurement theories that I have taught over the past 7 years. The Department of Learning and Instruction at the University at Buffalo has been consistently supportive of my teaching and research related to science assessment; I feel fortunate to be a member of this academic home.

Last but not the least, I thank Information Age Publishing for bringing this book into print, and Professor Calvin Kalman, editor-in-chief of the book series *Science & Engineering Education Sources*, for his support during the book preparation and final proof-reading along with valuable suggestions. Anonymous reviewers provided valuable suggestions to strengthen the book, I thank you. Ms. Nancy Wojcik edited the final version of the manuscript; I hope readers will find the book to be highly readable.

CHAPTER 1

ESSENTIAL CONCEPTS AND SKILLS FOR USING AND DEVELOPING MEASUREMENT INSTRUMENTS

Measurement is a process of quantifying observations. Measurement can be done in a variety of ways; using standardized instruments to conduct measurement is one way and an essential component of scientific inquiry in science education. A *measurement instrument* is a standardized tool with its associated procedures to quantify observations; it possesses empirical technical qualities. For example, in natural sciences a thermometer is a standardized measurement instrument; its making and use follow an international convention. As the result, temperature readings based on a thermometer are universally understandable and comparable. In science education, we also use measurement instruments to collect quantitative data on a wide variety of constructs. There are well-known measurement instruments in science education research, such as the TIMSS (Trend in International Math and Science Study) and PISA (Program of International Student Assessment) for measuring science literacy. Other measurement instruments, although less well-known, are routinely used and play important roles in science education research. Developing measurement instruments is a time-consuming and expensive process; it is important for science education researchers to become knowledgeable about a wide

Using and Developing Measurement Instruments in Science Education: A Rasch Modeling Approach, pp. 1–33

variety of measurement instruments currently available and be able to develop new measurement instruments for science education research when necessary. This knowledge begins with an appreciation of how measurement instruments have evolved throughout the history of science education.

EVOLUTION OF MEASUREMENT INSTRUMENTS IN SCIENCE EDUCATION

Using and developing measurement instruments have always been integral of the history of science education research. A brief overview of this history can help in understanding how using and developing measurement instruments closely relates to efforts to improve science education. Use and development of measurement instruments in science education began in the late nineteenth century and became popular in the early twentieth century. According to Travers (1983), the Boston Survey conducted in 1845 was the first use of printed tests for large-scale assessment of student achievement in science. Soon after, more school boards and states across the United States began to assess student achievement in science using standardized instruments. For example, in the early 1900s, the New York Board of Regents began to offer the Regents exams. According to Doran, Lawrenz, and Helgeson (1994), the second Curtis Digests, which reviewed science education research during the period from 1925-1930, showed that science educators began to use more "new" or standardized test questions such as completion, modified true-false, multiple-response, and modified multiple-response questions. Standardized achievement measurement instruments in science began to proliferate during the period from 1920s to 1930s. The purpose of introducing standardized measurement instruments into science achievement assessment was mainly to reduce errors in scoring, thus making assessment more scientific. The emergence of standardized measurement instruments was a cornerstone of the first generation of evaluation (Guba & Lincoln, 1989). One key characteristic of this first stage of using and developing measurement instruments in science education was to obtain objective measures about student science achievements.

The second stage of using and developing measurement instruments in science education was from the 1940s to the 1950s. This stage was characterized by expanding measurement targets beyond the cognitive domain and by explicitly tying measurement instruments to curriculum objectives, that is, ensuring the alignment between measurement instruments and curriculum objectives. As the result, paper-and-pencil measurement instruments for evaluation of laboratory instruction became available in the 1940s. The *Forty-Sixth Yearbook* (National Society for the Study of Education, 1947) recommended evaluation to include skills, interests, appreciation, attitudes, as well as the functional understanding of facts, large conceptions, and basic principles of science. As a result, measurement instruments in all those domains became available.

The third stage of use and development of measurement instruments in science education took place in the 1960s and 1970s. After the former Soviet Union's Sputnik launch in 1957, the need to evaluate National Science Foundation funded curriculum efforts such as BSCS (Biological Science Curriculum Study) Biology, Project CHEM, and PSSC (Physical Science Study Committee) Physics resulted in a new wave of using and developing measurement instruments in science education. Using measurement instruments to assess appropriate curriculum objectives continued. Measurement domains continued to expand to include measurement of science inquiry skills, attitude toward science, nature of science, as well as teachers' perceptions of science teaching and learning (Liu, 2008). For example, Tamir and Lunetta (1981) designed a comprehensive scheme for analyzing laboratory skills—the Laboratory Assessment Inventory (LAI). In addition, objectives-free measurement instruments were also advocated. Robert Stake's countenance of evaluation included explicit external standards or benchmarks for making judgment on the attainment of curriculum intents (Stake, 1967). In the past, evaluators were reluctant to judge that "gaining one skill is worth losing two understandings" (Stake, 1967, p. 95), or curriculum I objectives were more worthy than curriculum II objectives. Measurement instruments for externally formulated objectives became also valued in evaluation. Soon after, large-scale national and international science assessments emerged. Congress mandated the NAEP (National Assessment of Educational Progress) to be given to Grades 4, 8, and 12 students every 4 years beginning 1969. The International Association for the Evaluation of Educational Achievement (IEA) coordinated its first international science achievement study during 1970-1971, and the second during 1983-1984.

The fourth stage of using and developing measurement instruments in science education was during the 1980s and the 1990s. During this period, qualitative approaches to science education research became dominant, and use and development of measurement instruments retreated to a less prominent role. However, as the result of increasing interests in student alternative conceptions in science, use and development of diagnostic measurement instruments for assessing student alternative conceptions was a noticeable exception (Wandersee, Novak, & Mintz, 1994). A large number of assessment instruments for diagnosing student alternative conceptions were developed during this period. Also, non-paper-and-pencil based measurement instruments, that is, alternative science assessments, began to gain momentum (Mintzes, Wandersee, & Novak 1999). Alternative science assessment was a direct response to the limitations of paper-and-pencil based standardized measurement instruments using primarily selected response assessment methods, such as multiple choice. Performance assessment in particular received wide acceptance as an alternative assessment, and gradually became standardized for large-scale administration. For example, performance assessment was a part of national and international science assessments, such as the NAEP, and the 1994-1995 third International Mathematics and Science Study (Martin & Kelly, 1997). Performance assessment was perceived to be authentic because it approximated the scientific inquiry process.

Entering the twenty-first century, we are now in a new era of using and developing measurement instruments. This new era is characterized by a renewed interest in quantifying observations using measurement instruments. A number of factors have contributed to the revival of the use and development of measurement instruments in science education. The continuing interest in identifying student alternative conceptions has created a demand for more efficient and large-scale surveys of student alternative conceptions. Also, as standards-based science education reform is gaining momentum in the US and around the world, new demands for standardized measurement instruments for school accountability are emerging. Just as important as measuring student attainment of learning standards is the measurement of opportunities to learn in the classroom, at home and in school. "Students cannot be held accountable for achievement unless they are given adequate opportunity to learn science (National Research Council [NRC], 1996, p. 83). Consequences of using standardized measurement instruments for making high-stake decisions also need to be explicitly evaluated. In addition, a growing recognition of limitations of qualitative research methods and a call for randomized experimentation in education research (NRC, 2002) have created a conducive context for using and developing measurement instruments in science education. Today, use and development of measurement instrument in science education is becoming increasingly routine in all fields of science education research, including measurement of conceptual understanding, affective variables (e.g., attitude toward science), science inquiry, learning progression, and classroom and laboratory learning environments. Importantly, as the result of new advances over the past few decades in our knowledge about how student learn and in applications of technology for teaching and learning, as well as in measurement theories, a major change in approaches to developing measurement instruments is currently underway.

FUNDAMENTAL THEORIES FOR USING
AND DEVELOPING MEASUREMETN INSTRUMENTS

Underlying the evolution of using and developing measurement instruments in science education is change in conceptions of validity and reliability. *Validity* refers to the adequacy of claims made about a measurement process and outcome. The process of establishing validity of a measurement instrument is called *validation*. Validation used to be only based on correlations, which results in *criterion-related evidence* of validity. In order to establish criterion-related evidence of validity, a criterion variable must be identified, and measures of the criterion variable must be available and assumed valid. The correlation between the two sets of measures of a same group of examinees, one based on an instrument of the criterion variable and another on the instrument under validation, is then computed. If the correlation is statistically significant, then measures of the construct of the current instrument under validation may be claimed to be valid, and vice versa. For example, if we want to establish evidence for the validity of an instrument for measuring students' conceptual understanding of force and motion, the criterion variable may be identified as the students' physics achievement test. If we already know a group of students' physics achievement test scores based on a valid measurement instrument, then we can give the force and motion conceptual test to the same group of students, and compute the correlation coefficient between students' test scores on the physics achievement test and on the force and motion conceptual test. If the correlation coefficient is statistically significant, then we can claim that the force and motion test is valid. If measures of the criterion variable are collected after measures based on the instrument under validation, we call the criterion-related evidence as *predictive validity*. If measures of the criterion variable are collected about the same time as measures obtained from the instrument under validation, we call the criterion-related evidence as *concurrent validity*. For example, if we want to validate the force and motion conceptual test described above for ninth-grade students, then students' 12th grade physics course grades can be used to establish predictive validity, and students' ninth-grade physical science test grades can be used to establish concurrent validity.

Related to criterion-related evidence of validity are convergent validity and divergent/discriminant validity. *Convergent validity* is concurrent criterion-related validity when there is evidence to support the assumed statistically significant positive correlation between the measures based on the instrument under validation and measures based on an instrument of the criterion variable; *divergent/discriminant validity* is concurrent criterion-related validity when there is evidence to support an assumed statistically significant negative correlation between measures based on the instrument under validation and measures based on an instrument of the criterion variable. For example, if it is assumed that there should be a positive correlation between students' math achievement and science achievement, then a statistically positive correlation between students' science achievement test scores based on an instrument being developed and students' math achievement test scores based on an already validated instrument is considered as evidence for the convergent validity of the science achievement test. On the other hand, if it is assumed that there should be a negative correlation between students' test anxiety and science achievement, then a statistically negative correlation between students' science achievement test scores based on an instrument being developed and students' test anxiety based on an already validated instrument is considered as evidence for the divergent validity of the science achievement test.

Subsequently, evaluating the match between the intended content domain and the actual content domain of the measurement instrument became an acceptable approach to validation. This so-called *content-related validation* produces content-related evidence of validity. Content-related evidence may be established based on a table of test specification and the content coverage of test items. Typically, a panel of content experts reviews the table of test specification to decide if the test domain specified by the table of test specification provides adequate sampling of the content domain of the construct being measured. The expert panel may also review the test items of an instrument to see if they provide adequate coverage of the content domain of the construct being measured.

Since 1950s, the focus of standardized measurement instrument validation shifted from external, that is, criterion-related, and content-related toward the internal structure of test items. This approach of validation relied on construct related evidence of validity. *Construct validity* refers to the adequacy of claims about the actual measurement of the intended construct. Evidence for construct validity can be established through multiple approaches. Typically, a hypothesis is derived from a theory that defines the construct of measurement. Because the validity of the theory was assumed, accepting or failing to reject a hypothesis derived from the theory was considered evidence of the validity of the measurement instrument. One approach to construct validation is examination of correlation patterns of items of the measurement instrument. Items measuring a same construct should correlate with each other more than items measuring a different construct. In order to examine correlation patterns among items, a statistical method, called factor analysis, is commonly used. There are two approaches to factor analysis. Principal component factor analysis is an exploratory approach to examining item correlation patterns by creating distinct groups of items that are thought to measure different latent traits or factors. Items within the same group correlate highly with one common latent factor, but lowly with other latent factors. The number of factors that provides maximal discrimination among different factors is considered evidence for the number of constructs the items measure. If the number of factors and their corresponding distinct item groupings are consistent with the hypothesis based on the defined construct and instrument development, then there is evidence for construct related validity. Confirmatory factor analysis is an explicit hypothesis testing approach to examining item correlation patterns. First, an explicit hypothesis on the number of factors and item groupings according to the factors is formed and expressed as a structural equation model. The structural equation model is then submitted to structural equation modeling (SEM), another statistical analysis approach, to see if data fit with the model. If there is a good model-data-fit, then there is evidence to support the hypothesis, thus construct related validity. If there is not a good model-data-fit, then there is not sufficient evidence to support the hypothesis, and thus there is lack of construct-related validity.

For many years, validity evidence of standardized measurement instruments was conceptualized to be three types: criterion-related, content, and construct. Since the late 1980s, a unified theory of validity based on construct validity has become widely accepted. Messick (1989), in a seminal review of validity theories, defines validity as "an integrated evaluative judgment of the degree to which empirical evidence and theoretical rationales support the adequacy and appropriateness of inference and actions based on test scores or other modes of assessment" (p. 13). Under this *unified conception of validity*, evidential bases of validation, that is, criterion-related validation (predictive or concurrent), and content validation are all special cases of construct validation. Further, the consequence of standardized measurement instrument uses, i.e. the consequential base of validation, is also conceptualized as part of the construct validation. The *consequential basis of construct validation* attends to "the appraisal of both potential and actual social consequences of the applied testing" (Messick, 1989, p. 20). Thus, validation may be conducted through analyzing test content, response processes of examinees, internal structures of test items, relations of test scores to other variables, and consequences of testing (Joint committee of AERA, APA, and NCME, 1999).

One major limitation of the unified conception of construct validation is the lack of consideration of alternative hypotheses. Because a theory cannot be approved but can only be rejected, construct validation suffers from an apparent confirmatory bias of test developers (Kane, 2006). In order to address this limitation, current conceptions of validation, while still accepting the unified nature of validity, have expanded from a confirmatory hypothetical-deductive reasoning to a system of coherent arguments. That is, validation of a standardized measurement instrument is now considered a process of establishing evidence to argue for the validity of the proposed interpretations or uses of test scores, which is called the *argument-based approach to validation* or argument-based validity. A key difference between construct validity and argument-based validity is that argument-based validity goes beyond confirming the hypothesis for the construct by evaluating the viability of alternative hypotheses. Thus, argument-based validation no longer relies solely on hypotheses derived from a formal theory; it considers any evidence that may help support or counter-argue for the appropriateness of claims made about the test scores and uses.

Kane (2006) states that there are two types of arguments in argument-based validity: interpretative argument and validity argument. "The *interpretative argument* specifies the proposed interpretations and uses of test results by laying out the network of inferences and assumptions leading from the observed performances to the conclusions and decisions based on the performances" (p. 23). Kane (2006) further suggests that interpretive argument may be based on the following four interpretations: (a) trait interpretation, (b) theory-based interpretation, (c) qualitative interpretation, and (d) decision procedures. With the exception of qualitative interpretation, the above interpretations may be roughly considered as corresponding to the previously conceived content validation, construct validation, and consequence validation. The *validity argument* provides an evaluation of the interpretative argument in order to ensure that the interpretative argument is coherent and reasonable, and its assumptions are plausible.

Reliability of a standardized measurement instrument is concerned with the precision of test scores obtained from the instrument. The central concern of reliability is the consistency or replicability of scores across repeated applications of the measurement instrument. The classical test theory approach to reliability is to estimate the amount of errors due to various possible sources such as raters, different test forms, test-retest, etc. Accordingly, reliability may be classified into interrater reliability, equivalent form reliability, and test-retest reliability. Interrater reliability describes the consistency of scores given by two different scorers; equivalent form reliability describes the comparability of scores from two forms of the same test; test-retest reliability describes the stability of scores over time. The above three types of reliability can be quantified by a correlation coefficient. Specifically, *interrater reliability* can be established by calculating the correlation coefficient between two sets of scores given by two independent scorers to the same group of examinees; the *equivalent form reliability* can be established by calculating the correlation coefficient between two sets of scores obtained by the same group of examinees from two forms of the measurement instrument; and the *test-retest reliability* can be established by calculating the correlation coefficients between two sets of scores obtained by the same group of examinees from two successive administrations of the same measurement instrument.

Extending the concept of equivalent forms reliability by considering every item of a test as an equivalent form gives rise to the concept of internal consistency reliability. For internal consistency reliability, the most commonly used *Kuder-Richardson formula 20* **(KR-20)** provides an estimation of the degree of internal consistency among a set of multiple-choice questions in measuring a group of examinees' performances. *KR-20* can be calculated as follows:

$$KR_{20} = \frac{k}{k-1}\left(1 - \frac{\sum_{1}^{k} p_i q_i}{\sigma_x^2}\right)$$

Where k is number of items on the test, p_i is the percent of examinees answering item i correctly, q_i is the percent of examinees answering item i incorrectly, and σ_x^2 is the variance of test scores of examinees on the test. KR_{20} measures the percent of variation in examinees' test scores that are due to the variation in examinees' true abilities. KR_{20} ranges from 0 to 1; the higher the KR_{20} is, the more reliable the measurement instrument is.

A more generalized reliability measure for internal consistency among a set of any items (multiple choice, constructed-response, etc.) is the Cronbach's alpha. An *alpha coefficient* is a generalized KR_{20}; its value also ranges from 0 to 1, indicating the percentage of variance in a sample of examinees' scores due to the covariation among items caused by examinees' true abilities. An alpha coefficient may also be interpreted as the averaged correlation coefficient among all possible pairs of items of a test. The statistical measure for internal consistency is commonly the Cronbach's alpha. Cronbach's alpha is defined as

$$\alpha = \frac{k}{k-1}\left(1 - \frac{\sum_{1}^{k} \sigma_i^2}{\sigma_x^2}\right)$$

where k is the total number of questions on the test, σ_i^2 is the squared standard deviation (also called variance) of students' scores on item i, and

σ_x^2 is the squared standard deviation of students' scores on the entire test, that is, variance.

A more recent and comprehensive approach to reliability is the generalizability theory (Brennan, 2001; Haertel, 2006). While reliability is concerned with replicability of test scores across items, raters, times, and so on, *generalizability* is concerned with inferring scores from one test design to a universe of test designs. A test design consists of facets, such as items, raters, settings (e.g., performance test, paper-and-pencil test), time (pretest, posttest), test forms, and so on. Each facet may further be conceptualized as a random sample or an exhaustive list of its universe. For example, a set of items may be considered as a random sample of items from a large item pool; two raters may be considered as a random selection from a large pool of potential raters or as a fixed selection not to change from test to test. The generalizability theory approaches reliability as two sequential studies: the generalizability study (or G study), and the decision study (or D study). The G study first estimates the variance components corresponding to different facets in a given test design. Each variance component represents the amount of variation contributed by the facet. Based on the variance components, the G study continues by calculating the degree of generalizability of test scores from the given test design to the universe of all possible test designs. This degree of generalizability is in the form of a coefficient ranging from 0 to 1 that describes the percentage of total variance in examinees' observed test scores explained by the facets of the test design. Thus, following the G study, the D study investigates the effects of different test designs when varying the combination of facets on the generalizability coefficients, so that the most efficient test design (i.e., high generalizability but less costly) may be decided for future test implementation.

In order to develop a standardized measurement instrument that meets the above validity and reliability requirements, researchers follow a systematic process to create the instrument and to establish evidence of validity and reliability. This systematic process typically consists of the following 10 steps (Crocker & Algina, 1986):

1. Identify the primary purpose(s) for which the test scores will be used;
2. Identify behaviors that represent the construct or define the domain;
3. Prepare a set of test specifications by delineating the proportion of items for each type of behavior identified in step 2;
4. Construct an initial pool of items;
5. Have items reviewed (and revised, as necessary);

6. Hold preliminary item tryouts (and revise, as necessary);

7. Field-test the items on a large sample representative of the examinee population for whom the test is intended;

8. Determine statistical properties of item scores and, when appropriate, eliminate items that do not meet preestablished criteria;

9. Design and conduct reliability and validity studies for the final form of the test; and

10. Develop guidelines for administration, scoring, and interpretation of the test scores.

The above steps progress generally in sequence, but looping between steps 4 and 9 is also common. The ultimate goal of the above systematic process is to create a measurement instrument that meets expected standards of validity and reliability.

MEASUREMENT STANDARDS

The most current measurement standards are the *Standards for Educational and Psychological Testing* developed by a joint committee of the American Educational Research Association (AERA), the National Council on Measurement in Education (NCME), and the American Psychological Association (APA) (Joint Committee of the AERA, NCME, & APA, 1999). Published jointly by the three associations, the standards are updated regularly to maintain its relevance and reflect most recent measurement theories. The first version of standards was published in 1954. There have been five earlier versions of the standards before its current 1999 version. According to the standards, the purpose of the standards is to "provide criteria for the evaluation of tests, testing practices, and the effects of tests use" (Joint Committee of the AERA, NCME, & APA, 1999, p. 2). The standards document is organized into three parts. Part I deals with test construction, evaluation and documentation. This part includes the following standards: (a) Standard 1: validity, (b) Standard 2: reliability and error of measurement, (c) Standard 3: test development and revision, (d) Standard 4: scales, norms and score comparability, (e) Standard 5: test administration, scoring and reporting, and (f) Standard 6: supporting documentation for tests. Part II deals with fairness in testing. This part includes the following standards: (a) Standard 7: fairness in testing and test use, (b) Standard 8: rights and responsibilities of test takers, (c) Standard 9: testing individuals of diverse linguistic backgrounds, and (d) Standard 10: testing individuals with disabilities. Part III deals with testing applications. This part includes the following standards: (a) Standard 11:

responsibilities of test users, (b) Standard 12: psychological testing and assessment, (c) Standard 13: educational testing and assessment, (d) Standard 14: testing in employment and credentialing, and (e) Standard 15: testing in program evaluation and public policy.

Each standard is organized into two components; the first component is the background describing theoretical foundations for the standard, and the second component is the actual content of the standard. For example, the validity standard includes nine pages of review of validity theories that include sources of validity evidence, including evidence based on test content, response processes, internal structure, relations to other variables, convergent and discriminant evidence, test-criterion relationship, generalization, and consequences of testing.

Given the ultimate importance of validity and reliability in using and developing measurement instruments in science education, the 24 substandards for the validity and reliability standards are listed below. Each substandard is followed by a commentary. This list gives an overview of the scope of the standards that need to be considered; please refer to the original standards document for details.

Validity Standards

Standard 1.1: *A rationale should be presented for each recommended interpretation and use of test scores, together with a comprehensive summary of the evidence and theory bearing on the intended use or interpretation.*

Standard 1.2: *The test developer should set forth clearly how test scores are intended to be interpreted and used. The population(s) for which a test is appropriate should be clearly delimited, and the construct that the test is intended to assess should be clearly described.*

Standard 1.3: *If validity for some common or likely interpretation has not been investigated, or if the interpretation is inconsistent with available evidence, that fact should be made clear and potential users should be cautioned about making unsupported interpretation.*

Standard 1.4: *If a test is used in a way that has not been validated, it is incumbent on the user to justify the new use, collecting new evidence, if necessary.*

Standard 1.5: *The composition of any sample of examinees from which evidence is obtained should be described in as much detail as is practical, including major relevant sociodemographic and developmental characteristics.*

Standard 1.6: *When the validation rests in part on the appropriateness of test content, the procedures followed in specifying and generating test content should be described and justified in reference to the construct the test is intended to measure or the domain it is intended to represent. If the definition of the content sampled incorporates criteria such as importance, frequency, or criticality, these criteria should also be clearly explained and justified.*

Standard 1.7: *When a validation rests in part on the opinions or decisions of expert judges, observers or raters, procedures for selecting such experts and for eliciting judgments or ratings should be fully described. The qualifications, and experience, of the judges should be presented. The description of procedures should include any training and instructions provided, should indicate whether participants reached their decisions independently, and should report the level of agreement reached. If participants interacted with one another or exchanged information, the procedures through which they may have influenced one another should be set forth.*

Standard 1.8: *If the rationale for a test use or score interpretation depends on promises about the psychological processes or cognitive operations used by examinees, then theoretical or empirical evidence in support of those premises should be provided. When statements about the process employed by observers or scorers are part of the argument for validity, similar information should be provided.*

Standard 1.9: *If a test is claimed to be essentially unaffected by practice and coaching, then the sensitivity of test performance to change with these forms of instruction should be documented.*

Standard 1.10: *When interpretation of performance on specific items, or small subsets of items, is suggested, the rationale and relevant evidence in support of such interpretation should be provided. When interpretation of individual item response is likely but is not recommended by the developer, the user should be warned against making such interpretation.*

Standard 1.11: *If the rationale for a test use or interpretation depends on premises about the relationships among parts of the test, evidence concerning the internal structure of the test should be provided.*

Standard 1.12: *When interpretation of subscores, score differences, or profiles is suggested, the rationale and relevant evidence in support of such interpretation should be provided. Where composite scores are developed, the basis and rationale for arriving at the composites should be given.*

Standard 1.13: *When validity evidence includes statistical analyses of test results, either alone or together with data on other variables, the conditions under which the data were collected should be described in enough detail that users can judge the relevance of the statistical findings to local conditions. Attention should be drawn to any features of a validation data collection that are likely to differ from typical operational testing conditions and that could plausibly influence test performance.*

Standard 1.14: *When validity evidence includes empirical analyses of test responses together with data on other variables, the rationale for selecting the additional variables should be provided. Where appropriate and feasible, evidence concerning the constructs represented by other variables, as well as their technical properties, should be presented or cited. Attention should be drawn to any likely sources of dependence (or lack of independence) among variables other than dependencies among the construct(s) they represent.*

Standard 1.15: *When it is asserted that a certain level of test performance predicts adequate or inadequate criterion performance, information about the levels of criterion performance associated with given levels of test scores should be provided.*

Standard 1.16: *When validation relies on evidence that test scores are related to one or more criterion variables, information about the suitability and technical quality of the criteria should be reported.*

Standard 1.17: *If test scores are used in conjunction with other quantifiable variables to predict some outcome or criterion, regression (or equivalent) analyses should include those additional relevant variables along with the test scores.*

Standard 1.18: *When statistical adjustments, such as those for restriction of range or attenuation, are made, both adjusted and unadjusted coefficients, as well as the specific procedure used, and all statistics used in the adjustment, should be reported.*

Standard 1.19: *If a test is recommended for use in assigning persons to alternative treatments or is likely to be so used, and if outcomes from those treatments can reasonably be compared on a common criterion, then, whenever feasible, supporting evidence of differential outcomes should be provided.*

Standard 1.20: *When a meta-analysis is used as evidence of the strength of a test-criterion relationship, the test and the criterion variables in the* *local situation should be comparable with those in the studies summarized. If relevant research includes credible evidence that any other features of the testing application may influence the strength of the test-criterion relationship, the correspondence between those features in the local situation and in the meta-analysis should be reported. Any significant disparities that might limit the applicability of the meta-analytic findings to the local situation should be noted explicitly.*

Standard 1.21: *Any meta-analytic evidence used to support an intended test use should be clearly described, including methodological choices in identifying and coding studies, correcting for artifacts, and examining potential moderator variables. Assumptions made in correcting for artifacts such as criterion unreliability and range restriction should be presented, and the consequences of these assumptions made clear.*

Standard 1.22: *When it is clearly stated or implied that a recommended test use will result in a specific outcome, the basis for expecting that outcome should be presented, together with relevant evidence.*

Standard 1.23: *When a test use or score interpretation is recommended on the grounds that testing or the testing program per se will result in some indirect benefit in addition to the utility of information from the test scores themselves, the rationale for anticipating the indirect benefit should be made explicit. Logical or theoretical arguments and empirical evidence for the indirect benefit should be provided. Due weight should be given to any contradictory findings in the scientific literature, including findings suggesting important indirect outcomes other than those predicted.*

Standard 1.24: *When unintended consequences result from test use, an attempt should be made to investigate whether such consequences arise from the test's sensitivity to characteristics other than those it is intended to assess or to the test's failure fully to represent the intended construct.*

Reliability and Errors of Measurement Standards

Standard 2.1: *For each total score, subscore, or combination of scores that is to be interpreted, estimates of relevant reliabilities and standard errors of measurement or test information functions should be reported.*

Standard 2.2: *The standard error of measurement, both overall and conditional (if relevant), should be reported both in raw score or original scale* *units and in units of each derived score recommended for use in test inter-pretation.*

Standard 2.3: *When test interpretation emphasizes differences between two observed scores of an individual or two averages of a group, reliability data, including standard errors, should be provided for such differences.*

Standard 2.4: *Each method of quantifying the precision or consistency of scores should be described clearly and expressed in terms of statistics appro-priate to the method. The sampling procedures used to select examinees for reliability analyses and descriptive statistics on these samples should be reported.*

Standard 2.5: *A reliability coefficient or standard error of measurement based on one approach should not be interpreted as interchangeable with another derived by a different technique unless their implicit definitions of measurement error are equivalent.*

Standard 2.6: *If reliability coefficients are adjusted for restriction of range or variability, the adjustment procedure and both the adjusted and unad-justed coefficients should be reported. The standard deviations of the group actually tested and of the target population, as well as the rationale for the adjustment, should be presented.*

Standard 2.7: *When subsets of items within a test are dictated by the test specifications and can be presumed to measure partially independent traits or abilities, reliability estimation procedures should recognize the multifac-tor character of the instrument.*

Standard 2.8: *Test users should be informed about the degree to which rate of work may affect examinee performance.*

Standard 2.9: *When a test is designed to reflect rate of work, reliability should be estimated by the alternate-form or test-retest approach, using sep-arately timed administrations.*

Standard 2.10: *When subjective judgment enters into test scoring, evi-dence should be provided on both interrater consistency in scoring and within-examinee consistency over repeated measurements. A clear distinc-tion should be made among reliability data based on (a) independent panels of raters scoring the same performances or products, (b) a single panel scor-ing successive performances or new products, and (c) independent panels scoring successive performances or new products.*

Standard 2.11: *If there are generally accepted theoretical or empirical reasons for expecting that reliability coefficients, standard errors of measurement, or test information functions will differ substantially for various subpopulations, publishers should provide reliability data as soon as feasible for each major population for which the test is recommended.*

Standard 2.12: *If a test is proposed for use in several grades or over a range of chronological age groups and if separate norms are provided for each grade or each age group, reliability data should be provided for each age or grade population, not solely for all grades or ages combined.*

Standard 2.13: *If local scorers are employed to apply general scoring rules and principles specified by the test developer, local reliability data should be gathered and reported by local authorities when adequate size samples are available.*

Standard 2.14: *Conditional standard errors of measurement should be reported at several score levels if constancy cannot be assumed. Where cut scores are specified for selection or classification, the standard errors of measurement should be reported in the vicinity of each cut score.*

Standard 2.15: *When a test or combination of measures is used to make categorical decisions, estimates should be provided of the percentage of examinees who would be classified in the same way on two applications of the procedure, using the same form or alternative forms of the instrument.*

Standard 12.16: *In some testing situations, the items vary from examinees—through random selection from an extensive item pool or application of algorithms based on the examinee's level of performance on previous items or preferences with respect to item difficulty. In this type of testing, the preferred approach to reliability estimation is one based on successive administrations of the test under conditions similar to those prevailing in operational test use.*

Standard 12.17: *When a test is available in both long and short versions, reliability data should be reported for scores on each version, preferably based on an independent administration each.*

Standard 12.18: *When significant variations are permitted in test administration procedures, separate reliability analyses should be provided for scores produced under each major variation if adequate sample sizes are available.*

Standard 12.19: *When average test scores for groups are used in program evaluations, the groups tested should generally be regarded as a sample from a larger population, and even if all examinees available at the time of measurement are tested. In such cases the standard error of the group mean should be reported, as it reflects variability due to sampling of examinees as well as variability due to measurement errors.*

Standard 12.20: *When the purpose of testing is to measure the performance of groups rather than individuals, a procedure frequently used is to assign a small subset of items to each of many subsamples of examinees. Data are aggregated across subsamples and item subsets to obtain a measure of group performance. When such procedures are used for program evaluation or population descriptions, reliability analysis must take the sampling scheme into account.*

ESSENTIAL SKILLS FOR DEVELOPING MEASUREMENT INSTRUMENTS

A measurement instrument consists of individual tasks or items. The items can be in many different forms: multiple choice, checklist, rating scale, Likert scale, performance task, to name a few. Given that the most common item formats for standardized measurement instruments in science education are multiple-choice questions, true-false questions, and Likert-scale questions, this section provides an overview of basic skills for developing multiple-choice, true-and-false and Likert-scale questions.

Guidelines for Writing Multiple-Choice Questions

Multiple-choice (MC) questions are probably the most commonly used format for assessment in the cognitive domain. There are many advantages for using this format; Haladyna and Downing (1989a) summarize the following advantages:

1. Sampling of content can be very comprehensive, which generally leads to more content-valid test-score interpretation;
2. Reliability of test scores can be high when there are many high-quality MC items;
3. MC items are objective and efficient to score; and
4. MC items are flexible to be used to assess a wide variety of learning outcomes and contents such as both lower-order and high-order thinking skills.

Because of its popularity, writing MC questions has been a focus of scholarship for many years. Haladyna and Downing (1989a) reviewed 46 major measurement textbooks published since 1935 and summarized MC item-writing guidelines contained in the textbooks into 43 rules. Although agreements among the textbooks on these 43 guidelines vary, with some unanimously recommended by all textbooks and others only recommended by a few, the 43 guidelines have been either assumed to be good practices or studied empirically for its validity (Haladyna & Downing, 1989b). In a follow-up review, Haladyna, Downing, and Rodriquez (2002) revised the original 43-guideline taxonomy based on textbooks and empirical studies published after the original review. The revised taxonomy now has 37 rules organized into the following five categories: content concerns, formatting concerns, style concerns, writing the stem, and writing the choices. The 37 guidelines are as follows:

Content Concerns

1. Every item should reflect specific content and a single mental behavior, as called for in test specifications (i.e. test blueprint);
2. Base each item on important content to learn; avoid trivial content;
3. Use novel material to test higher level thinking skills;
4. Keep the content of each item independent from content of other items within a same test;
5. Avoid assessing over-specific and over-general content;
6. Avoid opinion-based items;
7. Avoid trick items; and
8. Keep vocabulary simple for the group of students being tested.

Formatting Concerns

9. Present MC items in a question, completion, true-false or the best answer format; avoid the complex format involving various combinations of choices; and
10. Format items vertically instead of horizontally.

Style Concerns

11. Edit and proof-read items;
12. Use correct grammar, punctuation, capitalization, and spelling; and
13. Minimize the amount of reading in each item.

Writing the Stem

14. Ensure that the directions in the stem are very clear;

15. Include the central idea in the stem instead of the choices;

16. Avoid window dressing (i.e. excessive verbiage); and

17. Word the stem positively. If negative words, such as NOT and EXCEPT, are used, use the word cautiously and always ensure that the word appears capitalized and boldface.

Writing the Choices

18. Develop as many effective choices as you can; in most situations three choices are adequate;

19. Make sure that only one of the choices is the right answer;

20. Vary the location of the right answer according to the number of choices;

21. Place choices in logical or numerical/alphabetical order;

22. Keep choices independent from each other; choices should not be overlapping;

23. Keep choices homogeneous in content and grammatical structure;

24. Keep the length of choices about equal;

25. *None-of-the-Above* choice should be used carefully;

26. Avoid the *All-of-the-Above* choice;

27. Phrase choices positively; avoid negatives such as NOT;

28. Avoid giving clues to the right answer, by such ways as

    (a) Specific determiners including *always, never, completely,* and *absolutely*;
    (b) Clang associations, choices identical to or resembling words in the stem;
    (c) Grammatical inconsistencies that cue the test-taker to the correct choice;
    (d) Conspicuous correct choice;
    (e) Pairs or triplets of options that clue the test-taker to the correct choice; and
    (f) Blatantly absurd, ridiculous options;

29. Make all distracters plausible;

30. Use typical errors of students to write distracters;

31. Use humor if it is compatible with the teacher and the learning environment.

Some of the above guidelines are universally or nearly universally promoted in measurement textbooks, such as including central ideas in the stem, avoiding clues to the correct answer, making all choices plausible, and making the choices relatively equal in length. Some of the above guidelines are not necessarily universally agreed on, such as presenting MC items in a question format. The following are examples to some of the above guidelines.

1. *Include central ideas in the stem instead of choices.*

Poor
    A plant...

    (a) Absorbs water.
    (b) Takes in nutrients.
    (c) Makes its own food.
    (d) Reproduces asexually.

Better
    How does a plant differ from an animal?

    (a) A plant absorbs water.
    (b) A plant takes in nutrients.
    (c) A plant makes its own food*.
    (d) A plant reproduces asexually.

2. *Avoid window dressing.*

Poor
    In Florida, which season of the year in which records indicate the maximum statistical occurrence of hurricanes?

    (a) Fall.*
    (b) Winter.
    (c) Summer.
    (d) Spring.

Better
    In Florida, which season has the most hurricanes?

    (a) Fall.*
    (b) Winter.
    (c) Spring.
    (d) Summer.

3.   *Make all choices plausible.*

Poor

What are electrons?

    (a) Mechanical tools.
    (b) Negative particles.*
    (c) Neutral particles.
    (d) Nuclei of atoms.

Better

What are electrons?

    (a) Negative particles.*
    (b) Neutral particles.
    (c) Positive particles.

4.   *Place choices in logical or numerical/alphabetical order.*

Poor

How many bonding electrons does a chlorine atom have?

    (a) a. 2
    (b) b. 3
    (c) c. 1*
    (d) d. 4

Better

How many bonding electrons does a chlorine atom have?

    (a) 1*
    (b) 2
    (c) 3
    (d) 4

5.   *Avoid giving clues to the right answer.*

Poor

Increasing the temperature will increase the pressure of a gas in a sealed container because

    (a) No container expansion.
    (b) Gas particles constantly move.
    (c) Gas particles collide with each other.

    (d) More gas particles collide with each other and with the container walls.*

Better

Increasing the temperature will increase the pressure of a gas in a sealed container because

    (a) Gas particles move more rapidly.
    (b) Gas particles expand bigger.
    (c) Gas particles collide more with each other.
    (d) Gas particles collide more with the container.*

6. *Avoid the complex format involving various combinations of choices.*

Poor

Which of the following is a renewable source of energy?
    1.   coal
    2.   hydro
    3.   wind
       (a) 1 & 2
       (b) 2 & 3*
       (c) 1 & 3
       (d) 3 only.

Better

Which of the following is a renewable source of energy?

    (a) coal
    (b) hydro*
    (c) natural gas
    (d) oil

Guidelines for Writing True-False Questions

1. *Avoid broad general statements if they are to be judged true or false.*

Rationale: General statements are often not directly relevant to the target construct of assessment. A general statement often contains many aspects, and it is possible that a respondent may agree with some aspects but not others. Thus, it is impossible to tell what exactly a respondent agrees or does not agree with.

Poor
>   Leaves are essential for plants   T   F

Better
>   Photosynthesis takes place in leaves   T   F

2.   *Avoid double negative statements.*

Rationale: Double-negative statements are difficult to compre-
hend, and may easily confuse respondents.

Poor
>   None of the senses is unnecessary in science experiments.   T   F

Better
>   All senses are necessary in science experiments.   T   F

3.   *Avoid complex sentences.*

Rationale: Complex sentences contain more than one idea, and it
is possible that a respondent may agree with one idea but not others.

Poor
>   Whales are mammals because they are large   T   F

Better
>   Whales are mammals.   T   F

4.   *Avoid long sentences.*

Rationale: Long sentences contain many ideas, and it is difficult
for a respondent to judge all ideas to be true or false.

Poor
>   Despite the theoretical and experimental difficulties of
>   determining the exact pH value of a solution, it is possible
>   to determine whether a solution is acidic by the red color
>   formed on litmus paper when it is inserted into the solution.
>   T   F

Better
>   It is possible to determine whether a solution is acidic by
>   blue litmus paper.
>   T   F

5.   *Avoid extraneous clues in the form of specific determiners.*

Rationale: Statements with such specific determiners as "always" and "absolutely" are usually considered unlikely to be true based on common sense statistics. Similarly, statements with such specific determiners as "Under some circumstances" and "may" are usually considered likely to be true by test-wise respondents based on common sense reasoning.

Poor
    Water always boils at 100 degrees Celsius.   T   F

Better
    Water boils at 100 degrees Celsius under STP.   T   F

6.   *If opinion is stated, attribute it to a source.*

Rationale: Opinions cannot be judged to be true or false as every respondent is entitled to hold a particular opinion. However, the source of an opinion is a fact, and it is appropriate to ask a respondent to judge if the source is true or false.

Poor
    Natural selection should be used to explain the evolution of living things.

    T   F

Better
    According to Charles Darwin, natural selection should be used to explain the evolution of living things.

    T   F

Guidelines for Writing Likert-Scale Questions

Likert-scale questions are commonly used in measurement instruments of noncognitive domains pertaining to attitudes, interests, preferences, and so on. A typical *Likert-scale question* consists of a statement and a few categories of choices corresponding to different degrees of endorsement of the statements. Categories are symmetrical with equal numbers of positive and negative categories around the middle or neutral category representing degrees of agreement. An example of five categories are: *"Strongly Agree"* (SA), *"Agree"* (A), *"Neutral"* (N), *"Disagree"* (D), and

"Strongly Disagree" (SD). Similarly, an example of three categories of agreements are: *"Agree"* (A), *"Neutral"* (N), and *"Disagree"* (D).

The Likert-scale question format was first proposed by Rensis Likert in 1932 (Likert, 1932). Over the past seven decades, many suggestions for writing Likert-scale questions, such as those in Likert (1967), have become conventions and are thus widely accepted. The following summarizes a few most common ones.

1.   *All statements should be expressions of desired behaviors, not statements of facts.*

Rationale: Validity of facts should not be subject to personal judgment.

Poor
> Science is an empirical approach to answering questions.
>   SA   A   U   D   SD

Better
> Science should only use data to answer questions.
>   SA   A   U   D   SD

2.   *Each statement should be clear, concise, and straight-forward; it should involve only one aspect rather than more than one aspect.*

Rationale: Higher than necessary reading comprehension can reduce the validity of responses. A respondent may have different opinions on different aspects, thus will have difficulty stating one same opinion to all the aspects.

Poor
> In order to improve student learning in science, the school should offer more elective courses in science, require more student labs in each course, and use only standardized assessment instruments.
>   SA   A   U   D   SD

Better
> The school should offer more elective courses in science.
>   SA   A   U   D   SD

3.　*Present statements in the present tense.*

Rationale: When a statement is in past tense, it presents more a fact than a value judgment.

Poor
> Pollution was a major concern to me.
> 　　　　SA　　A　　U　　D　　SD

Better
> Pollution is a major concern to me.
> 　　　　SA　　A　　U　　D　　SD

4.　*Have different statements worded so that about one half of them have one end of the attitude continuum corresponding to the left or upper part of the reaction alternatives and the other half have the same end of the attitude continuum corresponding to the right or lower part of the reaction alternatives.*

Rationale: Even distribution of statements toward the two opposite ends of the attitude continuum can avoid any space error or tendency to a stereotyped response.

Positive statement:
> Science classes are interesting.
> 　　　　SA　　A　　U　　D　　SD

Negative statement:
> Science classes are boring.
> 　　　　SA　　A　　U　　D　　SD

5.　*Have statements worded so that the modal reaction to some is more toward one end of the attitude continuum and to others more in the middle or toward the other end.*

Rationale: Statements worded this way can produce a more evenly distributed response pattern across the entire attitude continuum.

6.　*Avoid using statements that contain absolute qualifiers (e.g. always, never) and indefinite qualifiers (e.g., only, many, often).*

Rationale: Absolute qualifiers introduce extreme opinions, which decrease item discrimination. Similarly, indefinite qualifiers are ambiguous and can result in multiple interpretations, which also reduces item discrimination.

Poor
>   Technology design should never be part of a school science curriculum.
>
>   SA   A   U   D   SD

Better
>   Technology design should be part of a school science curriculum.
>
>   SA   A   U   D   SD

7. Avoid using too many choices.

   Rationale: Too many choices are difficult to decide, which reduces both validity, reliability and discrimination.

Poor
Science laboratories are interesting.
>   Negative   Positive
>   1   2   3   4   5   6   7   8   9   10

Better
Science laboratories are interesting.
>   SA   A   U   D   SD

LOCATING MEASUREMENT INSTRUMENTS

Because developing valid and reliable measurement instruments is time consuming and expensive, before developing a measurement instrument, science education researchers should first try to search if a suitable measurement instrument is available. There are various sources for locating standardized measurement instruments. The most comprehensive source is the *Mental Measurements Yearbooks* (MMY) published by the Buros Institute of Mental Measurement at the University of Nebraska, Lincoln. MMY contains a comprehensive collection and critical reviews of commercially available tests in many areas including achievement, personality, vocation, intelligence/scholastic aptitude, reading, mathematics, science, social studies, attitudes, and more. MMY was started by Oscar K. Buros in 1936; it has been periodically updated. The most recent version is the

16th Mental Measurements Yearbooks published in 2007. Although the actual copies of the tests are not included, pricing and ordering information is provided for every included test. Also published periodically by the Buros Institute is *Tests in Print (TIP)*. TIP provides a summary of tests reviewed in all the preceding mental measurement yearbooks. It contains a comprehensive bibliography of all known published tests, and classifies the reviewed tests in the MMY by author, subject, publisher, and so on. Essentially, TIP is an indexing system for MMY. MMY is currently available in electronic databases searchable by authors, publishers, publication years, subjects, key words, and so on.

Another well-known source for locating standardized measurement instruments is the ETS (Education Testing Services) Test Collection Catalog (ETS-TCC). Updated periodically, ETS-TCC contains information on both published and unpublished measurement instruments; it is published in six volumes: the achievement tests and measurements, vocational tests and measurements, tests for special populations, cognitive aptitude and intelligence tests, attitude tests, and affective measures and personality. Many tests are available for ordering from ETS. The ERIC Clearinghouse on Assessment and Evaluation (http://ericae.net/) is the host for the ETS test collection database.

As standardized measurement instruments are being continuously developed, many newer instruments may not be yet collected in MMY or ETC-TCC. Thus, it is always necessary to review major research journals in science education, such as *Journal of Research in Science Teaching*, *Science Education*, *International Journal of Science Education*, *School Science and Mathematics*, to name a few. Sometimes standardized tests are included in the appendices of journal articles; sometimes, only sample questions are provided. The authors can always be contacted for more information or the complete instrument when necessary.

CHAPTER SUMMARY

A measurement instrument is a standardized tool along with the accompanying procedures to quantify observations; they possess demonstrated technical qualities. In science education, the use and development of measurement instruments have been ongoing for over a century with identifiable stages. The first stage took place during the late nineteenth and early twentieth centuries; it marked the emergence of standardized measurement instruments for assessing science achievement. The second stage was during the 1940s and 1950s in which standardized measurement instruments were used to measure the attainment of curriculum objectives—the curriculum evaluation. The third stage was during the "curriculum reform" movement in the 1960s and 1970s in which measurement instruments were used to evaluate a wide variety of student and teacher outcomes associated with the new curriculums—the program evaluation. During the 1980s and 1990s, the use and development of measurement instruments in science education became less active due to the prevalence of qualitative approaches to science education research. Entering the twenty-first century, we are now in a new stage of use and development of measurement instruments. The current needs for using and developing measurement instruments are mainly due to our continuous interest in identifying student alternative conceptions, the worldwide standards-based movement toward science education, and a renewed call for scientific research in education.

Fundamental theories for using and developing measurement instruments are about validity and reliability. Theories of validity and reliability have evolved considerably. Validity used to be partitioned into various types, such as criterion-related, content, and construct validity. The current notion of validity is that validity is unitary, which may be called construct validity. Validity may be established through systematically collecting evidence and developing coherent arguments to support the intended interpretations and uses of test scores. Similarly, reliability used to be solely established by identifying sources of errors associated with items; our current notion of reliability is based on a systematic analysis of various sources of errors associated with not only items but also other facets of measurement (e.g., rater, testing setting) so that scores may be generalizable to all facets. This new notion of reliability is called the generalizability theory. As a result of our changing notions of validity and reliability, standards for educational and psychological testing have been updated. The most recent version of the standards was published in 1999 by the Joint Committee of AERA, APA and NCME.

Development of measurement instruments uses a wide variety of item formats, including multiple choice, true-false, constructed response, performance tasks, and the Likert scale. Writing high quality items is an essential skill science education researchers need to possess. Various guidelines are available for developing good multiple-choice, true-false, and Likert-scale questions. In addition to developing measurement instruments, there are also tools for locating previously developed measurement instruments. For example, the *Mental Measurements Yearbooks* (MMY) is a continuous and periodic publication to catalogue and review published measurement instruments; a searchable computer database is also available.

EXERCISES

1. For each of the following scenarios, indicate what validity evidence is of importance for the concerned measurement instrument.

    (a) A researcher is developing a standardized measurement instrument to measure the effectiveness of an experimental intervention for improving students' conceptual understanding of science concepts.

    (b) A program evaluator is developing a standardized measurement instrument to measure science teachers' satisfaction with a summer teacher professional development workshop.

    (c) A science teacher is developing an end-of-unit test to measure students' mastery of a science unit.

    (d) A doctoral candidate is looking for a measurement instrument on high school students' attitudes toward technology to help answer research questions about the relationship between science and technology.

    (e) A university placement test is used to measure students' readiness for taking calculus-based physics.

2. For each of the following scenarios, indicate what type of reliability is of concern for the used measurement instrument.

    (a) Two performance assessment tasks involving student hands-on problem solving tasks that are part of a state standardized achievement test.

    (b) A program evaluator is looking for a standardized measurement instrument for measuring students' mastery of a reform-based science curriculum.

    (c) An attitudinal survey is used to measure elementary school students' attitudes toward science.

    (d) A conceptual test will be used in both paper-and-pencil and online administrations.

    (e) A high school biology conceptual test consisting of 30 multiple-choice questions is used to assess students' understanding of evolution.

3. Use the *Mental Measurements Yearbooks* database to identify a standardized measurement instrument on a construct of your interest. Then read the reviews included in the MMY and locate the actual measurement instrument from the source. Finally, apply the validity and reliability standards to evaluate the adequacy of the measurement instrument.

REFERENCES

Brennan, R. L. (2001). *Generalizability theory.* New York, NY: Springer-Verlag.

Crocker, L., & Algina, J. (1986). *Introduction to classical & modern test theory.* Orlando, FL: Holt, Rinehart & Winston.

Doran, R. L., Lawrenz, F., & Helgeson, S. (1994). Research on assessment in science. In D. L. Gabel (Ed.), *Handbook of research on science teaching and learning* (pp. 388-442). New York, NY: Macmillan.

Guba, E. G., & Lincoln, Y. S. (1989). *Fourth generation evaluation.* Newbury Park, CA. Sage.

Haertel, E. (2006). Reliability. In R. L. Brennan (Ed.), *Educational measurement* (4th ed., pp. 65-110). Westport, CT: Praeger.

Haladyna, T. M., & Downing, S. M. (1989a). A taxonomy of multiple-choice item-writing rules. *Applied Measurement in Education, 2*(1), 37-50.

Haladyna, T. M., & Downing, S. M. (1989b). Validity of a taxonomy of multiple-choice item-writing rules. *Applied Measurement in Education, 2*(1), 51-78.

Haladyna, T. M., Downing, S. M., & Rodriguez, M. C. (2002). A review of multiple-choice item-writing guidelines for classroom assessment. *Applied Measurement in Education, 15*(3), 309-334.

Joint Committee of American Educational Research Association, American Psychological Association, & National Council on Measurement in Education (1999). *Standards for educational and psychological testing.* Washington, DC: American Psychological Association.

Kane, M. T. (2006). Validation. In R. L. Brennan (Ed.), *Educational measurement* (4th ed., pp. 17-64). Westport, CT: Praeger.

Likert, R. (1932). A technique for the measurement of attitudes. *Achieves of Psychology, 22,* 5-53.

Likert, R. (1967). The method of constructing an attitude scale. In M. Fishbein (Ed.), *Readings in attitude theory and measurement* (pp. 90-95). New York, NY: Wiley.

Liu, X. (2008). Standardized measurement instruments in science education. In M. -W. Roth & K. Tobin (Eds.), *World of science education: North America* (pp. 649-676). Rotterdam, The Netherlands: Sense.

Martin, M. O., & Kelly, D. L. (1997). *Third international mathematics and science study: Technical report (vol. II), implementation and analysis—Primary and middle school years.* Chestnut Hill, MA: Boston College

Messick, S. (1989). Validity. In R. L. Linn (Ed.), *Educational measurement* (3rd ed., pp. 13-103). New York, NY: Macmillan.

Mintzes, J. J., Wandersee, J. H., & Nova, J. D. (999). *Assessing science understanding: A human constructivist view.* San Diego, CA: Academic Press.

National Research Council. (1996). *National science education standards.* Washington, DC: National Academy Press.

National Research Council. (2002). *Scientific research in education.* Washington, DC: National Academic Press.

National Society for the Study of Education. (1947). *The forty-sixth yearbook: Part I: Science education in American schools.* Chicago, IL: University of Chicago Press.

Stake, R. (1967). The countenance of educational evaluation. *Teachers College Record, 68*, 523-540.

Tamir, P., & Lunetta, V. N. (1981). Inquiry related tasks in high school science laboratory handbooks. *Science Education, 65*, 477-484.

Travers, R. M. W. (1983). *How research changed American schools*. Kalamazoo, MI: Mythos Press.

Wandersee, J. H., Mintzes, J., & Novak, J. (1994). Research on alternative conceptions in science. In D. Gabel (Ed.), *Handbook of research on science teaching and learning* (pp. 177-210). New York, NY: Macmillan.

CHAPTER 2

APPROACHES TO DEVELOPING MEASUREMENT INSTRUMENTS

Although various measurement instruments in a wide variety of science education research areas are now available, the approaches to developing them have not varied much. Specifically, the approaches to developing measurement instruments in science education fall into two broad categories, one based on the classical test theory (CTT), and the other based on the item response theory (IRT). CTT has a long history, as long as that of developing measurement instruments. On the other hand, IRT is only 4 decades old, with routine applications of IRT for developing measurement instruments in science education only since the early 1990s. This chapter will first review the CTT; it will then discuss the IRT, specifically Rasch modeling, to develop measurement instruments.

CLASSICAL TEST THEORY AND GENERALIZABILITY THEORY

The *classical test theory* (CTT) is an approach to modeling measurement data; it has been the dominant approach to developing measurement instruments in science education for a long time; it remains largely so even today. The popularity of CTT is attributable to its conceptual simplicity and relatively less technical complexity in application. Conceptu-

Using and Developing Measurement Instruments in Science Education: A Rasch Modeling Approach, pp. 35–66
Copyright © 2010 by Information Age Publishing

ally, CTT assumes a test score to be a random observation of a subject's true ability. If X represents the observed score, T represents the subject's true ability or true score, and e represents a random error, then for any person i, there exists a relationship as follows:

$$X_i = T_i + e \tag{1}$$

Since we can only observe X_i although our objective is to obtain T_i, the accuracy (validity) and precision (reliability) of using X_i to represent T_i depend on estimation of the magnitude of e. One fundamental assumption when estimating e is that e is distributed randomly among all subjects within the population. There are many ways to minimize and estimate e for a target population, such as creating items based on a test blueprint, test-retest, internal consistency among items, and so on. No matter how e is estimated, CTT has the following important characteristics:

1. X_i is a total score, that is, the sum over all individual item scores;
2. e is estimated for the entire population and is the same for all individuals of the population;
3. T_i is a range, not a fixed score. That is, T_i can only be described with probability not certainty. For example, a 95% confidence interval of T_i can be expressed as:

$$T_i = X_i \pm 1.96\, \sigma_{xx} \tag{2}$$

Where σ_{xx} is the standard error of measurement for the measurement instrument. Depending on sources of errors, the value of σ_{xx} can be estimated in various ways. For example, if the test could be unreliable due to scoring as represented by its interrater reliability coefficient r_{xx}, then the standard error of measurement can be estimated as follows:

$$\sigma_{xx} = \sigma_x \cdot \sqrt{1 - r_{xx}} \tag{3}$$

Where σ_x is the standard deviation of the observed scores.

Two item properties affect validity and reliability measures; they are item difficulty and item discrimination. *Item difficulty* is the percent or proportion of students that have answered a question correctly. If 100 students answer a test question, but only 80 students answer the item correctly, then the item difficulty is 80% or 0.80. *Item discrimination* refers to an item's capability to differentiate between students whose overall abilities are high and those whose overall abilities are low. There are many indices for measuring item discrimination. One index is based on the correlation between students' scores on the item and their overall performance on the test. That is, for each item, there is a set of students' scores (e.g., 1s or 0s if the item is a multiple-choice question). Also, for the test, there is a set of students' test scores. A correlation between these two sets of scores can be used as an index of item discrimination. This correlation is also called biserial (if the item is scored on an ordinal scale based on a continuous construct) or point-biseral (if the item is scored dichotomously) correlation. Item discrimination index is typically expected to be above 0.3; the highest discrimination occurs when item difficulty is 0.5.

The reliability coefficient, r_{xx} can be estimated by various methods, such as internal consistency, test-retest, and equivalent forms. One key task when developing a measurement instrument following CTT is to estimate the reliability coefficient r_{xx} so that the standard error of the measurement instrument can be quantified.

One major recent extension to the CTT, specifically to the concept of reliability, is generalizability theory. Within the conceptual framework of generalizability, scores of subjects are generalizable when a large percentage of observed variance is due to true differences among subjects. In order to estimate the degree of generalizability, the observed variance can be partitioned into various components associated with differences among subjects, items, errors, and other measurement designs (e.g., multiple raters, multiple-forms, etc.). The conventional testing situation involving one sample of subjects answering all items of a test is called the one-facet measurement design; the measurement situation involving one sample of subjects answering all items of a test and multiple raters is called a two-facet measurement design. Facets may be fixed (i.e., representing themselves) or random (i.e., representing a larger population). For the one-facet measurement design, if the variance component among subjects or persons is σ_p^2, the residual component (i.e., errors) is σ_{res}^2, and n_j is the number of items on the test, then the generalizability coefficient (ρ_p^2) is:

$$\rho_p^2 = \sigma_p^2/(\sigma_p^2 + \sigma_{res}^2/n_i) \tag{4}$$

In the above one-facet measurement design, ρ_p^2 is identical to the reliability coefficient r_{xx}. For a two-facet measurement design involving items and raters, the coefficient of generalizability is:

$$\rho_p^2 = \sigma_p^2/(\sigma_p^2 + \sigma_{pi}^2/n_i + \sigma_{pr}^2/n_r + \sigma_{res}^2/n_i n_r) \tag{5}$$

where σ_{pj}^2 is the variance component due to the interaction between persons and items, σ_{pr}^2 is the variance component associated with the interaction between persons and raters, and n_r is the number of raters.

Within the generalizability theory framework, there are two sequential studies: the generalizability study (G-study) to estimate the variance components associated with subjects and various measurement design facets, and the decision study (D-study) to estimate the generalizability coefficient and to identify the most efficient measurement design. The G-study is conducted through Analysis of Variance (ANOVA). The D-study is conducted by computing the coefficient of generalizability and studying the effect of varying measurement design facets, such as increasing the number of items or raters, on the coefficient of generalizability. The purpose of the D-study is to identify the best combination of facets, that is, the best measurement design, that results in an acceptable coefficient of generalizability with minimal cost (e.g., minimal number of raters, or shortest test).

While reliability describes the extent to which X_is are consistent, validity describes the relationship between X_is and T_is, that is, the extent to which X_is qualitatively represent T_is. For example, the relationship between X_is and T_is may be examined as the degree to which observed scores (X_is) represent subjects' performance in a content domain (T_is)—content validity, or as the extent to which the observed scores (X_is) describe a latent construct (T_is)—construct validity, or as the ability of observed scores (X_is) to predict subjects' performances on different measurement instruments because of (T_is)—criterion related validity. Fundamentally, CTT is a theory of reliability, but it has major implications for test validation, because one necessary condition for validity is that scores are reliable.

There are a number of fundamental limitations with the above approach, that is, CTT, to developing measurement instruments. They are:

1. T_is are dependent on X_is;
2. e is the same for every subject in the population; and
3. T_is and X_is are not interval.

There are many consequences of the above limitations. Specifically, limitation #1 implies that T_is are always tied to the entire measurement instrument; changing items (e.g., removing or adding an item) to the instrument will result in changes in T_is. The reverse is also true. Thus, the true abilities of subjects are dependent on observed scores (X_is) based on an instrument. For example, an easier test will increase observed scores, thus true ability estimates, while a more difficult test will decrease observed scores of a sample, thus lowering their true ability estimates.

Similarly, a sample of subjects with higher abilities produces higher observed scores on the instrument, which makes the instrument easier; and a sample of subjects with lower abilities produces lower observed scores on the instrument, which makes the instrument more difficult. Common sense tells us that a person's true ability should not change from test to test. Thus, CTT is, in fact, counterintuitive.

The mutual dependence between subject ability and test difficulty is a classic paradox that makes measurement in science education fundamentally different from measurement in science and engineering. In science and engineering, a measurement instrument and the measurement target are always independent from each other. For example, a thermometer's degree scale does not change no matter what target the thermometer is used to measure, being water, alcohol, oil, and so on; similarly, the temperature of water is not going to change no matter what kind of thermometer, being alcohol or mercury, is used to measure. It is highly desirable to separate measures of targets from the instrument used to measure them if we want measures in science education to be more valid. Subject abilities at a given time should be considered as constants no matter what instrument is used to measure them; and an instrument's difficulty or measures should be considered as constants no matter what sample of subjects it is measuring.

The consequence to limitation #2 is that we can not have precise measures for individual subjects. Common sense tells us that different subjects may react to the same measurement instrument differently, thus should have different measurement errors. A same measurement error for all subjects is counterinitutive, and undermines measurement precision for individual subjects. It is highly desirable to identify individualized measurement errors for different subjects if we want measures in science education to be more reliable.

The consequence to limitation #3 is that theoretically we can not apply inferential statistics such as t test and F test to measurement data, because inferential statistics assume that data to be analyzed are interval. Although in science education research we routinely treat measurement data based on CTT as if they were interval, scores from a measurement instrument in the form of a total score or a percentage are in fact only ordinal. For example, a subject who scored 85 on an achievement test out of a total possible score of 100, thus 85%, should only be considered to have scored higher than a person who scored 80. The difference score between these two persons, that is, 5, does not reflect the same amount of achievement difference as that between two other persons who scored 55 and 50. This inequality in difference can be appreciated from another perspective. That is, it is always more difficult to score even one more point for a person whose score is close to the highest possible score (e.g.

100) than a person whose score is close to the other end (e.g., 0) or to the middle point (e.g., 50). The floor (minimal possible score, e.g., 0) and ceiling (maximal possible score, e.g., 100) effects are one other indication that total scores or its percentage conversions are not truly interval, because there is no differentiation among subjects when their scores have reached the floor or ceiling. Pretending raw scores to be interval when applying inferential statistics would reduce the statistical power to reject null hypotheses because of higher error variance in raw scores. It is highly desirable to use interval scores if we want to have more power in statistical testing in science education research.

RASCH MODELS AND ITEM RESPONSE THEORY

Rasch models are a family of probabilistic models to describe response patterns of examinees to individual items; they originated from the pioneering work of the Danish mathematician Georg Rasch who developed a simple Rasch model, commonly called the Rasch model, for a test of items that can be scored correctly or incorrectly (Rasch, 1960/1980). The Rasch model assumes that there exists a linear measure common to both items and examinees. For items, such a measure is the item difficulty; for examinees, such a measure is the ability. Both *difficulty* and *ability* are the likelihood for examinees to answer items correctly; difficulty is a property of items, and ability is a property of examinees. Both difficulty and ability measures are unidimensional, that is, only increasing and decreasing along one dimension. In a testing situation, the probability of a particular examinee answering a particular item correctly is solely determined by the difference between the ability and difficulty measures. The higher the ability is, the higher the likelihood for the examinee to answer the item correctly; similarly the higher the item difficulty is (i.e., more difficult), the lower the likelihood for the examinee to answer the item correctly. Applying the model to develop measurement instruments, that is, Rasch modeling, is to create a set of items that uniquely define such a linear measure. This process is also called Rasch calibration, which is analogous to constructing a meter stick. In order to construct a meter stick from a blank wooden stick, we need to place marks along the stick so that together they form a linear measure. Once a set of items are calibrated to define a linear measure, the set of items can then form a measurement instrument and be applied to any sample of examinees to produce ability measures. What are unique about these ability measures is that they are truly interval, not dependent on the set of items used to measure them, and they have individualized standard errors of measurement, which have overcome the three limitations identified with CTT discussed earlier.

Essentially, Rasch modeling applies a statistical model to raw data (no matter if they are nominal or ordinal) to produce measures of item difficulties and student abilities.

According to Rasch, for any item i with a difficulty D_i that can be scored as right ($X = 1$) or wrong ($X = 0$), the probability (P) of a person n with an ability B_n to answer the item correctly can be expressed as

$$P(X = 1 \mid B_n, D_i) = \frac{e^{(Bn - Di)}}{1 + e^{(Bn - Di)}} \tag{6}$$

Equation 6 is the well-known Rasch model for dichotomously scored items. Because the likelihood or log-odds for an event is the ratio of the probability of happening over the probability of not happening, we can thus show that the likelihood or odds for the person to answer item i correctly is

$$\frac{P}{1 - P} = \frac{e^{(Bn - Di)}}{1 + e^{(Bn - Di)}} \Bigg/ \left(1 - \frac{e^{(Bn - Di)}}{1 + e^{(Bn - Di)}} \right)$$
$$= e^{(Bn - Di)} \tag{7}$$

If L is the natural logarithm of the likelihood or odds, which is commonly called log-likelihood or log-odds or simply logit, then

$$L = \ln \left(\frac{P}{1 - P} \right) = B_n - D_i \tag{8}$$

Equation 8 states how the log-odds (logit) for a person to answer a question correctly is simply the difference between that person's latent ability and the item's latent difficulty. The bigger the difference, the more likely the person will answer the question correctly.

In the equations above B_n and D_i have some important properties. First and foremost B_n and D_i are expressed on a true interval scale, because both have an important property called linearity. This linearity property can be shown as follows. If Person n_1 has a higher ability (B_{n1}) than person n_2 (B_{n2}), then the difference in log-odds between person n_1 and person n_2 to answer the same item D_i correctly is

$$L_{n1} - L_{n2} = (B_{n1} - D_i) - (B_{n2} - D_i) = B_{n1} - B_{n2} \tag{9}$$

Therefore, only the difference in latent abilities determines the difference in log-odds, regardless of the difficulty of the item. Similarly, we can show that the difference in log-odds for the same person with an ability B_n to answer two questions with different difficulties (D_{i1} and D_{i2}) correctly is solely determined by the difference in item difficulties, regardless of the person's ability:

$$L_{i1} - L_{i2} = (B_n - D_{i1}) - (B_n - D_{i2}) = D_{i2} - D_{i1} \qquad (10)$$

The linearity of B_n and D_i implies that ability and item difficulty measures are mutually independent, which is called item invariance property and person invariance property; they are unique properties of Rasch measures.

Another important property of B_n and D_i is that they are latent, that is, not direct observations or counts. Referring to Equation 6 above, we see that only X, which is the score of the person on an item, is observable from the test. B_n and D_i need to be derived from Xs, or the response patterns of a test. Because of this, B_n is also called person or examinee ability parameter estimate and D_i item difficulty parameter estimate. Parameter estimates are calculated based on algorithms using computer programs described later.

Last, from equation 8, we see that the difference between B_n and D_i are on a logarithmic scale of the likelihood or odds or logit. The values of logits vary from $-\infty$ to $+\infty$, thus there is no upper and lower limits, that is, no ceiling or flooring effect in measures. If the difference between B_n and D_i is 0, that is, the person's latent ability is the same as the item's difficulty, according to Equation 6, we obtain that the probability (P) for the person to answer the question correctly is .5 or 50%. Because the person has an equal chance of answering the question correctly to answering the question incorrectly, the odds are 1 to 1, and the log-odds is 0 (Equation 8). Similarly, if the difference between B_n and D_i is +3, then the person has a probability of 95% to answer the question correctly (Equation 6), the odds are 19 to 1, and the log-odds is 2.20. On the other hand, if the difference between B_n and D_i is −3, then the person has a probability of 5% to answer the question correctly, the odds are 0.053 to 1, and the log-odds is −2.94.

Because of their unique properties above, B_n and D_i are also called measures. Almost 50 years ago, Thurstone (1959) considered linearity a fundamental property of measures. Linearity can be best understood by a meter stick's measurement scale (Liu & Boone, 2006). If Mike is 10 centimeters taller than Jane, and if Jane is 15 centimeters taller than Janet, then because the centimeter scale is a linear one, Mike should be 25 centimeters (10 cm + 15 cm) taller than Janet. In order to obtain linear measures, Thurstone had to use a large number of judges to sort a large number of items. Based on the grouping of items by the judges, each item was assigned a measure, and only the items that formed a linear progression by increasing measure of an equal distance were retained and used to form the measurement instrument. By applying Rasch modeling, however, fewer judges and items are needed to develop a measurement instrument, making the process more efficient.

Measures are also unidimensional. *Unidimensionality* refers to the fact that measures describe only one attribute of that which is observed. The following cites another example from Liu and Boone (2006). When evaluating the attitudes of ninth-grade students taught with a reform physics curriculum, one should strive to insure that the measures are only about the students' one construct—the attitudes toward the physics curriculum. It would be important not to devise a measurement instrument that also considers each student's attitudes toward (a) the school and (b) their teachers. That would be a case in which three dimensions would be combined together, and a unidimensional measure would not result.

Last but not the least, measures are based on abstract units. Data directly resulting from observations, called raw data, are not based on abstract units; they are based on counts—how many items have or have not been correctly answered on a test. Raw scores or counts are not measures. Consider how one compares apples at the market (Liu & Boone, 2006). If one wishes to compare apples, one does not do so by just counting apples. Some apples may be bigger than others. An improvement upon the concept of counts is to weigh apples, because weight is a measure of mass contained in the apple. Weight is a derived measure through the scale calibration and on an abstract unit. The general problem with the counting of apples is present when one wishes to measure a construct in science education. If counts are utilized, and such counts are not measures, then analysis of such data may be flawed. By utilizing Rasch modeling, measures can be created from raw data or counts.

Wright (1999) succinctly summarized *measures* to be: (a) linear, (b) inferences by stochastic approximations and on abstract units, (c) of unidimensional quantities, and (d) impervious to extraneous factors. We have considered the first three of these, the fourth characteristic can be viewed as the goal of a measure not being compromised by factors unrelated to the core meaning of the measures. For example, a meter stick being used to measure the height of students is not affected by the materials, legibility of numbers, or width of the stick. This issue will be further elaborated when we compare the item response theory to Rasch modeling later. In summary, Rasch measurement is an approach to modeling data from observations in order to produce measures that demonstrate the above four characteristics.

Since the development of the Rasch model by Georg Rasch for dichotomously scored items (i.e., correct or incorrect), many extensions to the original model have been developed. Major extensions to the dichotomous Rasch model are: (a) Rasch rating scale model, (b) Rasch partial credit model, and (c) Many-facet Rasch model. The Rasch rating scale model takes the following form (Andrich, 1978):

$$L = \ln \left(\frac{P}{1-P}\right) = B_n - (D_i + F_k) \tag{11}$$

where D_i is the difficulty of an item, F_k is the threshold difficulty or transition point between two categories of an item, and P is the probability of a person with ability B_n to choose category k of an item.

For example, the most commonly used Likert scale has five categories, *strongly agree* (SA), *agree* (A), *neutral* (N), *disagree* (D), and *strongly disagree* (SD). Among the five categories of each item, there are four between-category transition points or thresholds, thus $k = 4$. For example, $k = 1$ refers to the threshold between SA and A. In a rating scale such as a Likert scale, because all items have the same category structure (i.e., number of categories), F_k is the same for all items.

Both the dichotomous and rating-scale Rasch models assume that all items of a measurement instrument have the same structure (e.g., all multiple choice, or all Likert scale). However, in practice, it is more common to have a mixture of question formats within a same measurement instrument. For example, a conceptual test may contain both multiple-choice questions and constructed-response questions using a scoring rubric. In this situation, it is necessary to have a model containing characteristics of both the dichotomous and rating-scale Rasch models. This mixture of Rasch models is the partial credit Rasch model (Wright & Masters, 1982). The partial credit Rasch model allows each item to have its own structure (e.g., dichotomous, rating, etc.). The partial credit Rasch model takes the following form:

$$L = \ln \left(\frac{P}{1-P}\right) = B_n - D_{ik} \tag{12}$$

where D_{ik} is the difficulty of category k of item i. For dichotomous items, $k = 0$. For rating scale, k is equal to the number of thresholds.

In all the above Rasch models, only examinees and items are considered. In complex measurement designs, there may be more than one rater, or more than one setting involved. For measurement scenarios like this, the many-facet Rasch model (Linacre, 1989) has been developed. The many-facet Rasch model extends a two-facet Rasch model (e.g., the dichotomous and rating-scale models) into a many-facet Rasch model. The general form of a many-facet Rasch model is as follows:

$$L = \ln \left(\frac{P}{1-P}\right) = B_n - D_i - C_j \dots \tag{13}$$

where C_j is the difficulty of facet C category $_j$ (e.g., rater 1).

In addition to the above extensions, multidimensional extensions of the Rasch models have also been made. As discussed earlier, one key characteristic of Rasch measures is that items measure one construct—the requirement of unidimensionality. Although unidimensionality is theoretically sound, it may not be the most efficient in application. This is because in many testing situations, particularly in large scale assessment such as the Trend in International Math and Science Study (TIMSS) and the National Achievement of Educational Progress (NAEP), it is necessary to measure multiple constructs in a single test administration. For example, science achievement is a complex or composite construct; it likely contains a number of subdimensions or subconstructs. For example, depending on the number of content areas (biology, chemistry, physics, etc.) and cognitive reasoning levels (formulating hypothesis, developing explanation, etc.), students' scientific achievement may not be a unitary construct and may contain many dimensions: physical science achievement, life science achievement, and earth science achievement. A student may be strong in one dimension, but weak in others. From a measurement point of view, differentiating the dimensions and variance as well as covariance among them could greatly increase the reliability—the variance explained by the model. Based on this rationale, various multidimensional extensions of the Rasch model have also been developed (Briggs & Wilson, 2004). One multidimensional Rasch model is the Multidimensional Random Coefficients Multinomial Logit (MRCML) model (Wang, 1997). MRCML allows for the estimation of item and ability parameters based on clusters of items (dimensions), and calculate the correlations among the dimensions.

Concurrently, yet independently from the development of the Rasch model in the 1960s, American psychometrician Allan Birnbaum (1968) developed a set of logistic models to analyze item responses, the commonly known 1-parameter, 2-parameter, and 3-parameter logistic models. These logistic models form a family called item response theory (IRT) models. One-parameter models assume that only the item difficulty parameter is necessary and sufficient to describe items; they are identical to the Rasch models. Two-parameter models assume that both item difficulty and item discrimination parameters are necessary to describe items; and three-parameter models assume that, in addition to item difficulty and item discrimination parameters, the item guessing parameter is also necessary to fully describe items. The two-parameter and three-parameter logistic models are as follows:

$$L = \ln\left(\frac{P}{1-P}\right) = A_i(B_n - D_i) \tag{14}$$

$$L = \ln\left(\frac{P - C_i}{1-P}\right) = A_i(B_n - D_i) \tag{15}$$

It can be seen that the 2-parameter (i.e., difficulty D_i and discrimination A_i) and 3-parameter (i.e., difficulty D_i, discrimination A_i, and guessing C_i) IRT models appear similar to the Rasch model. Mathematically, the Rasch model can be derived from the above 2- and 3-parameter models when A_i is assumed to be 1 (all items have the same discrimination power) and C_i is assumed to be 0 (no guessing involved). In fact, popular IRT books (e.g., Embretson & Reise, 2000; Hambleton, Swaminathan, & Rogers, 1991) refer Rasch models as 1-parameter logistic models, and consider the Rasch models to be a special case of the more complex IRT models.

However, there are fundamental differences between Rasch models and IRT models. In the literature particularly during 1980s and early 1990s, there was intensive debate on the advantages and disadvantages of Rasch vs. IRT models. As the result, two camps, the Rasch camp and the IRT camp, have formed. Proponents of Rasch measurement demonstrated that B_n and D_i estimates from IRT models are not interval measures. Wright (1999) argues that the Rasch model is the only parsimonious model to construct linear measures. Adding additional parameters to the Rasch model, such as item discrimination A_i and item guessing C_i parameter as in 2-parameter and 3-parameter IRT models will not result in linearity in B_n and D_i, because additional parameters are always entangled in the estimates of B_n and D_i.

Wilson (2005) states that fundamental requirements of a measurement model are: (a) it must enable one to interpret the distance between an examinee and an item, and (b) it must enable one to interpret difference between different items and the difference between different examinees. The above two requirements can be met by constructing a combined Examinee and Item Map—the Wright map if a Rasch model is used (Wilson, 2005). A *Wright map* is a combined item difficulty and examinee ability diagram showing the distribution of items and examines along a same unidimensional logit scale. This combined diagram can not be constructed if IRT models are used. Fischer and Molenaar (1995) claim that Rasch modeling is currently the only way to convert ordinal observations into linear measures.

In addition to the above technical differences, there is also an important conceptual difference between Rasch models and IRT models when they are applied to develop measurement instruments. For Rasch models, the approach to measurement is to design appropriate items to form an instrument in order for data to fit a Rasch model so that the unique properties of B_n and D_i (e.g., linearity) can be obtained; for IRT, the approach is to find the best model (e.g., 1-parameter, 2-parameter, 3-parameter, etc.) to fit the data so that variance in data can be maximally explained. Clearly, applications of Rasch models are top-down or measure-oriented. On the other hand, applications of IRT models are bottom-up or variance explanation oriented. This fundamental conceptual difference has been called paradigm incompatibility (Andrich, 2004). Construction of measures must be based on theories, particularly cognitive theories (National Research Council Committee, 2001; Wilson, 2005). Rasch modeling is such a theory-based approach to developing measurement instruments. Given the above technical and conceptual differences, although 1-parameter IRT models are mathematically the same as Rasch models, the application of Rasch models to develop measurement instruments requires a quite different approach than that of 1-parameter logistic models; it is best not to equate the Rasch models with 1-parameter IRT models.

USING RASCH MODELING
TO DEVELOP MEASUREMENT INSTRUMENTS

Using Rasch models to develop measurement instruments is a systematic process in which items are purposefully constructed according to a theory and empirically tested through Rasch models in order to produce a set of items that define a linear measurement scale. The Rasch approach to developing measurement instruments consists of the following 10 steps:

1. Define the construct that can be characterized by a linear attribute or construct;
2. Identify the behaviors corresponding to different levels of the defined construct;
3. Define the outcome space of the behaviors;
4. Field-test with a representative sample of the target population;
5. Conduct Rasch modeling;
6. Review item fit statistics and revise items if necessary;
7. Review the Wright map and add/delete items if necessary;
8. Repeat (4) to (7) until a set of items fit the Rasch model and define a scale;

9. Establish validity and reliability claims for the measurement instrument; and

10. Develop documentation for the measurement instrument.

The 10-step process parallels the 10-step general test development process described in chapter 1. The 10-step process described in chapter 1 is applicable to developing measurement instruments following CTT. When applying Rasch modeling to develop measurement instruments, there are specific considerations pertaining to the 10-step general process. One key consideration in the development process based on Rasch modeling is the role of theories. The task for developing a measurement instrument is to create a set of items that produce data consistent with the theory. This process follows logical-hypothetical deductive reasoning commonly used in natural sciences. However, developing measurement instruments using Rasch is not to reject a hypothesis; rather, it is to construct items that result in data to agree with the hypothesis. This approach is also used in natural sciences. For example, developing a temperature scale (e.g., thermometer) is based on the theory of thermodynamics. Developing a temperature scale has nothing to do with validating or rejecting the thermodynamic theory; rather its purpose is to construct a device to generate measures consistent with the theory of thermodynamics. In science education, we can follow the same rationale to develop measurement instruments. In measuring students' understanding of the nature of science, initially we must have a good theory about the nature of science. Otherwise, the measures obtained may be irrelevant. This theory-based approach is the essence of construct validity; using Rasch modeling to develop measurement instruments ensures that the measures produced will have high construct validity.

Step 1: Define the Construct

When defining the construct to be measured, one important consideration is that the construct has a theoretically unidimensional progression from a lower level to a higher level. For example, if the construct to be measured is attitude toward science laboratories, then there must be a good theory or research literature to suggest that there is a unidimensional progression in students' attitude toward science laboratories from less favorable to more favorable. It is possible that student attitude toward science laboratories may be multifaceted or multidimensional. But each measurement scale must be related to only one facet or dimension, although a measurement instrument may contain more than one scale in administration. The theory is the starting point for developing a measurement instrument. If no such a theory is available, then consider postponing developing a measurement instrument. For example, if little had been known about the nature of temperature or there had been no commonly agreed-upon theories on temperature, there would have been no need to develop a measurement instrument to measure temperature, because any instrument developed would have been arbitrary and lacked credibility. In science education, the same should be expected when developing an instrument to measure a construct. If a construct is unknown, then developing an instrument to measure the construct is premature.

Step 2: Identify the Behaviors of the Defined Construct

Once the construct is defined in terms of a progression, the next step is to develop a test specification that defines the type of items to solicit examinees' responses. The test specification describes the attributes involved in the defined construct, and will directly inform the development of items. Because the construct is unidimensional, the attributes must also be hierarchical. For example, to measure students' conceptual understanding about the concept of energy, there must exist a hierarchy of content from easiest to most difficult, such as from energy phenomena/activities to energy sources and forms, energy transfer, energy degradation, and energy conservation. There must also exist a hierarchy in terms of cognitive reasoning involved, such as a progression from knowing to creating.

Step 3: Define Outcome Space of Items

Once a test specification is defined, an initial item pool is then created and item scoring keys and/or rubrics are developed. These items and their scoring keys/rubrics define the outcome space of items. Typically, more items than needed in the final measurement instrument should be prepared in anticipation for deletion of nonfitting items (described later). When developing items, limited try-out with a small purposefully selected sample of subjects should be conducted. Qualitative studies such as think-aloud may be helpful as well. The final initial items will then make a draft measurement instrument for field testing.

Step 4: Conduct Field Testing

Field testing is to administer the draft measurement instrument to a representative sample of the target population so that data can be collected for Rasch modeling. Although a random sample from the population is ideal, what is important for Rasch modeling is the spread of examinees along the measured construct. That is, an important consideration is to ensure that the range of examinees' abilities on the measured construct matches the range of item difficulties.

Step 5: Conduct Rasch Modeling

After the field testing, examinees' responses to items are entered into the computer, and Rasch modeling begins. There are a variety of computer programs available that are specifically developed for Rasch modeling. Bond and Fox (2001) point out that although

> each of the Rasch software programs has its own disciples, but no one program incorporates the advantages of all the packages, or avoids the tolerable shortcomings of its own particular estimation procedure.... The usual Rasch analytical procedures ... produce estimates that are generally equivalent, for all practical analytical purposes. (p. 210)

These commonly used Rasch modeling programs are: Winsteps, Facets, Quest/ConQuest, and RUMM.

Winsteps (Linacre, 2003) is a Windows-based program and the most popular Rasch modeling program in the United States. It handles a variety of data types, including dichotomous, multiple choice, rating, partial credit, rank order, and paired comparison. Different item types may also be combined in one analysis. The structure of the items and persons can be examined in depth, which facilitates exploration. For example, it identifies unexpected data points, as well as multidimensionality through principal component analysis of residuals. Measures can be fixed (anchored) at preset values. Its DOS-based predecessor, Bigsteps, with a capacity of 20,000 persons and 1,000 items, can be downloaded for free (http://www.winsteps.com). Also from the same developer, the Facet (Linacre, 1997) computer program extends the Rasch measurement into more complex measurement designs such as judged performances, and subtests of items replicated across tasks. For example, Facet can analyze the ratings awarded by judges to examinees who are being tested on their performance on a number of different skill items for each of several tasks. The second version of the Bond and Fox (2007) book includes a simplified version of Winsteps and Facet that produce essential output tables, graphs and statistics sufficient for common measurement instrument development needs.

Quest (Adams & Khoo, 1998) is a multiplatform program that runs on PC, Mac, and Vax/VMS. According to the information posted on its website (http://www.assess.com/Software/quest.htm), Quest offers a comprehensive analysis of data based on both the Rasch measurement theory and classical test theory. Quest can be used to construct and validate variables based on both dichotomous and polytomous observations from multiple-choice tests, Likert-type rating, short answer items and partial credit items. The outputs from Quest include item estimates, person estimates, fit statistics, as well as traditional statistics such as counts, percentages, and point-biserials. A variety of reliability indices are also available. ConQuest is an expanded version of Quest (Wu, Adams, & Wilson, 1997). ConQuest does analysis based on a wider range of item response models than Quest. While Quest does not have a GUI (graphical user interface), ConQuest has a GUI for Windows and Windows NT.

RUMM, Rasch Unidimensional Measurement Model, software (Sheridan, 1998) is a Windows-based computer program. According to information posted on the website (http://www.rummlab.com.au/), RUMM provides a powerful and flexible means of performing Rasch item analysis. With each analysis, RUMM produces tables, displays, plots and graphics to assist in the interpretation of items in relation to the latent trait under construction. All displays in RUMM can be saved to files for importing into a word processor (to enhance reports) and spreadsheet (for further analysis and plotting). RUMM implements user-friendly features, such as instant graphic displays, editing of invalid responses, data entry errors, rescoring of category responses after inspecting the category characteristic curves, multiple data sets, batch file creation, and anchoring item parameters from a previous analysis.

The issue of sample size for Rasch modeling has been a focus of research for many years. The current consensus is that the required minimal sample size for Rasch modeling can be as small as 50. As Wright and Tennant (1996) indicated, with a reasonably targeted sample of 50 persons, there is a 99% confidence that the estimated item difficulty is within ± 1 logit of its stable value, which is close enough for most practical purposes, especially when persons take 10 or more items. This is because Rasch models contain only one item parameter—difficulty, and the estimation of Rasch parameters does not depend on a sampling distribution. In response to common misconceptions about the minimal sample size for Rasch modeling, Wright and Tennant (1996) states that a large required minimal sample size for Rasch modeling (e.g., 200) is based on a misconception that Rasch parameter estimation requires a normally distributed sample. In fact, Rasch modeling escapes from such an awkward requirement by focusing on the separation between item parameters and person parameters.

Keep in mind that the issue of required minimal sample size is essentially an issue of standard error of measures (Rasch person and item parameter estimates). Wright (1977) shows that for a typical test with a raw score between 20% and 80% correct, that is, a 5-logit difference range, the minimal sample size is

$$N = 6/SE^2$$

where SE is the standard error of Rasch measures. For example, if we want our SE to be smaller than 0.35, which is typically adequate for pilot testing, then the required minimal sample size is 50; for SE to be smaller than 0.25, which is typically considered acceptable for low-stakes testing situations, the required minimal sample size is 96; for SE to be smaller than 0.15, which is typically considered excellent for most testing situations, the required minimal sample size is 267.

Step 6: Examine Model-Data-Fit for Items

Although different computer programs may use different formats to report fit statistics, there are many commonalities in reported statistics on items. Common item fit statistics include the mean square residual (MNSQ) and the standardized mean square residual (ZSTD). Both MNSQ and ZSTD are based on the difference between what is observed and what is expected by the Rasch model. MNSQ is a simple squared residual, while ZSTD is a normalized Z score of the residual. There are two ways to sum MNSQs and ZSTDs over all persons for each item, which produce four fit statistics. INFIT statistics (Infit MNSQs an Infit ZSTDs) are weighted means by assigning more weights for those persons' responses close to the probability of 50/50, while OUTFIT statistic (Outfit MNSQs and Outfit ZSTDs) are simple arithmetic means of MNSQs and ZSTDs over all persons. Thus, Outfit statistics are more sensitive to extreme responses –outliers. The rule of thumb is that items with good model-data-fit have Infit and Outfit MNSQ within the range of 0.7–1.3, and Infit and Outfit ZSTD within the range of –2 to +2.

Keep in mind that MNSQ and ZSTD are sensitive to sample sizes. Increasing the sample size will reduce MNSQ toward the expected value of 1, which may result in underdetecting misfitting items; similarly, increasing the sample size will increase ZSTD, which may result in over-detecting mis-fitting items. This is a well-known dilemma in Rasch modeling. Through a simulation study, Smith, Schumacker and Bush (1998) found that when sample size was over 500, corrections to commonly used mean square fit statistics criteria (e.g., MNSQ to be within 0.7–1.3) were needed. Overall, ZSTD is not as sensitive to sample sizes as MNSQ.

Table 2.1 shows a sample fit statistics table for an elementary science concept test. The dichotomous Rasch model was applied because all the 15 items were multiple-choice questions.

In Table 2.1, measures are item difficulties in logits– the bigger the measure is, the more difficult the item is. SE is the standard error of measurement for the item difficulty measure. INFIT and OUTFIT statistics

Table 2.1. Fit Statistics for an Elementary Science Concept Test

Item	Measure	S.E.	INFIT MNSQ	INFIT ZSTD	OUTFIT MNSQ	OUTFIT ZSTD	PTMEA
Q1	0.06	0.46	1.09	0.7	1.07	0.4	0.21
Q2	0.26	0.45	0.93	−0.5	0.90	−0.5	0.42
Q3	−2.01	0.75	0.91	0.0	0.80	0.0	0.29
Q4	0.87	0.46	1.26	1.6	1.38	1.8	−0.02
Q5	−0.61	0.50	0.87	−0.5	0.78	−0.6	0.45
Q6	−0.61	0.50	0.99	0.0	0.92	−0.1	0.30
Q7	−0.38	0.48	1.11	0.7	1.65	2.0	0.03
Q8	1.32	0.49	1.06	0.3	1.03	0.2	0.27
Q9	−0.15	0.47	0.99	0.0	1.06	0.3	0.29
Q10	0.06	0.46	1.09	0.7	1.04	0.3	0.21
Q11	3.01	0.76	0.80	−0.2	0.53	−0.4	0.50
Q12	1.56	0.51	0.73	−1.1	0.62	−1.3	0.68
Q13	−2.01	0.75	1.05	0.3	0.90	0.2	0.13
Q14	−2.01	0.75	1.00	0.2	0.78	0	0.21
Q15	0.67	0.45	0.91	−0.6	0.88	−0.7	0.45

are reported in both MNSQ and ZSTD. Finally, PTMEA is the point-measure correlation, indicating how the item contributes to the item difficulty. From Table 2.1, we can see that Q4, Q7, Q11, and Q12 may not fit the Rasch model well because some of their fit statistics are beyond the acceptable ranges. The negative point-measure correlation for Q4 also indicates that the question does not contribute to the measure. A graph called the bubble chart (Figure 2.1) can visually display both the item fit status and standard error of measurement, which also helps identify potential mis-fitting items.

In Figure 2.1, items are plotted based on their difficulty measures (y-axis) and their Infit ZSTD statistics (x-axis), along with their standard errors of measurements (the size of circles or bubbles). Plots outside the range -2 to +2 indicate potential item mis-fitting, and the bigger the circles are, the more errors in their difficulty measures. From Figure 2.1, we can see that all items are within the −2 and −2 range, but Q11 has a big circle, indicating that Q11 may not be fitting the model well.

Another aspect related to model-data-fit for items is item categories. For multiple-choice questions, item categories are concerned with this question: are all choices functioning? For rating scales (e.g., Likert scale),

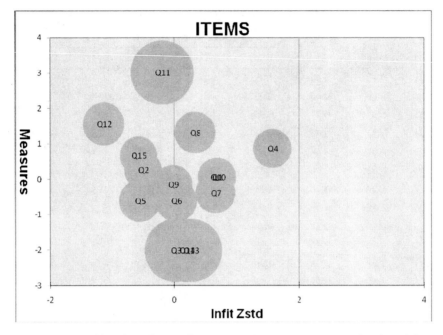

Figure 2.1.   Bubble chart for an elementary science concept test. The size of the circle for an item is determined by its standard error of measurement; items outside the ±2 Zstd range are potentially misfitting.

item categories are concerned with the question: do the choices progress in the expected order? Table 2.2 shows a partial output table for three multiple-choice questions. As we can see from the table, for Q8, no one selected choice D, and only one person selected B. For Q11, all choices were selected, although most (77%) selected the wrong choice D. PTMEA for incorrect choices should be negative and for correct choices positive. However, PTMEA for D of Q11, an incorrect choice, is positive. The above information suggests that the choice D for Q8 and Q11 may need improvement.

Figure 2.2 is the category probability curve for an attitude survey using the following categories: *Strongly agree* (1), *agree* (2), *slightly agree* (3), *slightly disagree* (4), *disagree* (5), and *strongly disagree* (6). The *x* axis represents the subjects' attitude measures in logits, and *y* axis represents the probability of choosing a particular category. It shows that, as the difference between subjects' attitude and item difficulty increases, it becomes more likely for subjects to choose category 6 (*strongly disagree*). However, categories 2, 3, 4, and 5 are buried under categories 1 and 6, indicating

Table 2.2. Item Choice Statistics

Item	Choices	Score	Count (%)	Measure	S. E.	OUTFIT MNSQ	PTMEA
Q8	B	0	1 (5%)	−0.93	0.0	0.2	−0.41
	A	0	14 (64%)	0.44	0.20	1.2	−0.08
	C	1	7 (32%)	0.78	0.26	1.0	0.27
Q11	A	0	2 (9%)	−0.38	0.55	0.4	−0.36
	B	0	1 (5%)	−0.19	0.0	0.4	−0.19
	D	0	17 (77%)	0.49	0.15	1.0	0.01
	C	1	2 (9%)	1.67	0.76	0.5	0.50

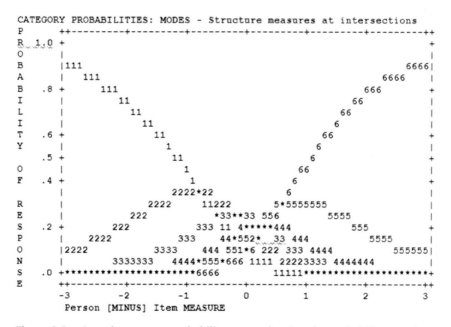

Figure 2.2. Sample category probability curves showing the probability associated with different differences between examinee abilities and item difficulties.

that the subjects are likely to respond with either category 1 (*strongly agree*) or category 6 (*strongly disagree*) depending on their overall attitude. Other categories become redundant, thus may be eliminated. The revised survey may no longer need six categories; instead only *agree* and *disagree* categories may be enough.

Step 7: Examine the Wright Map and Dimensionality Plots

The Wright map shows how items target persons. Figure 2.3 is a Wright map for the elementary science concept test mentioned earlier.

In the Wright map shown in Figure 2.3, both item difficulties and person abilities are shown along the same linear scale in logit units (the

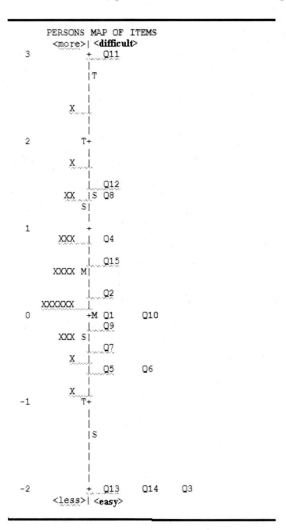

Figure 2.3. Wright map for an elementary science concept test. Both item difficulties and examinee abilities are arranged along a same logit scale shown on the far left.

middle line enumerated on the far left). A good measurement instrument should be able to target the intended population by matching its difficulty distribution with the sample's ability distribution. Any mismatch, i.e., gap, indicates that subjects within that gap can not be accurately differentiated because of the lack of items at that level. In Figure 2.3, a number of gaps exist: between Q11 and Q12, between Q8 and Q4, between Q2 and Q15, and between Q5/Q6 and Q13/Q14/Q3. Also keep in mind that this sample has only 22 students, which is quite small. On the other hand, the sample does have a good spread in the distribution of student abilities.

Item dimensionality is another important aspect to examine. A measurement instrument should be unidimensional. The *unidimensionality* requires that only one latent trait exists in item responses. This does not necessarily mean that only one latent trait exists among the examinees when they respond to the items; it is sufficient if one dominant factor exists in explaining the variances in item responses (Stout, 1990). There are various ways to examine dimensionality of data. First, fit statistics for items are examined and misfitting items could be measuring additional dimensions. Next, the dimensionality of Rasch residuals is examined. Rasch residuals are variances not explained by Rasch measures. If the items are unidimensional and fit the Rasch model well, then we should not expect a large variance of residuals left, and factor analysis of residuals should result in no dominant factors. On the other hand, if factor analysis of Rasch residual variances results in one or more dominant factors, than the items may be measuring more than one construct, and the unidimensionality does not hold well. Figure 2.4 shows the plot of factor analysis of residuals for the elementary science concept test described earlier.

In Figure 2.4, the scatterplots show how items are correlated with a potential additional construct not modeled by the Rasch model. If the original student response data are perfectly unidimensional, then the Rasch model would explain 100% variance. However, the Rasch model only explained 54% of total variance, leaving 46% variance unexplained—residuals. Among the 46% unexplained variance, it is possible that an additional construct could exist. Items with high correlations with the potential construct, that is, factor loadings <-0.4 and >0.4, may also measure the additional construct besides the intended construct explained by the Rasch model. In Figure 2.4, items A, B, C, a, b, c, and d (Q2, Q3, Q5, Q6, Q8, Q11, Q12, and Q13) are potential items that measure an additional construct because their factor loadings are beyond the -0.4 to +0.4 range. Those items need to be reviewed, modified or eliminated entirely if necessary.

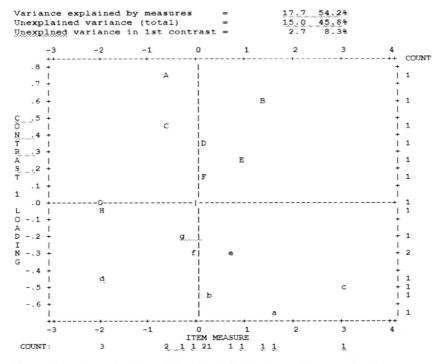

Figure 2.4.   Factor loadings of Rasch residual variance. Constrast loadings are correlation coefficients between an unintended construct and the items. scatterplots should be randomly distributed within the ±0.4 loading range if items are unidimensional.

Step 8: Examine Invariance Properties

When there is good model-data-fit and the instrument is unidimensional, item difficulty measures should be invariant from the sample used to calibrate the item difficulties, and person ability measures should be invariant from the set of items used to produce the ability measures. These two characteristics are called *item measure* and *person measure invariance properties*, or simply, item and person invariance properties. Thus, one final quality control when developing a measurement instrument is to examine the item and invariance properties.

In order to examine the item invariance properties, it is necessary to have two subsamples so that two sets of item difficulties are produced and compared for differences. The two subsamples are usually based on subject characteristics, such as gender, race, ability, etc. Because we expect that there should be no significant difference in item difficulty measures obtained from the two samples, any difference found may indicate bias in items, which is called item differential functioning (DIF). Bias due to DIF for gender or any meaningful group characteristics should be avoided. Rasch modeling provides various statistics to help identify DIF items.

Similarly, when the same sample of subjects taking two different tests that measure the same construct, person measures obtained from the two different tests should not be significantly different. However, because both item and person measures are interval instead of ratio, the 0 point of measures from different calibrations may be different. Thus, unless measures are obtained from the same calibration, before examining item or person invariance, measures from different calibrations should be equated through linear transformation first. Also, because item and person measures contain errors, the invariance should also be interpreted within the possible random sampling distribution.

Figures 2.5 shows the scatterplots between two sets of item difficulty measures based on two subsamples. Both x and y axes are in logits. The scatterplots are pairs of difficulty measures from two subsamples, and

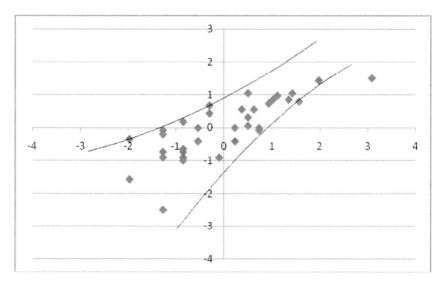

Source: Data are from Bond and Fox (2001/2007, p. 74).

Figure 2.5. Invariance of item difficulty measures obtained from two samples of examinees. The smaller the band is, the better the invariance.

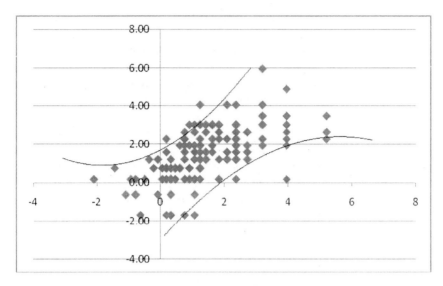

Source: Data are from Bond and Fox (2007, pp. 96-99).

Figure 2.6.   Invariance of examinee ability measures obtained from two sets of items or tests. The smaller the band is, the better the invariance.

the two trend lines define a 95% confidence interval around the mean and combined standard error of the two sets of difficulty measures. We can see that most scatterplots are within the band, indicating that the two sets of item difficulty measures are, in general, invariant from samples.

Similarly, Figure 2.6 shows the invariance property of person measures from two forms of a measurement instrument. Once again, we see that most subjects' measures are within the 95% confidence interval band, indicating that, overall, the person ability measures from two different forms of the instrument are invariant.

After examination of model-data-fit of items, the Wright map, dimensionality, as well as invariance properties, some items may be revised or deleted, and a new set of items may be created. This new set of items will form a revised version of the measurement instrument. The revised measurement instrument will then go for another cycle of field-testing and Rasch modeling until all items and the measurement instrument as a whole meet the quality expectations. The final measurement instrument consisting of the finalized items are now ready for validity and reliability studies.

Step 9: Conduct Valid and Reliable Studies

Reliability and validity are properties of measures, essential for any measurement instrument. The person separation index indicates the overall precision in person measures as compared to errors. A person separation index is the ratio of true standard deviations to error standard deviations in person measures. Thus, a ratio greater than 1 indicates more true variance than error variance in person measures, and the bigger this ratio is, the more precise the person measures. This person separation index can also be converted to a Cronbach's alpha equivalent value from 0 to 1. In the elementary science concept test mentioned earlier, the person separation index was only 0.53, and alpha was only 0.22, indicating that person measures have poor reliability—it is unlikely to produce the same person measures if another equivalent sample retook the test.

Because Rasch modeling can also estimate a standard error of measurement (SEM) for every individual person and item, reliability in Rasch measurement becomes a property of individual persons and items, thus more precise. Different persons and items have different SEMs; persons and items with measures closer to the mean have smaller SEMs than those further from the mean. Based on individual SEMs for persons and items, it is also possible to calculate the overall SEMs for an entire instrument.

Validation of the measurement instrument may be conducted through analyzing test content, response processes, internal structures, relations to other variables, and consequences of testing (Joint Committee of the AERA, APA, and MCME, 1999). All of the validation processes support a coherent argument for the construct validity of the measures. First, because the Rasch approach to developing measurement instruments is theory-based, items have been purposely developed according to the progression of the defined construct; they should represent the content domain of the construct. Also, the initial phases of defining the linear construct, that is, identifying student behaviors and defining the outcome space, typically involve content experts, thus content validity can be further ensured. Second, Rasch measurement can provide detailed analysis of individual response patterns that reflect the reasoning processes of individuals involved in answering each question. Think-aloud may also be used during the measurement development process to ensure that response processes of examinees are consistent with expectations. Third, when data fit the Rasch model and are unidimensional, then there is evidence that items measure the intended construct, thus person measures possess the construct validity. Fourth, because Rasch modeling produces interval measures of individual persons, using Rasch ability measures of individuals is likely to result in a strong correlation with measures of other variables. This is due to reduced error of measurement and increased statistical power for rejecting null hypotheses, which results in greater criterion-related validity. Comparing the rank order of individuals and items based on the Rasch ability and difficulty measures to that based on theories or other measures can also help establish criterion-related validity. Finally, consequence related to validation during Rasch modeling can be facilitated by providing clear interpretations of Rasch scale scores. For example, different competences related to a construct may be tied to specific ranges of Rasch scale scores.

Step 10: Develop Documentation for Test Use

The final stage in developing measurement instruments is documentation. The purpose of documentation is to provide information to facilitate users in their appropriate uses of the measurement instrument. Important information included in the documentation should cover such aspects as the intended uses of the measurement instrument, the definition of the construct, the process of developing the instrument including pilot-testing, field-testing, Rasch modeling, and guidelines for administering the measurement instrument and reporting individual scores. Because it is unrealistic to expect users to conduct Rasch modeling when using the measurement instrument, a raw score to Rasch scale score conversion table should be provided. By referencing the conversion table, users can find out the equivalent Rasch scale score for each raw score without conducting Rasch modeling. Users should only use Rasch scale scores in the subsequent statistical analyses. Table 2.3 is a sample raw score to Rasch scale score conversion table for the elementary science concept test mentioned earlier.

Table 2.3 demonstrates how each raw score corresponds to a Rasch scale score. Also, each Rasch scale score is associated with a standard error of measurement. Note that standard errors of measurement are bigger at the two ends of the scale, and smaller around the middle. This is because there are too few subjects at the two ends of the scale and there are more subjects around the middle to provide information for Rasch calibration.

It has to be noted that Rasch scale scores of individuals do not have to be negative. Because Rasch scale scores are interval, in order to make the Rasch scale score interpretation more intuitive, Rasch computer modeling programs allow users to specify any score range to report Rasch scale scores. For example, the score range can be from 0 to 100, or in a same range as the raw scores, or with a mean of 500 and a standard deviation of 100. The scaling process involves only simple linear transformation by including a few commands in Rasch calibration.

Table 2.3. Raw Score and Rasch Scale Score Conversion Table

Raw Score	Rasch Scale Score	SE
0	−4.65	1.87
1	−3.32	1.09
2	−2.44	0.83
3	−1.85	0.72
4	−1.37	0.67
5	−0.95	0.63
6	−0.56	0.61
7	−0.20	0.60
8	0.16	0.60
9	0.53	0.60
10	0.91	0.63
11	1.33	0.67
12	1.83	0.74
13	2.45	0.86
14	3.39	1.13
15	4.79	1.90

CHAPTER SUMMARY

There are two main approaches to developing measurement instruments; one is the classical test theory, and the other Rasch modeling. The classical test theory (CTT) has been the dominant approach to developing measurement instruments in science education. Within CTT, one main task for developing measurement instruments is to estimate and reduce measurement errors. Measurement errors may be due to inconsistency of items to detect subject abilities, or instability of scores over time, or incomparability of scores across different test forms. Different sources of measurement errors can be quantified as different types of reliabilities. The KR-20 and Cronbach's coefficient alpha are quantification of internal consistency among items of a test. Other reliabilities are interrater reliability and test-retest reliability. Once reliability of a test is estimated, the standard error of measurement of a test can be computed, and the true score of a subject can be estimated. The generalizability theory is an extension to the CTT, specifically to the reliability concept. The generalizability theory includes two types of studies: the G-study and the D-study. The G-study involves estimating variance components associated with subjects and various other measurement facets, and the D-study involves calculating the generalizability coefficient and studying the effects of varying measurement facets in order to identify a more efficient measurement design to achieve an acceptable generalizability.

A more recent approach to developing measurement instruments is to apply the Rasch models. Although Rasch models are mathematically identical to the one-parameter logistic Item Response Theory (IRT) models, they are conceptually different from IRT models. Applying Rasch models to develop measurement instruments is a theory-based approach. The process starts with a theory that describes a progression of a construct along a dimension. The purpose of Rasch modeling is to develop a set of items that produce data consistent with a Rasch model. When there is a good model-data-fit and unidimensionality in subjects' responses, then there is evidence for the construct validity of the subjects' measures. Rasch modeling also produces standard errors for individual items and subjects, in addition to measures of reliability for the entire instrument, such as the separation index and reliability coefficient.

EXERCISES

1. A research report includes the following information about a measurement instrument for measuring elementary school students' conceptions of scientists:

   The measurement instrument has 12 multiple-choice questions; it measures elementary school students' conceptions of scientists. The development of the instrument involved: (a) definition the construct—conceptions of scientists, (b) development of multiple-choice questions according to the definition, (c) review of items for its adequacy by a panel of science educators, (d) pilot-test of the instrument with 25 fifth-grade students in one school, and (e) field-test of the instrument with 250 students of Grades 3-6 from one school district. A principal component analysis of field-testing data indicated that all 12 items loaded highly on a same factor. The Cronbach's coefficient alpha was 0.82.

   Suppose that a researcher is looking for a measurement instrument on seventh-grade students' conceptions of scientists, and the above reported instrument is the closest the researcher could locate from the literature. What do you suggest the researcher to do?

2. Some people state that the classical test theory for developing a measurement instrument is a bottom-up approach, while Rasch modeling for developing a measurement instrument is a top-down approach. Discuss the possible meanings of the "bottom-up" and "top-down" approaches, and evaluate the appropriateness of this statement.

3. Read the following research report that involves both Rasch modeling and CTT:

Nehm, R. H., & Schonfeld, I. S. (2008). Measuring knowledge of natural selection: A comparison of the CINS, an open-response instrument, and an oral interview. *Journal of Research in Science Teaching, 45*(10), 1131-1160.

Questions:

1. Why do three assessment methods produce different findings about the same construct?

2. How are conclusions about the validity and reliability of CINS based on Rasch modeling and CTT similar and different?

3. What can you identify to be the advantages of Rasch modeling over CTT in developing measurement instruments?

REFERENCES

Adams R.J., & Khoo, S. -T. (1998). QUEST-Version 2.1 The Interactive Test Analysis System. *Rasch Measurement Transactions 11*(4), 598.

Andrich, D. A. (1978). A rating formulation for ordered response categories. *Psychometrika, 43*, 561-573.

Andrich, D. (2004). Controversy and the Rasch model: A characteristic of incompatible paradigms? In E. V. Smith, Jr., & R. M. Smith (Eds.), *Introduction to Rasch measurement* (pp. 143-166). Maple Grove, MN: JAP Press.

Birnbaum, A. (1968). Some latent trait models and their use in inferring an examinne's ability. In F. M. Lord & M. R. Novick (Eds.), *Statistical theories of mental thest scores* (pp. 397-479). Reading, MA: Addison-Wesley.

Bond, T. G., & Fox, C. M. (2007). *Appling the Rasch model: Fundamental measurement in the human sciences*. Mahwah, NJ: Erlbaum. (Original work published 2001)

Briggs, D. C., & Wilson, M. (2004). An introduction to multidimensional measurement using Rasch models. In E. V. Smith & R. M. Smith (Eds.), *Introduction to Rasch measurement* (pp. 322-341). Maple Grove, Minnesota: JAM Press.

Embretson, S. E., & Reise, S. P. (2000). *Item response theory for psychologists*. Mahwah, NJ: Erlbaum.

Fischer, G. H., & Molenaar, I. W. (Eds.). (1995). *Rasch models: Foundations, recent developments, and applications*. New York, NY: Springer-Verlag.

Hambleton, R. K., Swaminathan, H., & Rogers, H. J. (1991). *Fundamentals of item response theory*. Thousand Oaks, CA: Sage.

Joint Committee of the American Educational Research Association, American Psychological Association, and National Council for Measurement in Education. (1999). *Standards for educational and psychological testing*. Washington, DC: American Educational Research Association.

Linacre, J. M. (1989). *Many-faceted Rasch measurement*. Chicago, IL: MESA Press.

Linacre, J. M. (1997). *Facets* (version 3.08). Chicago, IL: MESA Press.

Linacre, J. M. (2003). *Winsteps* (version 3.4). Chicago, IL: Winsteps.

Liu, X., & Boone, W. (Eds.). (2006). Introduction to Rasch measurement in science education. In *Applications of Rasch measurement in science education* (pp. 1-22). Maple Grove, MN: JAM Press.

National Research Council. (2001). *Knowing what students know: The science and design of educational assessment* (Committee on the Foundations of Assessment. J. Pellegrino, N. Chudowsky, & R. Glaser, Eds, Division on Behavioral and Social Sciences and Education). Washington, DC: National Academy Press.

Rasch, G. (1980). *Probabilistic models for some intelligence and attainment tests*. Chicago, IL: University of Chicago Press. (Original work published 1960)

Sheridan, B. (1998). RUMM item analysis package: Rasch unidimensional measurement model. *Rasch Measurement Transactions, 11*(4), 599.

Smith, R. M., Schumacker, R. E., & Bush, M. J. (1998). Using item mean squares to evaluate fit to the Rasch model. *Journal of Outcome Measurement, 2*, 66-78.

Stout, W. (1990). A new item response theory modeling approach with applications to unidimensional assessment and ability estimation. *Psychometrika, 55*, 293-326.

Thurstone, L. L. (1959). *The measurement of values*. Chicago, IL: University of Chicago Press.

Wang, W. (1997). The multidimensional random coefficients multinomial logit model. *Applied Psychological Measurement, 21*, 1-23.

Wilson, M. (2005). *Constructing measures: An item response modeling approach*. Hillsdale, NJ: Erlbaum.

Wright, B. D. (1977). Misunderstanding the Rasch model. *Journal of Educational Measurement, 14*(3), 219-225.

Wright, B. D. (1999). Fundamental measurement for psychology. In S. E. Embretson & S. L. Hershberger (Eds.), *The new rules of measurement: What every educator and psychologist should know*. Hillsdale, NJ: Erlbaum.

Wright, B. D., & Masters, G. N. (1982). *Rating scale analysis*. Chicago, IL: MESA Press.

Wright, B. D., & Tennant A. (1996). Sample size again. *Rasch Measurement Transactions, 9*(4), 468.

Wu, M. L., Adams, R. J., & Wilson, M. (1997). *Conquest: Generalized item response modeling software—Manual*. Melbourne: Australian Council for Educational Research.

CHAPTER 3

USING AND DEVELOPING INSTRUMENTS FOR MEASURING CONCEPTUAL UNDERSTANDING

This chapter is concerned with conceptual understanding. Conceptual understanding is one of the primary objectives of science education, thus a common domain of measurement. Various theoretical frameworks about conceptual understanding are available. This chapter will first review these frameworks. It will then introduce standardized instruments for measuring conceptual understanding. Finally, this chapter will describe the process to developing new instruments for measuring conceptual understanding using the Rasch modeling approach.

WHAT IS CONCEPTUAL UNDERSTANDING?

The Webster's Encyclopedic Dictionary of the English Language defines *understanding* as "the ability to understand; the act of one who understands." It further defines *understand* as "to seize the meaning of; to be thoroughly acquainted with; expert in the use of practice of; to form a reasoned judgment concerning (something); to possess a passive knowledge of (a language); to appreciate and sympathize with; to gather and

Using and Developing Measurement Instruments in Science Education:
A Rasch Modeling Approach, pp. 67–108
Copyright © 2010 by Information Age Publishing

infer; to interpret, attribute a specified meaning to; to accept as fact, believe; to supply mentally (a word, idea, etc.); to have the power of seizing meanings, forming reasoned judgments etc; to feel and show sympathy, tolerance etc." Thus, understanding is primarily an act. In order to demonstrate understanding, an individual needs to perform or go through a process.

Wiggins and McTighe (2005) propose *six facets of understanding:* explanation, interpretation, application, perspective, empathy, and self-knowledge; all the six facets imply actions. According to Liu's (2009a, pp. 22-23) elaboration of the six facets, *explanation* is a person's ability to provide knowledgeable and justifiable accounts of events, actions, and ideas. An example of explanation is that the earth's tilt on its axis causes the season changes. *Interpretation* provides meanings of events or objects through narratives or translations. For example, an elementary student interprets the earth's season change by describing how hot the summer is and how cold the winter is. *Application* is the ability to use knowledge effectively in a new situation to solve a problem. For example, a middle school student uses his knowledge of simple circuits to find a faulty light bulb in a device. *Perspectives* are the ability to appreciate different points of views. For example, a student can see how a classmate made a mistake in solving a problem balancing a chemical reaction equation. *Empathy* is the ability to understand another person's feelings and worldviews. You may not agree with another person, but you respect the person's views and can feel how the person strongly holds the views. For example, you share the feeling of the environmental activists in their efforts to protect endangered animals, but may not necessarily agree with some of their extreme actions. Finally, *self-knowledge* is a person's ability to identify his/her own weaknesses and to actively seek improvement. For example, some students are better than others in self-evaluating their own learning and better able to look for additional resources to improve their learning. The six facets of understanding can function independently; however, the more facets a person's understanding involves, the better.

Besides the above conception of understanding, which is primarily process-oriented, researchers have also described understanding to be a mental state. For example, Mintzes and Wandersee (1998) define *understanding as meanings* that are (a) resonant with or shared with others; (b) without internal contradictions; (c) without extraneous or unnecessary propositions; and (d) justified by the conceptual and methodological standards of the prevailing scientific paradigm. Therefore, Mintzes and Wandersee's notion of understanding focuses mainly on the epistemological status of knowledge.

A both process- and state-oriented view about understanding is proposed by White and Gunstone (1992). White and Gunstone suggest that there can be six elements in which understanding of concepts may be stored and retrieved from long-term memory; they are proposition, string, image, episode, intellectual skill, and motor skill. Liu (2009a, p. 23) provides an elaboration of those six elements. *Propositions* are facts, opinions and beliefs. For example, the earth is one of the planets of the solar system. Facts, opinions, and beliefs, although distinct, may not be necessarily differentiable in student alternative conceptions. For example, students may think that it is a fact that plants take food from the soil, but this statement is only a personal belief that is scientifically incorrect. *Strings* are fundamental statements or generalizations that do not vary from situation to situation. Strings are usually in the form of proverbs, laws, and rules. For example, that matter can not be created or destroyed, thus is conserved, is a string, but that water is matter is a proposition. *Images* are mental representations of sensory perceptions. For example, a clear lake is an image of water. *Episodes* are memories of events experienced directly or vicariously. For example, swimming in a lake is an episode of the buoyancy force. *Intellectual skills* are mental processes performed to solve a problem or conduct a task. For example, comparing the differences between physical change and chemical change involves an intellectual skill of differentiation. Finally, *motor skills* are procedures followed to conduct a physical task. An example of motor skills is performing a measurement. Six elements of understanding are located in different regions of long-term memory; they may require difficult mental processes to access. A person may possess understanding as an episode, while another person may possess understanding as a proposition or string. The more elements of understanding a person possesses, the better the person's understanding.

All the above notions of understanding are general; conceptual understanding in science is also domain specific. There are various ways of defining domains of science, which is the task of a science content standard. For example, the document of *National Science Education Standards* (National Research Council, 1996) divides science content into three domains: the physical science, life science, and earth and space science. For the domain of physical science, students from K-4 are expected to understand properties of objects and materials, position and motion of objects, and light, heat, electricity, and magnetism. From Grade 5 to 8, students are expected to understand properties and changes of properties in matter, motions and forces, and transfer of energy. From Grade 9 to 12, students are expected to understand the structure of atoms, structure and properties of matter, chemical reactions, motions and forces, conservation of energy and increase in disorder, and interactions of energy and matter. For the domain of life science, at Grades K to 4, students are expected to understand characteristics of organisms, life cycles of organisms, and organisms and environments. From Grade 5 to 8, students are expected to understand the structure and function in living systems, reproduction and heredity, regulation and behavior, populations and ecosystems, diversity and adaptations of organisms. For Grade 9 to 12, students are expected to understand the cell, molecular basis of heredity, biological evolution, interdependence of organisms, matter, energy, and organization in living systems, and behavior of organisms. For the domain of earth and space science, at Grades K to 4, students are expected to understand the properties of earth materials, objects in the sky, and changes in earth and sky. From Grade 5 to 8, students are expected to understand the structure of the earth system, earth's history, and earth in the solar system. From Grade 9 to 12, students are expected to understand energy in the earth system, geochemical cycles, origin and evolution of the earth system, and origin and evolution of the universe. Measuring students' understanding of the above topics requires first of all a clear definition of types and levels of understanding on each of them, and use of appropriate assessment formats or tasks to solicit student understanding.

Consistent with the above conceptualizations that highlight three characteristics of conceptual understanding, that is, process-oriented, state-oriented, and domain specific, the revised Bloom's taxonomy of learning outcomes in the cognitive domain (Anderson & Krathwohl, 2001) consists of two dimensions, one dimension for types of knowledge and another for cognitive process skills. The *types of knowledge* include factual knowledge, conceptual knowledge, procedure knowledge, and meta-cognitive knowledge. The *cognitive process skills* include: (a) remember, (b) understand, (c) apply, (d) analyze, (e) evaluate, and (f) create. The *knowledge* in the original Bloom's taxonomy developed in the 1950s is elaborated into *factual knowledge* (content) and *remembering* (cognitive skill). Further, the *synthesis* in the original taxonomy has now become *create* and the highest cognitive skill in the revised taxonomy. Table 3.1 summarizes the meanings of the revised Bloom's taxonomy.

We can see that the revised Bloom's taxonomy defines "understand" in a specific way, narrower than that defined by Wiggins and McTighe (2005). It seems that the entire cognitive domain of the revised Bloom's taxonomy is conceptual understanding in the sense by Wiggins and McTighe.

INSTRUMENTS FOR MEASURING CONCEPTUAL UNDERSTANDING

A variety of standardized measurement instruments related to conceptual understanding are available in science education. Liu (2009b) has

Table 3.1.   Revised Bloom's Taxonomy: Cognitive Dimension

1. Remembering—Retrieve relevant knowledge from long-term memory.
1.1 Recognizing
1.2 Recalling

2. Understand—Construct meaning from instructional messages, including oral, written, and graphic communication.
2.1 Interpreting
2.2 Exemplifying
2.3 Classifying
2.4 Summarizing
2.5 Inferring
2.6 Comparing
2.7 Explaining

3. Apply—Carry out or use a procedure in a given situation
3.1 Executing
3.2 Implementing

4. Analyze—Break material into its constituent parts and determine how the parts related to one another and to an overall structure or purpose.
4.1 Differentiating
4.2 Organizing
4.3 Attributing

5. Evaluate—Make judgments based on criteria and standards
5.1 Checking
5.2 Critiquing

6. Create—Put elements together to form a coherent or functional whole; reorganize elements into a new pattern or structure.
6.1 Generating
6.2 Planning
6.3 Producing

Source: Anderson and Krathwohl (2001).

reviewed standardized measurement instruments developed by researchers in North America and published in refereed journals over the past 50 years (pp. 650-654). The following summative descriptions expand Liu's review by including instruments developed outside North America and most recently published instruments. The majority of the instruments have been developed based on CTT. They are for various intended uses and based on various theoretical frameworks of conceptual understanding. Please note, the following descriptions of the instruments are for readers' information only; whether or not a science education researcher will choose an instrument for a particular research question requires a critical review of the instrument by the researcher, which is beyond the scope of this book.

Misconceptions Test (Doran, 1972)

This instrument contains 77 multiple-choice items, covering eight types of misconceptions on the particle theory of matter. The target population is elementary students (i.e., Grades 2-6). Average item difficulty ranges from .39 to .89 across types of misconceptions. Mean point-biserial correlation as a measure of item discrimination ranged from .26 to .54. Pilot testing found that there was a statistically significant correlation between misconception scores and science achievement scores. Internal consistency reliability coefficients for the eight subtests were from .39 to .89 (adjusted to the 50-item length); and the alpha coefficient was .49 for all items together.

Misconception Identification Test (MIT) (Wheeler & Kass, 1978)

MIT contains 30 multiple-choice items for identifying high school chemistry students' misconceptions on chemical equilibrium. Each item asks students to predict the effect of changing certain variables, for example, temperature, pressure, and concentration, on the equilibrium conditions of selected chemical systems. The responses for all the questions are uniform, which include: (a) greater than at the first equilibrium, (b) less than at the first equilibrium, (c) the same as at the first equilibrium, and (d) insufficient evidence provided to decide. The test also asks students to write free responses to account for their reasoning of the predictions for five randomly chosen items. Two scores are obtained: (a) a performance score based on correct responses and (b) a misconception score based on certain misconceptions. Misconception scores were found to be statistically significantly related to students' performance on Piagetian formal operational tasks. KR-20 was found to be .57 for misconception scores.

What Do You Know About Photosynthesis and Respiration? (P&P) (Haslam & Treagust, 1987)

P&P is a 13-item, two-tiered, multiple-choice instrument for measuring secondary school (Grades 8 to 12) students' alternative conceptions on photosynthesis and respiration. The development of the instrument followed the following process: (a) description of science content in terms of propositional knowledge statements and concept maps, (b) development of items based on interviews, open-ended pencil-and-paper tests, and related literature, (c) the development of two-tiered test items. A series of five pilot-studies were conducted to validate the instrument. The Cronbach's coefficient alpha was 0.72. Item difficulties ranged from 0.12 to 0.78 with a mean of 0.38. Discrimination indices ranged from 0.36 to 0.60

with a mean of 0.48. There was a statistically significant difference among grade levels in student correct answers; there was no statistically significant gender difference and interaction effects between gender and grade level.

Physical Changes Concepts Test (PCCT) (Haidar & Abraham, 1991)

PCCT measures high school students' conceptions about dissolution, diffusion, effusion, and states of matter, as well as students' use of the particulate theory in their responses to questions about these concepts. It consists of two forms: The application form (A form) and the theoretical form (T form). The A form tests students' ability to utilize the concepts in everyday-life situations using everyday language. The T form tests students' scientific knowledge about these concepts using scientific language. In the T form, items cue students to use such terms as atoms and/or molecules. Validation involved reviews of items by science education professors and chemistry professors. Pilot-testing found that students' formal reasoning ability and their preexisting knowledge were associated with their conceptions and use of the particulate theory. Also, there was a statistically significant difference between students' applied and theoretical knowledge.

Force Concept Inventory (FCI) (Hestenes, Wells, & Swackmaher, 1992)

FCI contains 30 multiple-choice questions that require a forced choice between Newtonian concepts and common-sense alternatives. The FCI questions are based on analysis of interviews of students from ninth grade to university undergraduate and graduate physics majors. About half of the questions in the FCI came directly from another similar diagnostic test called Mechanics Diagnostic Test. The authors interviewed 20 students and found that students gave very similar responses to FCI questions as to previous diagnostic questions.

Test of Understanding Graphs in Kinematics (TUG-K) (Beichner, 1994)

TUG-K is for assessing high school and university students' understanding of graphs related to kinematics. Expert panels reviewed the list of objectives to be assessed, such as "given position-time graph, students will determine velocity." Three items were written for each objective. Open-ended questions were given to a small group of students first; common errors were used to create distracters. The instrument was revised a number of times based on pilot-tests with both high school and college students. Item discrimination index was >.30 for all items (average .36). KR-20 reliability coefficient was .83.

Diffusion and Osmosis Test (DOT) (Odom & Barrow, 1995)

DOT is a 12-item two-tiered multiple-choice test for measuring college introductory biology students' alternative conceptions of diffusion and osmosis. Correct responses to both tiers of a question are necessary to score a credit for the question. Validation of the test involved 240 students enrolled in a freshman biology laboratory course. Discrimination indices of the 12 items ranged from .2 to .69 with an average discrimination index of .45. Item difficulty indices ranged from .20 to .99 with an average difficulty of .53. Split-half internal consistency after the Spearman-Brown correction was .74. Post instruction test results showed that biology majors scored much higher than nonbiology majors.

Force and Motion Conceptual Evaluation (FMCE) (Thornton & Sokoloff, 1998)

FMCE is a 43-item multiple-choice test for university introductory physics students' alternative conceptions. Content validity was claimed to be high based on the fact that a group of physics professors reviewed the initial questions and considered them to be appropriate. Pre- and post-test results showed that 70%-90% of students answered questions from the Newtonian perspective at the end of the term after completing a reformed physics course, while only less than 20% of students did so at the end of a traditional physics course, suggesting that FMCE was very sensitive to new approaches to teaching physics for understanding.

Astronomy Diagnostic Test (ADT) (Hufnagel, Slater, Deming, Adams, Adrian, Brick, & Zeilik, 2000)

ADT, version 2, is a 21-question multiple-choice test, plus 12 additional demographic questions. Questions for ADT were mainly from two sources: the Project START Astronomy Concept Inventory (Sadler, 1998) and the Misconceptions Measure developed by one of the authors (Zeilik). The development of ADT 2.0 went through multiple cycles of pilot-testing and statistical analysis through the Collaboration for Astronomy Education Research (CAER), a multiinstitutional collaborative across the United States. Pilot-testing institutions included public and private 2-year and 4-year colleges, and public and private research universities. A database of the precourse ADT scores from 22 classes is also available to download from the website for comparison studies.

The Conceptual Survey of Electricity and Magnetism (CSEM)
(Maloney, O'Kuma, Kieggelke, & Heuvelen, 2001)

CSEM is a 32-item multiple-choice question test for 2-year college introductory physics students. The instrument went through three revisions based on trials and feedback. The final version included the questions related to the following topics: change distribution on conductors/insulators; Coulomb's force law; electric force and field superposition; force caused by an electric field; work, electric potential, field and force; induced charge and electric field; magnetic force; magnetic field caused by a current; magnetic field superposition; Faraday's law; and Newton's third law. Item difficulties ranged from .1 to a little over .8; item discriminations ranged from .1 to .55. Factor analysis revealed 11 main factors. KR-20 reliability coefficient was .75.

Conceptual Inventory of Natural Selection (CINS)
(Anderson, Fisher, & Norman, 2002)

CINS is a 20-item multiple-choice test for assessing pre- and post-instruction knowledge of university biology nonmajors and preinstruction knowledge of majors. The test items are based on actual scientific studies of natural selection. The difficulty of test items ranged from .15 to .81, with an average difficulty index of .46. The item discriminations indicated by point-biserial correlation ranged from .16 to .52. The principal component analysis suggested seven interpretable factors, with all the 20 items (except one) having a significant loading on one factor. The seven factors accounted for 53% of total variance. There was also a positive correlation between student scores on CINS and on interviews. KR-20 was .58 and .64 based on two samples of students.

Nehm and Schonfeld (2008) conducted additional validation of CINS. They found that CINS scores were statistically significantly correlated with student scores on both an open-ended survey and an oral interview of natural selection, providing additional evidence for the convergent validity. Discriminant validity was claimed based on statistically non-significant correlation with student test scores on an earth science achievement. Rasch modeling on student responses to CINS items showed that all items had a good fit with the unidimensional Rasch model, although principal component factor analysis still found 8 factors with 10 items loaded on the first factor. The instrument was overall easier for the biology-major students because about 15% of the sample had abilities above the most difficult item. They also found that although CINS contained significantly more alternative conceptions represented by the distracters, CINS could only identify 75% of the alternative conceptions noted by the open-ended survey, while the open-ended survey could reveal a similar variety of student alternative conceptions.

Chemistry Concept Inventory (CCI) (Mulford & Robinson, 2002)

CCI includes 22 multiple-choice questions. It covers all key concepts typically taught in a first-semester college chemistry course. Graduate chemistry students scored almost perfect on the test. Chemical education researchers determined the questions to be appropriate for first-year chemistry students. Interviews with a limited number of students also confirmed that they interpreted and responded to the questions as intended. The Cronbach's alpha based on the pretest results of 928 students was .704, and .716 on the posttest.

Symbolic, Application, Particulate Test (SAP) (Bunce & Gabel, 2002)

SAP is a 30-question multiple-choice test measuring students' understanding of major chemistry topics/concepts including states of matter, density, mixture/substance, conservation of mass, reaction type, moles, chemical reaction, solution, neutralization, and pH. There are three questions for each concept topic, with one related to the macroscopic representation, one related to symbolic representation, and one related to submicroscopic/particulate representation. KR-20 for SAP was 0.76.

Testing Students' Use of the Particulate Theory (TSUPT)
(Williamson, Huffman, & Peck, 2004)

TSUPT is a 36-item primarily constructed-response question test for university introductory chemistry courses. The questions followed the same format and content scope as *PCCT* (Haidar & Abraham, 1991). Six questions test each of the following concepts: (a) dissolution, (b) insolubility, (c) saturation, (d) diffusion, (e) states of matter, and (f) effusion. Two questions come directly from PCCT, and four are new. The six questions form a progression from everyday knowledge to more scientific knowledge by using scientific terms (molecules, atoms, particles, etc.). An independent evaluator randomly scored selected responses; interrater reliability was found to be 90%.

Determining and Interpreting Resistive Electric Circuit Concepts Test (DIRECT)
(Engelhardt & Beichner, 2004)

DIRECT is a 29-item multiple-choice question test for both high school and university introductory physics students on the understanding of direct current electric circuits. The multiple choices for each item are based on students' open-ended answers. Multiple cycles of expert review, pilot-testing with a large number of students across the country, and revision took place over the years. The discrimination index ranged from 0 to .43 with an average of .24; item-total correlation ranged from .07 to .46 with an average of .33; and difficulty ranged from .15 to .89 with an average of .49. No statistically significant difference in scores was found between university and high school students, but there was a statistically significant difference between male and female students. Factor analysis revealed 11 factors. KR-20 reliability coefficient was .70.

Brief Electricity and Magnetism Assessment (BEMA)
(Ding, Chabay, Sherwood, & Beichner, 2006)

BEMA is a 30-item multiple-choice test for college-level calculus-based introductory physics courses. Selected college faculty members reviewed the initial questions. A small number of students answered the questions with both the multiple-choice and short-answer formats. Students' common errors were used to construct the next version of the multiple-choice test. The draft instrument was then pilot-tested and revised. Item difficulty averaged .37, item discrimination averaged .34, and point biserial coefficient averaged .45. KR-20 reliability coefficient was .85.

The Geoscience Concept Inventory (GCI) (Libarkin & Anderson, 2006)

GCI is a multiple-choice test developed for use in entry-level college earth science courses. It contains 73 questions. These questions cover topics related to general physical geology concepts, as well as underlying fundamental ideas in physics and chemistry, such as gravity and radioactivity. All questions are based on interviews of students' alterative conceptions. Data used to validate the inventory came from a wide range of institutions representing entry-level college students nationwide. Rasch measurement was used to construct the inventory and to establish indices of validity and reliability. Although there are 73 questions in the inventory, it is not necessary to use all of them; instead one set of 15 questions may be used by following the suggestions to ensure appropriate composition of questions in order to provide equivalent content coverage and difficulty distribution to that using the entire inventory.

Quantum Physics Conceptual Survey (QPCS)
(Wuttiprom, Sharma, Johnston, Chitaree, & Soankwan, 2009)

QPCS is a 25-item multiple-choice test on university students' understanding of quantum physics. The initial development of QPCS included analysis of the syllabuses from eight universities in Thailand, consultation with physicists, and analysis of a group of postgraduate physics education students' responses to a physics exam. Four themes were found to be fundamental in underlying quantum physics: waves and particles, de Broglie wavelength, double slit interference, and the uncertainty principle. Wave function was dropped from the QPCS because introductory physics course students would not have studied this area yet. Further consultation with physics education researchers resulted in the addition of one more theme—the photoelectric effect.

The initial draft survey was administered to various groups of students, including experts at a university in Australia. Validation and revision of the items involved a Delphi study. The experts in the Delphi study were a group of five physicists who had more than 20 years experience, each in teaching physics. They met as a group each week for several weeks until they found no inconsistencies or unwarranted omissions left in the proposed survey questions. The experts agreed that the questions were all topics important to introductory quantum physics, and that the wording was unambiguous, with little cause for misunderstanding.

The main validation study took place in Australia. Item difficulties for the items ranged from slightly above 0.2 to slightly above 0.9, with most items around 0.3-0.7. The majority of the items (20 questions) had a discrimination index of 0.3 or greater and the average discrimination index was 0.35. KR-20 test reliability index for QPCS was 0.97.

Commentary

The most important consideration when choosing a measurement instrument is evaluation of the measured construct of conceptual understanding. Different instruments may define understanding in quite different ways; thus it is important to ensure the appropriateness of the defined conceptual understanding for the intended uses. This evaluation is essentially an issue of construct validity. Once the measured construct of conceptual understanding is deemed appropriate, the next consideration is the intended population of the measurement instrument. An instrument validated for one population may not be valid for a different population. Only after the evaluation of the above two issues, can the focus of instrument evaluation then shift to reported technical properties of items (e.g., item difficulty and discrimination) and the instrument (e.g., content validity, criterion-related validity, reliability, etc.).

Given that there can be a variety of different ways of establishing validity and reliability, it is important to examine the relevance of reported validity and reliability evidence to your intended use of the instrument. For example, an instrument validated through its ability to predict students' performances on a state test may not necessarily be appropriate for its use as a diagnostic test because the validity of a diagnostic test should more appropriately be established through the instrument's ability to assist in planning instruction. Similarly, if the reported reliability is solely based on the internal consistency (e.g., Cronbach's alpha), and your intended use is a repeated measurement of the targeted conceptual understanding for a same sample, then test-retest reliability should be expected.

Most of the above described instruments for assessing conceptual understanding are diagnostic tests. Diagnostic tests focus on analysis of students' selections of incorrect responses, and the analysis is typically done on the individual item level. If a diagnostic test is used for summative assessment for which analysis is typically based on total scores, then it is important to examine the evidence of unidimensionality—all items of the instrument measure the same construct. Evidence for unidimensionality is typically established based on findings of factor analysis. If no evidence for unidimensionality is reported, then a summative use of the instrument may be questionable. For example, Huffman and Heller (1995) found that fewer than six FCI items converged on any single factor, and that different samples produced different factor patterns, indicating lack of unidimensionality of FCI. If this is the case, then using total scores of FCI for summative assessment may be questionable. Some authors of diagnostic instruments explicitly warn against uses of diagnostic instruments beyond the diagnosing purpose. For example, Hufnagel et al. (2000) stated about ADT 2.0, a diagnostic test for astronomy concepts, that

> the ADT should *not* be used as a graded test, or to assess the abilities of individual students. It cannot reliably assess any one concept, as that would require multiple questions on one concept. It also may not predict student course success for a number of reasons.... The ADT is not intended to guide content selection, nor does it represent a fair sample of typical course content. (Hugnagel et al., 2000, p. 155).

If an instrument does not entirely meet your selection criteria, you may decide to modify the instrument and go through a validation process to establish its validity and reliability. It is common that an instrument does not meet all the criteria or conditions of an intended use, and it is necessary for researchers to further validate the instrument to justify its new use. One the other hand, because statistics based on CTT are always sample-dependent, and in many cases the samples used for validation are local or convenient samples, it is always necessary to continue validating an instrument even if it meets your selection criteria.

DEVELOPING INSTRUMENTS FOR MEASURING
CONCEPTUAL UNDERSTANDING

Identify the Primary Purpose(s) for Which
the Test Scores Will Be Used

The very first step in developing a standardized instrument for measuring conceptual understanding is to clearly identify the purpose for which the measurement instrument will be used. Stating clearly intended uses of the standardized measurement instruments not only helps users decide appropriate uses of the instrument, but also guides the development of the standardized measurement instrument. One way to think about the intended uses of the standardized measurement instrument is the timing of its use during instruction. There are three possible uses of measurement instruments: diagnostic test, formative test, and summative test. A diagnostic test measures students' conceptual understanding of a specific concept or topic in order to better plan for instruction. For example, it is important to understand student alternative conceptions when planning effective science teaching. A diagnostic use of a measurement instrument requires the instrument to be sensitive to specific areas of student misunderstanding when planning for instruction. A formative use of a measurement instrument requires the instrument to be able to differentiate different stages of conceptual understanding. Finally, a summative use of a standardized measurement instrument requires the instrument to be directly relevant to a targeted set of learning objectives. Of course, it is possible that a measurement instrument may be used for all the above three purposes. Generally speaking, the more diverse the intended uses are, the more complex the measurement instrument development process (e.g., validation) will be.

Another way to think about the potential uses of a standardized measurement instrument is in terms of criterion-referenced score interpretation or norm-referenced score interpretation. A criterion-referenced use of a measurement instrument is to use a test score to infer how a student may have understood a particular concept or topic that is found in the curriculum. A norm-referenced use of a measurement instrument is to use a test score to infer how a student is compared to other students in terms of conceptual understanding. Although it is not impossible to develop a measurement instrument for both of the above purposes, a better measurement instrument is the one that is clearly intended for one of the purposes. This is because development of a criterion-referenced standardized measurement can be very different from that of a norm-referenced standardized measurement instrument in terms of such aspects as item writing, test assembly, validation and so on. As discussed later, sometimes the requirements from criterion-referenced and norm-referenced uses are incompatible.

When stating the intended uses of the measurement instrument, it is also important to clearly identify the target population. This is because different populations have different abilities and expectations in terms of conceptual understanding; an instrument intended for elementary school students is certainly not appropriate for secondary school students. Of course, it is possible that an instrument can be intended for both elementary and secondary school students, but this instrument may not be expected to be relevant to university students.

Define the Construct to Be Measured

In order to develop an instrument to measure conceptual understanding of a concept, it is necessary to explicitly identify the construct and define it. The construct for a conceptual understanding measurement instrument is the understanding of a specific science concept, such as understanding of forces, understanding of evolution, and so forth. Because there are various theories about understanding, it is necessary to adopt a theory about understanding before a definition of the construct is developed. For example, if the revised Bloom's taxonomy is adopted as a framework of understanding and the measurement target is the concept of mechanical forces, then a two-dimensional table defining the construct of understanding of mechanical forces may be developed. The content dimension may consist of such topics as vectors and scalars, linear motion, projectile motion, circular motion, and springs. The cognitive dimension may consist of remembering, interpreting, and explaining. The next consideration is describing the internal hierarchy among specific elements of understanding. Because the purpose of developing a measurement instrument of conceptual understanding is to differentiate different levels of conceptual understanding among the target student population, there must be a theory suggesting which specific elements of understanding are more advanced and which specific elements of understanding are more primitive. For example, in terms of conceptual understanding of mechanic forces, a hierarchy of understanding may be conceptualized as follows (Figure 3.1).

Figure 3.1 suggests that students' understanding of mechanic forces can be differentiated along a linear dimension from remembering or recognizing different types of forces (gravitational, centripetal, mechanical, magnetic, etc.) to explaining various motions (e.g., linear, projectile, circular, spring, etc.). This defined construct explains difficulty levels of

```
┌────────────────────────────────────────────────────────────┐
│                                                            ▲   │
│              Explaining motions                            │   │
│                                                            │   │
│         Representing forces using diagrams                 │   │
│                                                            │   │
│            Interpreting force diagrams                     │   │
│                                                            │   │
│   Defferentiate Newtown's first, second and third laws     │   │
│                                                            │   │
│        Remembering types of forces and motions             │   │
└────────────────────────────────────────────────────────────┘
```

Figure 3.1.   A hierarchy of elements in mechanical forces understanding. The hierarchy is unidimensional from least competence at the bottom to most competent on the top.

assessment items and students' understanding levels, which will guide subsequent stages of the measurement instrument development.

Identify Behaviors That Represent the Construct

Based on the defined construct, the domain of the measurement target will then be defined. The domain of the measurement target is what the instrument will cover; it consists of specific observable behaviors subjects will exhibit. For example, the domain of students' conceptual understanding of the concept of mechanical forces may be defined as students' abilities to answer questions related to kinematics, Newton's first law, second law, and third law, the superposition principle, and kinds of forces.

Stating the observable behaviors of students in terms of the measurement target does not mean that the instrument will measure all the behaviors. One approach commonly taken in developing measurement instruments is domain sampling. That is, what a measurement instrument measures is a representative sample of the universe of behaviors that define the measurement target. Since it is impossible for any measurement instrument to measure all the behaviors of a target, if the measured behaviors are representative of all possible behaviors, then the instrument can still be used to make valid inferences about students' conceptual understanding of the target.

Take the concept of mechanical forces as an example again. If the measurement instrument is for diagnostic uses, then the universe of student behaviors should consist of all the known students' preconceptions or misconceptions that a given population of students typically demonstrate and are important to consider during curriculum and instructional planning.

This universe of students' preconceptions may be identified through a comprehensive review of the literature on students' alternative conceptions of forces. This results in a list of students' alternative conceptions related to such aspects as kinematics, Newton's first law, second law, and third law, the superposition principle, and kinds of forces.

However, if the intended use of the instrument is summative, then the domain of student behaviors for understanding of forces will be quite different. One possible way to define the domain is to analyze the expected content standards. In the content standards, the expected students' understanding of forces may be already specified. For example, the New York physics core curriculum specifies the expected students' conceptual understanding of forces in terms of the following observable behaviors:

Explain and predict different patterns of motion of objects (e.g., linear and uniform circular motion, velocity and acceleration, momentum and inertia).

1. Construct and interpret graphs of position, velocity, or acceleration versus time.
2. Determine and interpret slopes and areas of motion graphs.
3. Determine the acceleration due to gravity near the surface of earth.
4. Determine the resultant of two or more vectors graphically or algebraically.
5. Draw scaled force diagrams using a ruler and a protractor.
6. Resolve a vector into perpendicular components both graphically and algebraically.
7. Sketch the theoretical path of a projectile.
8. Use vector diagrams to analyze mechanical systems (equilibrium and nonequilibrium).
9. Verify Newton's Second Law for linear motion.
10. Determine the coefficient of friction for two surfaces.
11. Verify Newton's Second Law for uniform circular motion.
12. Verify conservation of momentum.
13. Determine a spring constant. (The University of the State of New York, 1996, p. 26)

If the intended use of the measurement instrument is formative, then the above identified universe of student behaviors may not be enough, because they do not reflect the progression of student learning. One possible description of such a learning progression is as follows:

Facet Cluster on Forces

00 Students can identify forces on an object and compare their relative sizes.
    01 Students can identify the sources of forces on an object.

02 Students can correctly identify the direction a force is acting.

03 Students can compare the relative sizes of forces on static objects.

40 The student reports that objects cannot exert forces along or parallel to its surface.

50 For an object at rest or moving horizontally, the student believes the downward force is greater than the upward force.

60 The student believes that force is a property of an object and its size is indicated by the magnitude of other properties of the object.

61 If an object has more mass than another object, it also has more force.

62 If an object is more active (moves faster) than another object, it also has more force.

70 The student reports an energy source as a force.

71 The engine or battery exerts a force on the object.

80 The student believes that passive objects cannot exert a force even though they touch another object.

81 For an object at rest on a surface (e.g., a book on a table), the surface (e.g., table) does not exert an upward force.

82 Passive objects (e.g., ropes) connecting two other objects do not exert forces, but instead transmit the active force. (For example, in the situation of a person pulling on a rope connected to a cart, the student identifies the person as exerting the force on the cart, not the rope).

90 The student believes that motion determines the existence of a force or forces.

91 If an object is moving there is a "force of motion".

92 When the "force of motion" runs out, the object will stop.

93 If an object is not moving, no forces are involved in the situation. (Diagnoser Tool, n.d.)

In the above facet cluster on force, explicit learning goals and various intermediate understandings, that is, different sorts of reasoning, conceptual, and procedural difficulties, form a learning progression. Each cluster contains the intuitive ideas students have as they move toward scientifically accurate learning targets. Each facet has a two-digit number. The 0X and 1X facets are the learning targets. The facets that begin with the numbers 2X through 9X indicate ideas that have more problematic aspects. In general, higher facet numbers (e.g., 9X, 8X, 7X) are the more problematic facets. The X0's indicate more general statements of student ideas. Often these are followed by more specific examples, which are coded X1 through X9. Therefore, nine categories of student performances are differentiated in this example. The nine categories may define the universe of student behaviors of conceptual understanding of force.

Similarly, for criterion-referenced and norm-referenced uses, the universe of student behaviors for a measurement instrument of conceptual understanding need to be defined accordingly. No matter for what use the measurement instrument will be, the universe of student behaviors should be defined in operational terms. Operationally defined domain is better to inform the development and validation of the measurement instrument.

Prepare a Test Specification

Once the measurement domain is defined, a sample of the domain, that is, what the measurement instrument will cover, will then be defined as a table of test specification. A table of test specification is also called a test blueprint. It consists of a topic dimension and a cognitive reasoning dimension. Because there may be different emphases given to different topics and different cognitive reasoning skills, it is necessary to assign different weights to different combinations of topics and cognitive reasoning skills. The above three components, that is, topic, cognitive reasoning skills, and weight, form a table of test specification. Table 3.2 is a sample table of test specification.

A table of test specification like Table 3.2 indicates two important aspects about the measurement domain: (a) what to assess (the intersections between rows and columns), and (b) how much emphasis (the cell values). In the example of Table 3.2, we see that the measurement will cover five topics: vectors and scalars, linear motion, projectile motion, circular motion, and spring; the above topics of content involve three cognitive reasoning skills: remembering, interpreting, and explaining. The cell values are determined by the product between weights of the corresponding topic and skill. The procedure for creating such a table is as follows: (a) identify topics to be assessed and their relative emphases in percentages—defining the rows; (b) identify cognitive skills expected and their relative emphases in percentages—defining the columns; (c) calculate the cell values by multiplying the row percentage by the column percentage; and (d) make adjustment to cell values to ensure that the total of cell values is equal to 100%.

A table of test specification intends to provide guidance in the next step—constructing items. In order for the specification to be more informative, a more detailed table of specification including type of items and

Table 3.2 A Sample Table of Test Specification on Forces

		Remembering	*Interpreting*	*Explaining*	
Weight (%)		*50%*	*30%*	*20%*	*Subtotal (%)*
Vectors and scalars	20%	10	6	4	20
Linear motion	30%	15	9	6	30
Projectile motion	15%	7.5	4.5	3	15
Circular motion	20%	10	6	4	20
Spring	15%	7.5	4.5	3	15
Subtotal (%)		50	30	20	100%

Table 3.3.   A Sample Table of Test Specification With Type of Items and Total Points

	Remembering	*Interpreting*	*Explaining*	
Number of Items (Points)	*Multiple-Choice*	*Short Constructed-Response*	*Extended Constructed-Response*	*Subtotal*
Vectors and scalars	5 (5)	2 (3)		
Linear motion	8 (8)	2 (4)		
Projectile motion	4 (4)	1 (2)	2 (10)	
Circular motion	5 (5)	1 (3)		
Spring	4 (4)	1 (2)		
Subtotal	26 (26)	7 (14)	2 (10)	35 (50)

total point of the instrument may be developed. Table 3.3 is a more detailed table of test specification.

Table 3.3 is derived from Table 3.2. It assumes a total of 50 points for the entire instrument. From Table 3.3 we see that the measurement instrument will include 35 items, among which 26 are multiple-choice, 7 short constructed-response, and 2 extended constructed-response questions. Each multiple-choice question is worth 1 point, each short-constructed response question is worth 1 to 3 points, and each extended constructed-response question is worth 1 to 10 points.

One important decision when developing a table of test specification like Table 3.3 is deciding the total number of items for the instrument, or test length. A general principle to follow is that a longer test is more reliable than a shorter test. The relationship between test reliability and test length is best demonstrated by the Spearman-Brown formula as follows:

$$\rho'_{xx} = L * \rho_{xx} / [1 + (L - 1) \rho_{xx}] \qquad (1)$$

Where ρ_{xx} is the reliability of the test, ρ'_{xx} is the reliability of the test when its length is increased by L times (L *may* be a fraction if the test length is to be decreased).

Therefore, a test with a reliability of 0.5 can have a reliability of 0.67 if its test length is doubled, that is, containing double its current number of items. As we know, the standard error of measurement for a measurement instrument is directly proportional to its reliability and score variance. Lord (1959) and Kleinke (1979) have shown an approximate relationship between the test length and the standard error of the measurement as follows:

$$\sigma_e = 0.43 \sqrt{K} \qquad (2)$$

$$\sigma_{e\%} = \frac{43}{\sqrt{K}} \qquad (3)$$

Where σ_e is the standard error of measurement in the raw score unit, $\sigma_{e\%}$ is the standard error of measurement in the percentage score unit, and K is the number of items in the measurement instrument. For example, a test with 30 items is expected to have a standard error of measurement of 2.4. That is, any observed total score out of 30 (assuming each item is worth 1 point) may be expected to contain an error of 2.4 points. Similarly, if the total score is in percentage, then any percentage score is expected to have a standard error of 7.9.

Construct an Initial Pool of Items and Define the Outcome Space of the Behaviors

Based on the table of test specification, a preliminary set of items may be constructed. Guidelines for writing different types of items, such as multiple choice and true-false are reviewed in chapter 1, and additional guidelines for other types of items such as constructed-response and performance assessment questions are available from other literature (e.g. Liu, 2009a). When writing items, it is important to follow the table of test specification. If a group of item writers are involved in this step, it is helpful for them to spend time discussing the table of test specification so that everyone understands what the table specifies. A sample item may be written for each of the cells, and agreed to be used as a reference for writing other items. The initial items, together with their scoring keys/rubrics, define the outcome space of subject behaviors on the measurement instrument.

Item Review

After the initial set of items are written, they should be reviewed for content accuracy, appropriateness or relevance to the test specifications, technical item-construction flaws, grammar, offensiveness or appearance of "bias", and level of readability (Crocker & Algina, 1986). Given the breadth of item review, a panel of experts is needed. The item review panel should possess a combination of expertise that includes content, pedagogy and measurement. The content expert is best suited to review the content accuracy of items; the pedagogy expert is best suited to review the appropriateness of items for the target population, and the measurement expert is best suited to review technical soundness of items. Additional experts may also be asked to review for other specific aspects of items such as readability and cultural bias. Item review may result in specific suggestions to revise items. Only after items have passed the item review will they then be put into pilot-testing.

Item Tryout

Once items are considered acceptable by a panel of experts, they may then be reviewed by select target students. This step is called item tryout or pilot-testing. The number of subjects involved in this step does not need to be high; 30 to 50 is adequate. One important factor in considering the sample for tryout is representativeness—how the subjects represent the variation in the target population in terms of the measurement construct. In order to obtain maximal feedback from subjects on quality of items, some additional questions may be posed to subjects to respond to as part of answering the items. For example, DeBoer, Dubois, Hermann, and Lennon (2008) used the following set of questions to accompany each item in their pilot-testing of items:

1. Is there anything about this test question that was confusing? Explain.
2. Circle any words on the test question you don't understand or aren't familiar with.

3. Is answer choice A correct?   Yes   No   Not Sure
4. Is answer choice B correct?   Yes   No   Not Sure
5. Is answer choice C correct?   Yes   No   Not Sure
6. Is answer choice D correct?   Yes   No   Not Sure

(Questions 3-6 are each followed by the statement: Explain why or why not.)

7. Did you guess? Yes No
8. Should there be any other answer choice?
9. Was the picture or graph helpful? Why or why not? [If there was no picture or graph...] Would a picture or graph be helpful?
10. Have you studied this topic in school?   Yes   No   Not Sure
11. Have you learned about it somewhere else?   Yes   No   Not Sure
    Where (TV, museum visit, etc)?

In addition to probing questions like those above, interviewing a few representative students about the items, that is, orally administering the items and asking for justification, may also be helpful. The purpose of the above processes is to obtain as much information, both qualitative and quantitative, about the processes of students answering the items in order to judge if the items operate as expected. Informal descriptive item analysis may also be conducted to get a general sense of item properties. Same as item review discussed above, item tryout may result in specific suggestions for revising the items. The revised items are then assembled in an instrument for field-testing.

Field Test of Items

After items are revised, they are then assembled into an instrument for field testing. The assembled instrument should include every element in the final form including instructions for subjects/examinees, instructions for test administrators, the entire set of items, and scoring guide. The mechanical aspects of test assembly to consider may include item ordering, item grouping, and answering format. In general, items should be grouped by major item formats, such as selected response questions, short constructed-response questions, and extended constructed response questions, and should be placed in order of increasing difficulty within each item group. For a longer test and for a population of older age (e.g., high school students and older), a separate answering sheet may be provided for students to mark on, but for a short test and for a younger population (e.g., elementary school students), answering may be done together with questions.

Field testing of items involves a larger sample of subjects than that used in the pilot-testing. One major consideration in selecting the field-testing sample is the match between the range of subjects' abilities and the range of item difficulties. The required sample size also depends on the number of items. Typically, the sample size is over 200, or 5 to 10 times as many subjects as items. Items for field testing should be assembled and presented in a format similar to that of the final instrument; thus items should not contain probing questions, as is the case in pilot-testing. The purpose of field-testing is to collect data from subjects in order to conduct Rasch modeling.

Conduct Rasch modeling

After field-testing, a data file containing subjects' responses to items is then prepared. The data file should include subjects' original response codes (e.g., A, B, C, D), not the scored points (e.g., 0, 1). The data file is then submitted to a Rasch modeling computer program to produce a series of tables and graphs that describe the degree of model-data-fit for items and the measurement instrument as a whole.

First, item fit statistics are reviewed, and potentially misfitting items are identified for possible revisions. Figure 3.2 is a portion of an output table based on a university general physics sample of students' responses to the Force Concept Inventory.

Figure shows that INFIT MNSQs, INFIT ZSTDs, and OUTFIT ZSTDs for all items are within the acceptable range, indicating that these items seem to have a good model-data-fit. However, OUTFIT MNSQs for items Q5, Q25, Q7, Q17 and Q9 are greater than 1.3, which are outside the acceptable range. Because OUTFIT MNSQs are unweighted mean residuals, these large fit statistics could be due to a few students' unusual response patterns. In addition to examining the fit statistics, PTMEA CORR (point-measure correlation) is a measure of the relationship between subjects' scores on the item and their Rasch measures; any negative correlation may signal potential misfitting as well. In order to further find out if these items are misfitting, or just simply not have been responded to normally by a few individuals, item characteristic curves (ICCs) and students' response patterns may be reviewed. Figure 3.3 is the ICC for Q5.

In Figure 3.3, the x-axis is the difference between students' ability measures and the item difficulty measure, and the y-axis is the probability of students responding to the item. The observed pattern is in scatterplots,

ENTRY NUMBER	RAW SCORE	COUNT	MEASURE	MODEL S.E.	INFIT MNSQ	ZSTD	OUTFIT MNSQ	ZSTD	PTMEA CORR.		ITEM
5	6	50	2.23	.49	1.19	.7	2.10	1.6	A	.22	Q5
25	4	50	2.81	.59	1.09	.3	1.95	1.2	B	.26	Q25
7	36	50	-1.46	.34	1.20	1.2	1.91	1.8	C	.16	Q7
17	4	50	2.81	.59	1.47	1.1	1.39	.7	D	.16	Q17
9	24	50	-.21	.32	1.21	1.6	1.40	1.5	E	.26	Q9
1	41	50	-2.13	.39	.92	-.3	1.28	.7	F	.32	Q1
2	21	50	.10	.32	1.07	.6	1.20	.9	G	.38	Q2
19	29	50	-.71	.32	1.19	1.6	1.15	.6	H	.28	Q19
29	19	50	.31	.33	1.13	.9	1.12	.6	I	.37	Q29
15	21	50	.10	.32	.98	-.1	1.11	.5	J	.45	Q15
22	24	50	-.21	.32	1.08	.7	1.07	.3	K	.38	Q22

Figure 3.2.   Sample item-fit statistics for selected FCI items. Fit statistics are within the highlighted columns. The entry number represents the item estimation order, raw score is the sum of total credits earned on the item by all examinees, count is the total number of responses by examinees, measure is the Rasch item difficulty, Model S.E. is the standard error of the Rasch item difficulty, and ptmea corr. is the correlation coefficient between examinees' item scores and their Rasch scale scores.

and the model expected pattern is in the smooth line. Students were grouped into 13 ability levels and are represented by "x" along the *x*-axis. As we can see that, Q5 is a very difficult question, as most students' abilities were below the item difficult level (the difference is below 0). For students whose ability measures higher than the item difficulty measure, we should expect their probability to answer the question correctly to be greater than 0.5, and the bigger the difference is, the closer to 1 their probabilities should be. As can be seen from Figure 3.3, only one group of students whose abilities are above the item difficulty, and their probability to answer this question correctly is close to 1, indicating a good fit. For the 12 groups of students whose abilities were below the item difficulty, we should expect their probabilities to answer the item correctly to be smaller than 0.5, and the lower their abilities were the closer to 0 their probability should be. Overall, observed probabilities should fall within the band around the expected smooth line. As can be seen from Figure 3.3, one group of stu-

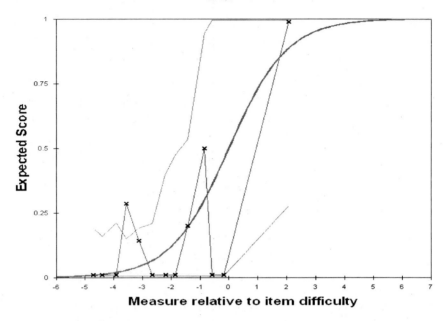

Figure 3.3.   Sample item characteristic curve. Scatterplots are actual observations, and the trace line is the expected pattern.

dents' probabilities was outside the band, indicating a misfit for this group of students. Because the sample size was 50, thus the size for each group was about 4 students. Based on this, about 4 out of 50 subjects were not fitting the model, indicating that, overall, the fit was good.

In Figure 3.4, items are arranged vertically from the easiest (Q6) to the most difficult (Q25). Horizontally, subjects are arranged from the most capable (person 46) to the least capable (person 10). Thus, diagonally we should expect correct responses (1s) in the upper left corner region and incorrect responses (0s) in the lower right corner region. Those 0s in the upper left corner region are unexpected, indicating irregular responses by particular subjects. Similarly, those 1s in the lower right region are unexpected, indicating irregular responses. Specifically for Q5, which is the fourth most difficult item on the FCI, persons 15, 23, 36, and 22 responded to the question in an unexpected manner, it is helpful to find out what reasons may have contributed to the irregularity. Could it be typo errors in data inputting? Is there any qualitative data available to help explain the irregularity? Would an interview of those subjects shed light on their responses?

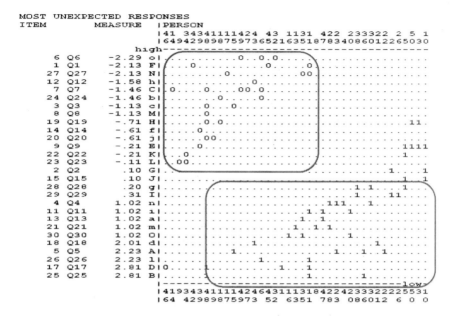

```
MOST UNEXPECTED RESPONSES
ITEM            MEASURE   |PERSON
                          |41  34341111424  43  1131  422  233322  2  5  1
                          |64942989875973652163518783408601226503 0
                     high--------------------------------------------
    6  Q6        -2.29  o |. . . . . . . . . .0. . .0. .0 . . . . .|. . . . . . . . . . . . . . .
    1  Q1        -2.13  F |. . . .0 . . . . . . . . . . . . .0 . . . . . .0 |. . . . . . . . . . . . . . .
   27  Q27       -2.13  N |. . . . . . . . . .0. . . . . . . . . . . . . .00 |. . . . . . . . . . . . . . .
   12  Q12       -1.58  h |. . . . . . . . . . . . . . . . . . .0 . . . .|. . . . . . . . . . . . . . .
    7  Q7        -1.46  C |0. . . . .0. . . . .00.0. . . .|. . . . . . . . . . . . . . .
   24  Q24       -1.46  b |. . . . . . .0. . . . .0. . . .|. . . . . . . . . . . . . . .
    3  Q3        -1.13  c |. . . . . .0. . .0. . . .|. . . . . . . . . . . . . . .
    8  Q8        -1.13  M |. . . . . . .0. . . . . .|. . . . . . . . . . . . . . .
   19  Q19        -.71  H |. . . . . .0.0. . . . . .|. . . . . . . . . . . . .11.
   14  Q14        -.61  f |. . . .0. . . . . . . .|. . . . . . . . . . . . . . .
   20  Q20        -.61  j |. . . . . .00. . . . .|. . . . . . . . . . . . . . .
    9  Q9         -.21  E |. . . .0. . . . . . . .|. . . . . . . . . .1111
   22  Q22        -.21  K |. .0. . . . . . . . . .|. . . . . . . . . .1. . . .
   23  Q23        -.11  L |.00. . . . . . . . . . .|. . . . . . . . . . . . . . .
    2  Q2          .10  G |. . . . . . . . . . . . .|. . . . . . . . .1. . . .1
   15  Q15         .10  J |. . . . . . . . . . . . .|. . . . . . . . . . . . . .1
   28  Q28         .20  g |. . . . . . . .|. . . . . . . . . . .1.1. . . .1.
   29  Q29         .31  I |. . . . . . .|. . . . . . . . . .1. . .11. . .
    4  Q4         1.02  n |. . . . . . .|. . . . . . . . .111. . .1. . . . . .
   11  Q11        1.02  i |. . . . . . .|. . . . . . .1.1. . .1. . . . .
   13  Q13        1.02  a |. . . . . . .|. . . . . . . .1. .1. . . . . .
   21  Q21        1.02  m |. . . . . . .|. . . . .1. . .1.1. . . . .
   30  Q30        1.02  O |. . . . . . .|. . . . . . .1.1. . . . .1. . . .
   18  Q18        2.01  d |. . . . . . .|. . . .1. . . . . . . . . . .1. . . .
    5  Q5         2.23  A |. . . . . . .|. . . .1. . . . . . .1. . .1. .1. .
   26  Q26        2.23  l |. . . . . . .|. . . . . . . . . .1. . . . . .1. . .
   17  Q17        2.81  D |0. . . . .|. . . . . . . . . . . .1. . .1. . . . . .
   25  Q25        2.81  B |. . . . .|. . . . . . . . . . . . . .1. . . . . .1. . . . . . .low.
                          |-------------------------------------------------
                          |41934341111424643111318422423333222255 31
                          |64  42989875973  52  6351  783  086012  6  0  0
```

Figure 3.4. Sample most unexpected response patterns. The 0s and 1s in the circled ranges are unexpected.

Another way to identify unusual response patterns is through examination of the Guttman scalogram. A Guttman scale (Guttman, 1944) is a set of items that produce an orderly response pattern from correct to incorrect when subjects are arranged from most capable to least capable and items are arranged from easiest to most difficult. Figure 3.5 is a portion of the Guttman scalogram of responses by a sample of university students on the FCI test.

In Figure 3.5, subjects are arranged vertically from the most capable (person 46) to the least capable (person 40); items are arranged horizontally from the easiest (Q6) to the most difficult (Q25). It shows that overall the pattern is a gradual change diagonally from 1s in the upper left to 0s in the lower right. Most subjects' response patterns contain occasional irregularities such as person 46's response to Q17, person 14's response to Q7, and person 9's responses to Q23, Q11, Q30 and Q5. Because the Rasch model is a stochastic model, it treats occasional irregularities as random effects. However, extensive irregularities such as those circled for person 34 and person 6 are treated as errors; they will result in high OUTFIT MNSQs. Identifying those extensive irregularities can help pinpoint problematic items for revisions or extreme behavior subjects for deletion. For example, person 6 seems to have responded randomly; this

```
GUTTMAN SCALOGRAM OF RESPONSES:
PERSON |ITEM
       |  21 21    1112 22 122 11231 212
       |61727403869409232589413108567 5
       |-------------------------------
    46 +1111111111111111111111111111101
    14 +1111011111111111111111111110000
     9 +1111111111111011111011010100
    34 +111111111111(001)1111110010010
    39 +1111111111010111010111100100
    42 +1011111111111110110011110100 0
    19 +1111111111101011101010100000
    48 +1111011001010111111110000010111
    15 +1111111011111001011101001010 00
    17 +1101111111111111101010000000 0
    18 +1111101111011010111011101000 00
    33 +1111111111111011101000001000000
    25 +1111111101111001001001010000 0
    27 +1111011111101111010100010000 00
    49 +0111011111111011000001111000 00
    12 +1111111101111000010001010000 0
    43 +11101101110110110101000010100 00
     6 +0111000111011100111100010001 00100
    40 +1111111110111101100000000000000
```

Figure 3.5.   A sample guttman scalogram. persons are arranged from most able (top) to least able (bottom), and items are arranged from easiest (left) to most difficult (right). the expected response patterns should be from 1s on the upper left to 0s on the lower right. The circled responses are unexpected.

subject might not be taking the test seriously and his/her responses could be removed from analysis.

One final aspect of examination of model-data-fit for items is the difficulty order of item choices (for multiple-choice questions) or scoring categories (for scoring rubrics). For multiple-choice questions, we should expect the correct choice, that is, the answer key, to be the most difficult among all choices; similarly, scores on a scoring rubric should gradually increase in difficulty from the lowest score to the highest score. Figure 3.6 is a sample Rasch modeling output table showing the difficult measures of item choices for four FCI questions.

Figure 3.6 shows that the correct answer B for Q7 is actually easier than choice E—an incorrect answer, indicating that choice B may need to be revised, or indeed choice E might be better made as the correct answer. Similarly, choice B for Q17 is also problematic. Another aspect to look at in terms of item choices or scoring categories is the distribution of obser-

ENTRY NUMBER	DATA CODE	SCORE VALUE	DATA COUNT	%	AVERAGE MEASURE	S.E. MEAN	OUTF MNSQ	PTMEA CORR.	ITEM
5 A	C	0	9	18	-1.03	.30	.4	-.30	Q5
	E	0	15	30	-.54	.21	.6	-.16	
	D	0	16	32	.05	.29	1.6	.16	
	A	0	4	8	.43	.52	1.8	.16	
	B	1	6	12	.49	.89	2.3	.22	
25 B	B	0	10	20	-.74	.25	.4	-.20	Q25
	E	0	6	12	-.69	.34	.4	-.14	
	A	0	1	2	-.44		.4	-.02	
	D	0	29	58	-.11	.22	1.2	.12	
	C	1	4	8	.85	1.24	2.1	.26	
7 C	A	0	3	6	-1.71	.39	.3	-.30	Q7
	C	0	1	2	-.63		.9	-.04	
	D	0	3	6	-.46	.61	1.4	-.05	
	E	0	7	14	-.09	.51	3.5	.05	
	B	1	36	72	-.11*	.21	1.1	.16	
17 D	E	0	1	2	-.63		.4	-.04	Q17
	D	0	43	86	-.33	.19	2.0	-.19	
	A	0	2	4	.63	.31	1.4	.14	
	B	1	4	8	.43*	.52	1.4	.16	

Figure 3.6. Sample Rasch output for item choice difficulties. the correct answer should be most difficult, while distractors may have various difficulties.

vations – how many subjects have selected each of the choices or scored each of the score categories. Ideally, there should be about an even distribution of subjects over the choices or categories. Unusually low observations could indicate that the choices were flawed—either containing clues or being too obvious to be incorrect. Choices A for Q25, C for Q7, and E for Q17 only had 1 observation, indicating that those questions may not need these choices. In fact, every item had a few choices with quite low observations (smaller than 10); those choices may need to be revised.

One last aspect for model-data-fit for items is the examination of differential item functioning (DIF). When items are biased, their difficulty measures will be statistically significantly different between subsamples. Figure 3.7 presents sample DIF statistics from the Rasch modeling of FCI on two subsamples: males and females.

Figure 3.7 shows that item difficulty measures for males and females are different with varying sizes. For Q1, the difference between the difficulty measures is 1.31 logit in favor of females, that is, the item is more difficult for males than for females. Although the t test shows that the difference is not statistically significant, the probability for Mantel Haenszel test, a chi-square statistics, is statistically significant ($p = 0.032$, which is <.05), indicating that Q1 is potentially gender biased. For other items, although there are differences in difficulty measures between males and

PERSON CLASS	DIF MEASURE	DIF S.E.	PERSON CLASS	DIF MEASURE	DIF S.E.	DIF CONTRAST	JOINT S.E.	t	d.f.	Prob.	MantelHanzl Prob.	Size	ITEM Number	Name
F	-2.98	.77	M	-1.67	.47	-1.31	.91	-1.45	48	.1540	.0320	-	1	Q1
M	-1.67	.47	F	-2.98	.77	1.31	.91	1.45	48	.1540	.0320	+	1	Q1
F	.23	.50	M	.01	.43	.22	.65	.34	48	.7344	.8174	.00	2	Q2
M	.01	.43	F	.23	.50	-.22	.65	-.34	48	.7344	.8174	.00	2	Q2
F	-.96	.49	M	-1.26	.44	.30	.66	.45	48	.6535	.5378	.00	3	Q3
M	-1.26	.44	F	-.96	.49	-.30	.66	-.45	48	.6535	.5378	.00	3	Q3
F	.75	.52	M	1.29	.53	-.54	.74	-.73	48	.4672	.7013	-	4	Q4
M	1.29	.53	F	.75	.52	.54	.74	.73	48	.4672	.7013	+	4	Q4

Figure 3.7. Sample Rasch modeling statistics for differential item function. Statistics in the circled columns show the statistical significance of the difference between the measures obtained from different groups.

females, the differences are not statistically significant based on both *t* tests and Mantel Haenszel tests, thus those items are not gender biased.

Following examination of model-data-fit of items, an examination of model-data-fit for the entire instrument is next. First, the Wright map should be examined for the match in distributions between person abilities and item difficulties, and any gaps should be identified. Figure 3.8 shows the Wright map for the FCI test based on a sample 50 university introductory physics students' responses.

Figure 3.8 shows that although overall students' abilities spread about evenly over a range from −2.5 to 4.5 logits, there are a few gaps in items. First, there are no items for one very advanced student with an ability about 4.5 logit. Second, there is a large item gap between 0.5 logit and 1.0 logit, and another large gap between 1.0 logit and 2.0 logit. Subjects whose abilities fall within those gaps will not be differentiated well, which will result in large measurement errors. Addition of items at the corresponding difficulty levels is necessary.

Third, the dimensionality of items should also be examined. This is usually through examination of factor loadings of items on a potential additional dimension within the item residuals. Figure 3.9 is the dimensionality map that shows how items are correlated with a potential additional construct within the item residuals. Any items with a high correlation (the absolute loading or correlation coefficient is greater than 0.4) may indicate that those items measure more than one construct, thus need to be revised.

Figure 3.9 shows that most items fall within the range of small factor loadings (−0.4, +0.4). However, a few items, items A, B, C, and *a* are outside the

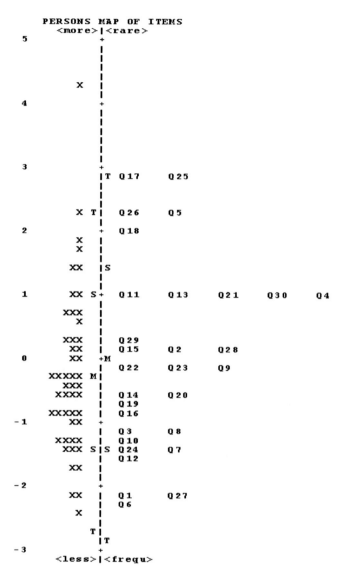

Figure 3.8.   Wright map for the FCI test. numbers on the left define a Rasch scale. Items and persons are distributed along the rasch scale according to their relative measures.

range. Those items are Q25, Q17, Q26, Q2, and Q27; they may measure more than one construct, thus need to be revised. Overall, the 30-item FCI is unidimensional, because it explains 71% of total observed variance.

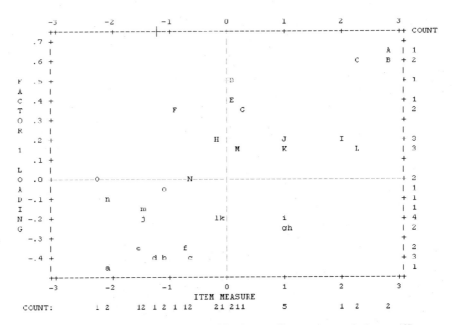

Figure 3.9.   Dimensionality of item residuals. Loadings are correlation coefficients between item measures and their measures on an additional dimension. Items with correlation coefficients beyond the ±0.4 range are potentially measuring an additional dimension.

One last aspect to examine is the overall person separation and reliability. Figure 3.10 shows a summary of Rasch modeling for the FCI test based on a sample of 50 subjects. We can see that overall the test differentiated subjects well—with a separation index of 2.24 based on the observations, or 2.36 based on model expectations if there was a perfect model-data-fit. Those separation indices are equivalent to the Cronbach's alpha of 0.83 and 0.85.

Design and Conduct Validity and Reliability Studies

Validity Study

Validity study includes two components: establishing interpretative arguments, and establishing validity arguments. Interpretative arguments include collecting evidence related to test content, response processes, internal structure, external structure, and consequence.

```
+------------------------------------------------------------------------+
| PERSONS      50 INPUT      50 MEASURED            INFIT        OUTFIT   |
|           SCORE    COUNT    MEASURE   ERROR    IMNSQ  ZSTD  OMNSQ  ZSTD |
| MEAN      13.9     30.0       -.24     .49      .99   -.1   1.06    .1  |
| S.D.       5.5      .0        1.23     .10      .28    1.3   .68    1.2 |
| REAL RMSE  .50  ADJ.SD       1.13  SEPARATION  2.23  PERSON RELIABILITY .83 |
|------------------------------------------------------------------------|
| ITEMS       30 INPUT      30 MEASURED            INFIT        OUTFIT    |
| MEAN      23.1     50.0        .00     .38      .99   -.1   1.06    .1  |
| S.D.      11.7      .0        1.44     .09      .15    .8    .36    .7  |
| REAL RMSE  .40  ADJ.SD       1.39  SEPARATION  3.51  ITEM  RELIABILITY .93 |
+------------------------------------------------------------------------+
```

Figure 3.10.   Summary of Rasch modeling statistics. Separation index is the ratio of adjusted standard deviation over root mean square error.

Test Content. Evidence for the validity related to test content may be established by examining the agreement between the coverage of the test items and the assessment domain as defined by the construct and the table of test specification. The alignment between the domain defined by the test specification and the domain of the test items may be examined qualitatively and/or quantitatively. Qualitative analysis involves experts' judgment on the match between the two. Quantitative analysis may involve calculating an alignment index (e.g., Porter, 2002). If the alignment is significantly high, then the test scores can be generalized into the target assessment domain. In Rasch modeling, the person and item invariance properties should also provide additional evidence of test content representing the content domain of the defined construct.

Response Processes. Rasch modeling provides various statistics and graphical representations to help evaluate examinees' response patterns. In addition, qualitative studies may also help establish evidence related to the validity of response processes. Qualitative studies seek to understand how the measurement instrument works in specific context and with individual subjects. A case study of a few subjects taking the measurement instrument may be conducted to help understand how individuals perform on the test in specific context, which may have already been part of the item try-out. The data of a qualitative validity study are often in the form of narrative observations, or interpretative descriptions of subject behaviors on the measurement instrument. The qualitative data may then be categorized in order to identify common themes. The themes may further be analyzed to identify relationships among them. The categories, themes, and relationships identified from the qualitative interpretation can greatly enhance the validity arguments.

Internal Structure.   Rasch modeling for developing a measurement instrument specifically adopts a theory-based interpretation approach. When applying Rasch models to develop measurement instruments, the first step is to identify a valid theory. Based on the theory, a number of inferences are then derived. The inferences include linearity of a latent construct, the hierarchy of behaviors of items, and the overall coherence of the items, that is, undimensionality. Items and the measurement instrument are specifically constructed according to the above inferences that are consistent with characteristics of Rasch models, so that the probability of a subject answering an item correctly is solely determined by the difference between an item's latent difficulty and a subject's latent ability. Fit statistics, the Wright map, dimensionality map, DIF, and other statistics and graphs can help establish evidence related to instrument's internal structure.

External Structure.   External structure is concerned with if the subjects' Rasch measures are correlated with other relevant variables. For conceptual understanding measurement, relevant variables may be subjects' course performance, achievement, and future tests of conceptual understanding, etc. Establishing validity related to external structure typically involves collection of additional data related to the relevant variables, and statistical analysis usually involves correlation or regression. For example, if the person ordering based on the Rasch measures is consistent with the teacher's ordering of the students, then there is evidence for the criterion-related validity of Rasch measures.

One powerful design for validity study related to extrapolation is the Multitrait-Multimethod (MTMM) design (Campbell & Fiske, 1959). Table 3.4 is a hypothetical design and its results.

In the validity study represented in Table 3.4, conceptual understanding of two concepts, Concept 1 and Concept 2, are involved, and two methods, Method A (e.g., multiple-choice test) and Method B (e.g., constructed response test), are used. This design implies that collection of three additional data sets is necessary for the same sample of subjects, one for conceptual understanding of another concept using two different test methods, and another for conceptual understanding of the same concept using a different test method. Each subject will now have four test scores, corresponding to the four scenarios of the design: same test method but with two different concepts and same concept but with two different meth-

Table 3.4. A Hypothetical MTMM Validation Design

	Method A		*Method B*	
	Concept 1 (A1)	*Concept 2* (A2)	*Concept 1* (B1)	*Concept 2* (B2)
A1	(.80)			
A2	.60	(.85)		
B1	.76	.22	(.90)	
B2	.20	.85	.50	(.83)

ods (A1, A2, B1, and B2). Correlation between two sets of subjects' scores can be computed and the results may be presented in the format of Table 3.4. In Table 3.4, values on the diagonal in parentheses refer to the reliability of each test. Values in bold are correlation coefficients between scores on the same concept based on two different methods. A validity claim may be made if this correlation is high. This type validity is also called convergent validity. Values in italic are correlation coefficients between two sets of scores on two different concepts based on a same assessment format. This type correlation should be moderate (may or may not be statistically significant depending on the nature of the two concepts), and should definitely be lower than the previous correlation for the same concept with different test formats. Finally, values in normal font are correlation coefficients between two sets of scores for two different concepts based on two different test methods, and should not be significant. This type validity is also called discriminant validity or divergent validity. As can be seen, a MTMM design can help make a variety of validity claims pertaining to external structure.

Consequences. Consequences are related to uses of measurement results. For example, a conceptual understanding test may be used to place subjects into different levels of courses, or different instructional approaches. Two types of evidence are needed: one pertaining to the decision making process and the other to the intended and unintended consequences. A decision-making process based on test scores must be based on a clearly stated rationale and procedure. Evidence may come from the literature or from some commonly accepted theories. New empirical evidence to justify the decision-making process may also be established. Similarly, evidence for the intended and unintended consequence should be established empirically when possible, but may also be done through literature.

Although establishing evidence related to consequences requires additional data collection, enhancing interpretation of Rasch measures, that is, translating quantitative measures into qualitative categories, can help produce positive evidence related to consequences. Interpretation of Rasch measures may be enhanced using both internal and external criteria. Internal criteria include review of the clarity of the qualitative categories, justification of cut-off scores, and distribution of subjects among different categories. External criteria include correlation studies between categorization of subjects and their performances on other relevant measures.

Establishing Validity Arguments.   While it is important that a variety of validity evidence is collected about a measurement instrument as described above, it is also important to examine the consistency among this variety of validity evidence. Thus, in addition to establishing interpretative arguments, a validity claim for a measurement instrument must also involve evaluation of the interpretative arguments as a whole. Important aspects to consider when evaluating interpretative arguments are: (a) clarity, (b) coherence, (c) plausibility of both inferences and assumptions. A claim about the validity of a measurement is sound when all the interpretative arguments are clearly stated, coherent, and plausible and the assumptions underlying the arguments are sound. Because of the potential complexity of the interpretative arguments, it is unlikely that a validity claim can be made in a binary fashion, that is, either having validity or having no validity. It is possible that a validity claim is categorical with specific qualifiers or conditions.

Reliability Study

Reliability study is an important component of applying Rasch models to develop measurement instruments. Rasch modeling provides various statistics pertaining to reliability of items, persons, and the entire measurement instruments. Specifically, the standard errors of measurement (SEs) for individual items and subjects are calculated, and large SEs are indications of item misfitting. Reliability of the entire measurement instrument is examined based on the person separation index and its equivalent Cronbach's alpha. A high separation index (e.g., > 2.0) and alpha (e.g., >.80) are indications of high reliability.

In addition to the reliability study as part of Rasch modeling, traditional reliability studies may also be conducted. For example, interrater reliability may be established during the item writing process involving scoring rubrics. If more than one form of an instrument is available, then the equivalence between two sets of subjects' scores from two forms can be established by calculating the correlation coefficient. Further, inconsistency to scores may also be caused by the timing of a test. This reliability study involves administering the same instrument twice within a certain time interval, and the correlation coefficient between subjects' scores on the two test administrations is calculated as a measure of reliability. The final potential source for subjects' score inconsistency is the media used to present the test. For example, a paper-and-pencil test may be converted into a computer-administered test, or an instrument in English for one culture may be translated into another language for another culture. In these cases, a same sample of subjects must take both forms of the test and the correlation coefficient between the two sets of scores is computed as a reliability measure.

In fact, all the above traditional reliability studies may be incorporated into Rasch modeling by examining person measures invariance. This is because Rasch modeling can produce two sets of person ability measures that are invariant from time to time, or from test form to test form if model-data-fit is good and the instrument is unidimensional. This property of Rasch measures is called person measure invariance property. The same method as described in chapter 2 on item measure invariance property can be used to examine the person measure invariance property.

Develop Guidelines for Use of the Instrument

The final step in developing a measurement instrument is the creation of a user's manual or guide. In addition to the actual measurement instrument that consists of items, a user's guide should also state the purpose or uses of the instrument and the test domain including the table of test specification, and document item properties, and validity and reliability evidence. The user guide may also include item scoring rubrics, and rules for determining performance categories based on total test scores. If relevant, the user's guide should also suggest ways for making valid decisions based on total scores, and when possible point out the potential invalid decisions made based on total scores. The overall purpose of a user's guide is to help users decide if the instrument is appropriate for the intended use and, if so, how to use it.

When a measurement instrument has been developed by applying Rasch models, another important consideration is score reporting. Because Rasch modeling requires application of computer programs, we should not expect users to conduct Rasch modeling in order to obtain subjects' ability measures. A raw-score to Rasch measure conversion table should be provided as part of the user's guide. With this conversion table, users will still score subjects using scoring keys/rubrics and obtain raw total scores for the subjects. Users will then consult the score conversion table to find out equivalent Rasch ability measures, which is also called Rasch scale scores. Rasch scale scores will then be used in subsequent sta-

Table 3.5.   Raw Total Score to Rasch Scale Score Conversion Table

SCORE	MEASURE	S.E.	SCORE	MEASURE	S.E.	SCORE	MEASURE	S.E.
0	-5.39E	1.85	11	-.82	.44	22	1.40	.49
1	-4.13	1.04	12	-.63	.44	23	1.65	.51
2	-3.35	.76	13	-.44	.44	24	1.92	.54
3	-2.87	.65	14	-.25	.44	25	2.23	.57
4	-2.49	.58	15	-.06	.44	26	2.57	.61
5	-2.18	.54	16	.13	.44	27	2.98	.67
6	-1.91	.51	17	.33	.44	28	3.51	.79
7	-1.67	.48	18	.52	.45	29	4.32	1.06
8	-1.44	.47	19	.73	.46	30	5.60E	1.86
9	-1.23	.46	20	.94	.47			
10	-1.02	.45	21	1.16	.48			

tistics analysis. Table 3.5 is a sample score conversion table from raw total scores to Rasch ability measures or scale scores for the FCI test.

In Table 3.5, raw total scores range from 0 to 30, because FCI is a 30-multiple-choice-item test with each item worth one point. Each raw total score is correspondent with one Rasch scale score, that is, measure, together with its standard error of measurement. By consulting this table, users of FCI can find out their subjects' Rasch scale scores based on their raw total scores, and use Rasch scale scores for subsequent statistical analysis. Once again, although measures in Table 3.5 contain negative values, ranging from −5.39 to 5.6, Rasch measures can be scaled to any range with any mean.

CHAPTER SUMMARY

Conceptual understanding can be defined many ways. One way is to conceptualize it as a process. An example of this conceptualization is the six facets of understanding that include explanation, interpretation, application, perspective, empathy, and self-knowledge. Understanding may also be defined as a state, for example, as meanings that are (a) resonant with or shared with others; (b) without internal contradictions; (c) without extraneous or unnecessary propositions; and (d) justified by the conceptual and methodological standards of the prevailing scientific paradigm. Understanding may further be conceptualized as both a process and a state. A representative definition of this conceptualization is the six elements of understanding; they are proposition, string, image, episode, intellectual skill, and motor skill. Besides the above conceptualizations, understanding is also domain specific, that is, specific to content domains. There are various domains of science, such as physical science, life science, and earth and space science. Each domain consists of a list of fundamental concepts with specific conceptual understanding. The revised Bloom's taxonomy can represent the three characteristics of conceptual understanding, that is, process-oriented, state-oriented, and domain specific. The revised Bloom's taxonomy of learning outcomes in the cognitive domain consists of two dimensions, one dimension for types of knowledge and another for cognitive process skills. The types of knowledge include factual knowledge, conceptual knowledge, procedure knowledge, and meta-cognitive knowledge. The cognitive process skills include: (a) remember, (b) understand, (c) apply, (d) analyze, (e) evaluate, and (f) create.

Science educators have developed various instruments for measuring conceptual understanding. When using an instrument to measure a conceptual understanding, it is important to review the intended uses of the measurement instrument and the evidence for validity and reliability. Many current measurement instruments for conceptual understanding may not possess the needed validity and reliability, because our notions of validity and reliability have been evolving; continuously validating a current measurement instrument is always necessary.

Using Rasch models to develop a measurement instrument for conceptual understanding starts with a theory about conceptual understanding of a concept. The theory must be valid, and should imply a linear construct that differentiates different levels of conceptual understanding among subjects. Based on the defined construct and different levels of performances of conceptual understanding, a test specification table is then created to guide the development of an item pool. Items will be reviewed by a panel of experts for content validity. Items may then be tried-out with a small number of subjects to see if the items function as expected. The final set of items is then administered to a representative sample of subjects whose ability range matches the difficulty range of items; this process is called field-testing. Field-testing data form the basis for Rasch modeling. During Rasch modeling, model-data-fit of items, Wright maps, item dimensionality, as well as differential-item-function are examined. Rasch modeling may result in revisions of items and possibly further field-testing. The final set of items demonstrating a good fit with a Rasch model and being unidimensional forms a measurement instrument. Although much of the evidence for the validity and reliability of the measurement instrument is obtained during the Rasch modeling, additional validity and reliability studies may also be conducted. The final step in developing a measurement instrument for conceptual understanding is development of documentation for measurement instrument uses. Score reporting should be an important component of documentation.

EXERCISES

1. Force Concept Inventory (FCI) (Hestenes, Wells, & Swackhamer, 1992/1995) is one of most popular conceptual tests in science education. Based on principal component factor analysis, Huffman and Heller (1995) found that only fewer than 6 FCI items converged on any single factor, and that the two samples suggested different factors. Huffman and Heller interpreted their results to suggest that FCI is not unidimensional. However, Hestenes and Halloun (1995) counterargued that a single factor solution of factor analysis consistent with the Newtonian force concept could be expected if a non-novices (that is, those who scored 60%–80% on the inventory) or a physicist data sample were used. What are your views on the nature of unidimensionality of FCI? What are implications of this debate on the application of FCI for educational research?

2. Figure 3.9 was based on a group of college students' responses to a FCI pretest at the beginning of the introductory college physics course. What does Figure 3.9 suggest in terms of dimensionality of FCI? Is the suggestion consistent with Huffman and Heller's (1995) conclusion? If there is a discrepancy between the two, explain why?

3. Locate one instrument introduced in this chapter and any technical documentation or reports containing information on the validity and reliability of the instrument. Apply the validity and reliability standards described in chapter 1 to review the instrument; is the instrument valid and reliable? Administer the instrument to a group of intended subjects to collect data, and then conduct Rasch modeling based on the collected data. Are the conclusions about the validity and reliability of the instrument based on Rasch modeling of your data different from what were reported by the author(s)? If yes, explain why?

REFERENCES

Anderson, D. L., Fisher, K. M., & Norman, G. J. (2002). Development and evaluation of the conceptual inventory of natural selection. *Journal of Research in science Teaching, 39*(10), 952-978.

Anderson, L. W., & Krathwohl, D. R. (2001, Eds.). *A taxonomy for learning, teaching, and assessing: A revision of Bloom's taxonomy of educational objectives*. New York, NY: Longman.

Beichner, R. J. (1994). Testing student interpretation of kinematics graphs. *American Journal of Physics, 62*(8), 75-762.

Bunce, D. M., & Gabel, D. (2002). Differential effects on the achievement of males and females of teaching the particulate nature of chemistry. *Journal of Research in Science Teaching, 39*(10), 17.

Campbell, D. T., & Fiske, D. W. (1959). Convergent and discriminant validation by the multitrait-multimethod matrix. *Psychological Bulletin, 56*, 81-105.

Crocker, L., & Algina, J. (1986). *Introduction to classical & modern test theory.* Fort Worth, FL: Holt, Rinehart and Winston.

Deboer, G. E., Dubois, N., Hermann Abell, C., & Lennon, K. (2008, March-April). *Assessment linked to middle school science learning goals: Using pilot testing in item development.* Paper presented at the Paper presented at the National Association for Research in Science Teaching Annual Conference, Baltimore, MD.

Ding, L, Chabay, R., Sherwood, B., & Beichner, R. (2006). Evaluating an electricity and magnetism tool: Bried electricity and magnetism assessment. *Physical Review Special Topics—Physics Education Research, 2*, 010105.

Diagnoser Tool. (n.d.). *Instructional tools for science and mathematics.* Retrieved from http://www.diagnoser.com/diagnoser/index.jsp

Doran, R. L. (1972). Misconceptions of selected science concepts held by elementary school students. *Journal of Research in Science Teaching, 9*, 127-137.

Engelhardt, P. V., & Beichner, R. J. (2004). Students' understanding of direct current resistive electric circuits. *American Journal of Physics, 72*(1), 98-115.

Guttman, L. (1944). A basis for scaling qualitative data. *American Sociological Review, 9*, 139-150.

Haidar, A. H., & Abraham, M. R. (1991). A comparison of applied and theoretical knowledge of concepts based on the particulate nature of matter. *Journal of Research in Science Teaching, 28*, 919-938

Haslam, F., & Treagust, D. F. (1987). Diagnosing secondary students' misconceptions of photosynthesis and respiration in plants using a two-tier multiple choice instrument. *Journal of Biological Education, 21*, 203-211.

Hestenes, D., & Halloun, I. (1995). Interpreting the force concept inventory: A response to Huffman and Heller. *The Physics Teacher, 33*, 502-506.

Hestenes, D., Wells, M., & Swackmaher, G. (1992). Force concept inventory. *The Physics Teacher, 30*, 141-158.

Huffman, D., & Heller, P. (1995). What does the force concept inventory actually measure? *The Physics Teacher, 33*, 138-143.

Hufnagel, B., Slater, T., Deming, G., Adams, J., Adrian, R. L., Brick, C., Zeilik, M. (2000). Pre-course results from the astronomy diagnostic test. *Publication of the Astronomical Society of Australia, 17*, 152-155.

Kleinke, D. (1979). Systematic errors in approximations to the standard error of measurement and reliability. *Applied Psychological Measurement, 3*, 161-164.

Libarkin, J. C., & Anderson, S. W. (2006). The geoscience concept inventory: Application of Rasch analysis to concept inventory development in higher education. In X. Liu & W. J. Boone (Eds.), *Applications of Rasch measurement in science education* (pp. 45-73). Maple Grove, MN: JAM Press.

Liu, X. (2009a). *Essentials of science classroom assessment.* Thousands, CA: Sage.

Liu, X. (2009b). Standardized measurement instruments in science education. In M. -W. Roth & K. Tobin (Eds.), *The world of science education: Handbook of research in North America* (pp. 649-677). Rotterdam, The Netherlands: Sense.

Lord, F. M. (1959). Tests of the same lengths do have the same standard error of measurement. *Educational and Psychological Measurement, 19*, 233-239.

Maloney, D. P., O'Kuma, T. L., Hieggelke, C. J., & van Heuvelen, A. (2001). Surveying students' conceptual knowledge of electricity and magnetism. *Physics Education Research, American Journal of Physics Supplement, 69*(7), S12-23.

Mintzes, J. J., & Wandersee, J. H. (1998). Reform and innovation in science teaching: A human constructivist view. In J. J. Mintzes, J. H. Wandersee & J. D. Novak (Eds.), *Teaching science for understanding: A human constructivist view*. San Diego, CA: Academic Press.

Mulford, D. R., & Robinson, W. R. (2002). An inventory for alternate conceptions among first-semester general chemistry students. *Journal of Chemical Education, 79*(6), 739-744.

National Research Council. (1996). *National science education standards*. Washington, DC: National Academy Press.

Nehm, R. H., & Schonfeld, I. S. (2008). Measuring knowledge of natural selection: A comparison of the CINS, an open-response instrument, and an oral interview. *Journal of Research in Science Teaching, 45*(10), 1131-1160.

Odom, A. L., & Barrow, L. H. (1995). Development and application of a two-tier diagnostic test measuring college biology students' understanding of diffusion and osmosis after a course of instruction. *Journal of Research in Science Teaching, 32*(1), 45-61.

Porter, A. C. (2002). Measuring the content of instruction: Uses in research and practice. *Educational Researcher, 31*(7), 3-14.

Sadler, P. M. (1998). Psychometric models of student conceptions in science: Reconciling qualitative studies and distractor-driven assessment instrument. *Journal of Research in Science Teaching, 35*(3), 265-296.

Thornton, R. K., & Sokoloff, D. R. (1998). Assessing student learning of Newton's laws: The force and motion conceptual evaluation and the evaluation of active learning laboratory and learning curricula. *American Journal of Physics, 66*(4), 338-352.

The University of the State of New York. (1996). *Physical setting/physics core curriculum*. Albany, NY: New York State Department of Education.

Wheeler, A. E., & Kass, H. (1978). Student misconceptions in chemical equilibrium. *Science Education, 62*(2), 223-232.

Wiggins, G., & McTighe, J. (2005). *Understanding by design*. Alexandria, VA: Association for Supervision and Curriculum Development.

White, R., & Gunstone, R. (1992). *Probing understanding*. London: The Falmer Press.

Williamson, V., Huffman, J., & Peck, L. (2004). Testing students' use of the particulate theory. *Journal of Chemical Education, 81*(6), 891-896.

Wuttiprom, S., Sharma, M. D., Johnston, I. D., Critaree, R., & Soankwan, C. (2009). Development and use of a conceptual survey in introductory quantum physics. *International Journal of Science Education, 31*(5), 631-654.

CHAPTER 4

USING AND DEVELOPING INSTRUMENTS FOR MEASURING AFFECTIVE VARIABLES

Affective variables are both outcomes and processes in science education; they form an important domain of measurement. This chapter will first review various theoretical frameworks related to affective variables. It will then introduce standardized instruments for measuring affective variables. Finally, this chapter will describe the process for developing new instruments for measuring affective variables using the Rasch modeling approach.

WHAT ARE AFFECTIVE VARIABLES?

One most influential conceptualization of affective variables is the *taxonomy of affective education objectives* (Krathwohl, Bloom, & Masia, 1964). This taxonomy perceives affective variables as a continuum from external influences to internal driving forces. This continuum is also hierarchical. A lower degree of feeling and emotion is characterized by passively attending to external stimuli, and a higher degree of feeling and emotion is characterized by proactively acting and creating external stimuli. Figure 4.1 presents the Krathwohl et al.'s taxonomy of affective educational objectives.

Using and Developing Measurement Instruments in Science Education:
A Rasch Modeling Approach, pp. 109–163
Copyright © 2010 by Information Age Publishing
All rights of reproduction in any form reserved.

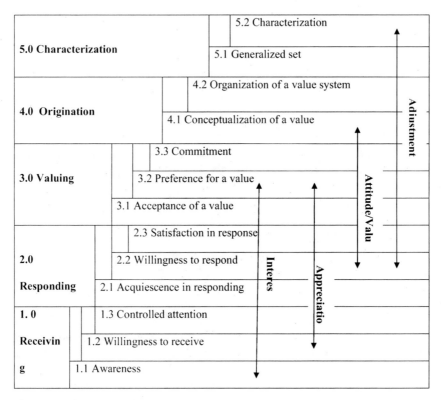

Figure 4.1.   Taxonomy of affective educational objectives (adapted from Hopkins, 1998, p. 274). The hierarchical progression from receiving (1.0) to characterization (5.) is internalization.

Figure 4.1 shows that the entire affective domain is conceptualized as a continuum of internalization from receiving to responding, valuing, organization and characterization. The continuum is hierarchical, that is, higher categories subsume all lower categories. Each category also contains a few hierarchical subcategories. Specifically, interest relates to subcategories 1.1 to 3.2; appreciation relates to subcategories 1.3 to 3.2; attitude and valuing relate to subcategories 2.2 to 4.1, and adjustment relates to subcategories 2.2 to 5.2.

Definitions of the categories and subcategories are as follows:

1.0 Receiving

At this category, a person is only sensitive to the existence of certain phenomena, and is willing to receive or to attend to them. The role of the person is mainly passive. For example, in schools, a receiving level of interest is demonstrated by a student's willingness to attend to the school's environmental club.

1.1 Awareness: At this subcategory, a person is simply aware of the existence of a phenomenon, but may not be able to verbalize it or recall its specifics, not to mention understanding it. For example, as an indication of interest in environmental conservation, a student is aware of the value of participating in an environmental science club.

1.2 Willingness to Receive: At this subcategory, a person is already aware of the existence of a phenomenon, and the person does not try to avoid it when the phenomenon is presented to him/her. For example, as an indication of interest in environmental conservation, a student is willing to attend an environmental science club activity when asked by a friend.

1.3 Controlled or Selected Attention: At this subcategory, a person consciously or semiconsciously shows a preference to attend to one phenomenon over others. However, at this level, the person remains passive in receiving stimuli. For example, as an indication of interest in environmental conservation, a student is willing to attend an environmental club activity when asked by a friend although there are other activities going on simultaneously.

2.0 Responding

Different from the previous category—receiving, responding is characterized by actively participating in various activities instead of passively attending to them. Various degrees of active participation define the following three subcategories of responding:

2.1 Acquiescence in Responding: At this subcategory, a person is reluctantly participating in a given activity, such as participation due to some pressure. For example, as an indication of interest in environmental science, a student is participating in the school recycling program because it is a school requirement.

2.2 Willingness to Respond: At this subcategory, a person is voluntarily participating in a given activity. For example, as an indication of interest in environmental conservation, a student is voluntarily participating in a school recycling program without any outside pressure.

2.3 Satisfaction in Response: At this subcategory, a person is not only voluntarily participating in a given activity, but also feeling a sense of satisfaction as the result of participation. For example, as an indication of interest in environmental conservation, a student is voluntarily participating in a school recycling program and at the same time developing a feeling that she/he is making a positive difference to the environment.

3.0 Valuing

At this category, a person can appreciate values of a given phenomenon. Within previous categories, a person simply receives or responds to a given phenomenon with no appreciation of values. People differ in their appreciation of values from receiving external values to personally attaching values to a phenomenon.

3.1 Acceptance of a Value: At this subcategory, a person accepts the value assigned from external sources. For example, as an indication of interest in environmental conservation, a student agrees with the claim that recycling is good to environmental conservation.

3.2 Preference for a Value: At this subcategory, a person not only accepts a given value, but also has internalized the value to become a personal belief. For example, as an indication of an interest in environmental conservation, a student believes that recycling is benefitting environmental conservation.

3.3 Commitment: At this subcategory, a person has a strong conviction on and a certainty beyond doubt about the value of a phenomenon. There is a real motivation for the person to act. For example, as an indication of the attitude toward environmental conservation, a student believes strongly in the benefit of recycling to environmental conservation and is personally devoted to implementing the recycling program in the school.

4.0 Organization

At this level, a person has developed a value system. Different from the previous category—valuing, a person at this category sees more than one value relevant to a particular phenomenon, and is able to compare different values and understand how they are related to each other.

4.1 Conceptualization of a Value: At this subcategory, a person is able to conceptualize the value developed over the previous categories in an abstract way and relates it to other values the person already holds. For example, as an indication of a person's attitude toward environmental conservation, the person considers involvement in a recycling program in school as an act of a responsible citizen.

4.2 Organization of a Value System: At this subcategory, a person is able to develop a complex and internally coherent value system. For example, as an indication of a person's adjustment toward environmental conservation, the person is able to articulate a sophisticated and coherent value system that environmental conservation is a universal ethic without boundaries of country, gender, language, race, culture, and so on.

5.0 Characterization By a Value or a Value Complex

At this category, a person has demonstrated two characteristics: (a) a way of life that is governed by a value system; and (b) a philosophy of life or worldview that is demonstrated consistently over time and across contexts. At this category, due to the internalized value system, the person has developed certain characteristics related to a phenomenon.

5.1 Generalized Set: At this subcategory, a person decides to act according to an organized value complex. For example, as an indication of a person's adjustment to environmental conservation, the person is able to reduce his consumption of plastic materials and reuse many other household objects.

5.2 Characterization: At this subcategory, a person's entire lifestyle and everyday behaviors are governed by the developed coherent value system. In other words, a person has now characterized himself/herself by both a philosophy of life or a worldview and a new lifestyle. For example, as an indication of a person's adjustment toward environmental conservation, a person has adopted a naturalist lifestyle that is consistent with his naturalist philosophy of life.

As can be seen from the above illustrations, the Krathwohl et al.'s taxonomy of affective educational objectives is based on a continuous process of internalizing values to form a coherent value system, which in turn governs a person's behaviors. The whole taxonomy can be considered as a spiral consisting of multiple cycles of the behavior → internalized value → behavior process. Therefore, although the taxonomy is for the affective domain, it also involves the other two domains—the cognitive and psychomotor domains. This is because without reasoning, it is impossible to internalize values in order to form a value system; similarly, without action (which involves psychomotor skills), it is impossible for a person to act according to his/her value systems.

Affective outcomes are typical expectations in science curriculums for students. For example, the *Benchmarks for Science Literacy* (American Association for the Advancement of Science, 1993) state that by the end of 12th grade, students should "know why curiosity, honesty, openness, and skepticism are so highly regarded in science and how they are incorporated into the way science is carried out; exhibit those traits in their own lives and value them in others" (p. 287); students should also "view science and technology thoughtfully, being neither categorically antagonistic nor uncritically positive" (p. 287). In science education, two of the most researched affective variables are attitude and motivation.

Attitude

Various definitions of attitude are available. One definition is by Eagly (1992) who defines attitude as a tendency or state internal to a person that biases or predisposes the person toward favorable or unfavorable responses. Simpson, Koballa, Oliver, and Crawley (1994) define *attitude* as a predisposition to respond positively or negatively to things, people, places, events, or ideas. Science education researchers have studied various constructs related to attitude. In general, these attitudinal constructs can be grouped into two categories: those that are related to students, and those that are related to teachers. Examples of constructs of attitude related to students are student attitude toward school science, student attitude toward science and technology, student attitude toward science labs, student attitude toward science teaching, and student attitude toward science careers. Examples of constructs of attitude related to teachers are teachers' attitude toward inquiry, elementary teachers' attitude toward teaching science, teachers' attitude toward science curriculum, and teachers' attitude toward computer integration. Regardless of the attitude being measured, it is important to note that "attitude cannot be separated from its context and the underlying body of influences that determine its real significance" (Osborne, Simon, & Collins, 2003, p. 1055).

Research in science education has differentiated between "attitude towards science" and "scientific attitude" (Gardner, 1975). *Scientific attitude,* or *science attitude,* refers to evidence-based reasoning and argumentation, search for clarity and internal consistency, open-mindedness and skepticism, and willingness to change when data contradict their own views. On the other hand, *attitude toward science* refers to feelings, beliefs and values held by a person about science. Attitude toward science is not a unitary construct; it consists of a number of interrelated subconstructs such as perception of the science teacher, anxiety toward science, the value of science, self-esteem related to science, motivation towards science, enjoyment of science, attitude of peers and friends toward science, attitude of parents toward science, the nature of the classroom environment, achievement in science, and fear of failure in courses (Osborne et al., 2003). Similarly, Simpson and Troost (1982) identified 15 categories of attitudes toward science, including science affect, science self-concept, general self-esteem, locus of control, achievement motivation, science anxiety, emotional climate of the science class, physical environment of the science class, other students in the science class, science teacher, science curriculum, family-general, family-science, friends and science, and school. Further, attitudes toward science are students' expressed preferences and feelings; they are not necessarily student behaviors related to science (Osborne et al., 2003).

As for teachers, research has shown that teachers' beliefs affect their attitudes. For example, based on a sociocultural model of beliefs, science teachers' attitudes toward science are strongly influenced by science teachers' epistemological beliefs, while science teachers' beliefs are closely linked to teachers' content knowledge, confidence, self-efficacy, experience, and social context (Jones & Carter, 2007).

A related concept to attitude is values. While attitude primarily deals with things, people and places, values deal with abstract ideas such as science and technology. Values emphasize more on affect and cognition and less on immediate behavior (Simpson et al., 1994).

Motivation

Although there is no universally agreed upon definition of motivation (Jones & Carter, 2007), *motivation* may be considered as "an internal state that arouses, directs, and sustains students' behavior" (Koballa & Glynn, 2007, p.85). According to Koballa and Glynn (2007), there are four *approaches to defining motivation*: the behavioral, humanistic, cognitive, and social. The behavioral approach to motivation focuses on extrinsic and material incentives and reinforcement; the humanistic approach focuses on human's intrinsic needs such as self-actualization and self-determination; the cognitive approach emphasizes goals, plans, expectations, and attributions; and finally the sociocultural approach focuses on individuals' identities and interrelations with others within a community. Motivation focuses on the desire to act or not to act; it relates to the behavior component (Simpson et al., 1994). For example, taking primarily a cognitive approach, Zusho, Pintrich, and Coppola (2003) conceptualize motivation processes in relation to student science achievement to include four components: the self-efficacy beliefs, task value beliefs, goal orientation, and affects. The self-efficacy beliefs are students' judgments of their capabilities to perform a task, as well as their beliefs about their agency in the course. Task value beliefs refer to students' beliefs on the utility and importance of a course. Goal orientations are individuals' purposes when approaching, engaging in, and responding to achievement situations. Specifically, two achievement goals, that is, mastery and performance goals, are found to be important determinants of students' motivation and performance. Finally, affects refer to students' interests and anxiety. Science educators study motivation in order to explain why students strive for particular goals when learning science, how intensively they strive, how long they strive, and what feelings and emotions may characterize them in these processes. Like attitude, there are various constructs related to motivation, such as motivation to learn, motivation to teach, motivation to implement a new curriculum, to name a few. Motivation is influenced by attitude.

INSTRUMENTS FOR MEASURING STUDENT AFFECTIVE VARIABLES

A variety of standardized measurement instruments related to affective variables are available in science education. Liu (2009) has reviewed standardized measurements developed by researchers in North America and published in refereed journals over the past 50 years (pp. 650-654). The following summative descriptions expand Liu's review by including instruments developed outside North America and most recently published instruments. The majority of the instruments have been developed based on classical test theory. They are for various intended uses and based on various theoretical frameworks of affective variables. Please note, the following descriptions of the instruments are for readers' information only; whether or not a science education researcher will choose an instrument for a particular research question requires a critical review of the instrument by the researcher, which is beyond the scope of this book.

Instruments for Measuring Student Attitudes

Science Support Scale (Tri-S) (Schwirian, 1968)

Tri-S is a 40-item Likert-scale survey of university nonscience major students' attitudes toward science. Attitude toward science is conceptualized as particular cultural values which are more conducive to the growth and development of the scientific institution in a society than are their opposites. Specifically, these values are (a) rationality, (b) utilitarianism, (c) universalism, (d) individualism, and (e) a belief in progress and meliorism. An initial list of 60 questions were created corresponding to the above five values. This original scale was tried with 196 university non-science majors. Item analysis based on item discrimination and subscale internal consistency reduced the original number of items to 40 (8 items per subscale). Split-half internal consistency reliability corrected by the Spearman-Brown formula for the five subscales ranged from 0.59 to 0.87.

The Scientific Attitude Inventory (SAI and SAI-II)
(Moore & Sutman, 1970; Moore & Foy, 1997)

SAI measures high school students' attitude toward science. It consists of six positive and six corresponding negative intellectual and emotional attitudes toward science. These six pairs of attitudes are: (a) nature of the laws and/or theories of science—changeable versus unchangeable truths, (b) the basis of scientific explanation—observation vs. authority, (c) characteristics needed to operate in a scientific manner—independence of thought versus group thinking, (d) the type of activity engendered in science—idea generating versus technology developing, (e) dependent on public understanding versus no need for public understanding, and (f) science as a career—interesting and rewarding versus dull and uninteresting. Validation involved expert panel reviews and pilot-testing by 10th-grade students in three sequences of biology courses. Analysis of variance controlling for IQ and science GPA showed that the groups who received instruction relevant to the attitudes scored significantly higher on the posttest than on the pretest. The final form of SAI consists of 60 items with 5 items for each of the six pairs of attitude subscales. The test-retest reliability based on pre- and posttest scores was .934.

SAI-II is a revision of SAI; it consists of 40 items. SAI-II contains improvement in readability and elimination of gender-biased language. SAI-II has also replaced the four-category Likert responses in SAI with five-category Likert responses. The intended attitudes to be measured in SAI-II remain to be six pairs of opposing attitudes. The alpha reliability was 0.78. However, factor analysis did not result in the hypothesized 12-attitude structure.

Although SAI as well as SAI-II has been widely used in science education research, there are questions about its construct validity both conceptually (Munby, 1983a, 1997) and empirically (Lichtenstein et al., 2008; Moore & Foy, 1997). Munby (1983a) conducted a conceptual analysis of items in SAI and concluded that many SAI items may not tap into attitude related to science, raising doubt about its construct validity. Revisions to SAI to produce SAI-II failed to address the issue of construct validity (Munby, 1997). In a recent validation study through both exploratory and confirmatory factor analysis, Lichtenstein et al. failed to produce the claimed constructs corresponding to the 12 attitudes or 6-pairs of attitudes. At most, Lichtenstein could only identify 2 meaningful constructs that may be called "science is rigid" (6 items, $\alpha = 0.59$) and "I want to be a scientist" (8 items, $\alpha = 0.85$).

Specific Interest in Biological, Physical and Earth Sciences (SIBPE)
(Skinner & Barcikowski, 1973)

SIBPE measures intermediate level (Grades 7 and 8) students' attitudes toward specific disciplines. The items ask students to indicate how many times they had done each of the 70 activities during a specific time period. The instrument contains 12 general science questions with 12 items from each of the science subject areas (i.e., biology, chemistry, physics, and earth science). Validation of the instrument involved panel reviews and pilot-testing with 2,137 seventh- and eighth-grade students participating in a National Science Foundation-funded science program. Factor analysis was conducted in subsamples of seventh grade males, females, and eighth grade males and females. Eight similar main factors were present in all the subsamples.

The Biology Attitude Scale (BAS) (Russell & Hollander, 1975)

BAS is a 30-item instrument for measuring university students' attitudes toward biology. The scale was given consecutively once a week for seven weeks to a group of students taking a biology course, and the stability of students' scores was very high (averaged .80 over seven weeks). The reliability of the Likert scale was consistently over .90. Biology majors scored significantly lower after the biology course; the life science majors scored no statistically significantly different from pre- to postcourse; and education majors scored statistically significantly higher on the postcourse survey. Correlation between BAS and another scale based on semantic differential was high ($r = .80$).

The Environmental Concern Scale (ECS) (Weigel & Weigel, 1978)

ECS is composed of 16 statements focusing on a wide range of conservation and pollution issues. The general public is the target audience. The statements are presented in a 5-point Likert-scale ranging from *"strongly agree"* to *"strongly disagree."* Each item had a high correlation with the scale score (.12 to .42). The correlation between the scale scores and scores on a criterion measure was .58. Prediction validity was established based on correlation between scale scores and behaviors on petitioning ($r = .5$, $p < .01$), the litter pick-up ($r = .36$, $p < .05$), recycling ($r = 0.39$, $p < .01$), and the comprehensive behavioral index ($r = 0.62$, $p < .01$). Six week test-retest reliability was .83. Alpha internal consistency was .85.

Test of Science-Related Attitudes (TOSRA) (Fraser, 1978)

TOSRA is a 70-item Likert-scale instrument measuring junior high school students' science related attitudes. It has seven scales: social implications of science, normality of scientists, adoption of scientific attitudes, enjoyment of science lessons, leisure interest in science, and career interest in science. TOSRA is an extension of a previous instrument by adding two new scales, and by providing uniform instructions, number of items across scales and response formats. Initial items were reviewed by a group of science teachers for content validity, and field-tested for item quality. The main validation study involved 1,337 Grades 7-10 students in Australia. Cronbach's alpha coefficients for the above seven scales ranged from

0.66 to 0.93 for the Grade 7 sample, from 0.64 to 0.93 for the Grade 8 sample, from 0.69 to 0.92 for the Grade 9 sample, and from 0.67 to 0.93 for the Grade 10 sample. Intercorrelations among TOSRA scales were calculated as indices of discriminant validity. The correlations were generally low ranging from 0.10 to .58 ($M = 0.33$).

The Simpson-Troost Attitude Questionnaire (STAQ) (Simpson & Troost, 1982)

STAQ is one of a series of measurement instruments developed as part of a large-scale longitudinal study on relationships between affective variables and student achievements. It is a 60-item Likert-scale survey of secondary school (Grades 6-10) students' attitude toward science. It contains 15 subscales related to: student attitude toward science, motivation to achieve in science, science anxiety, attitude toward science teachers, and attitude toward science curriculums. The validation of the instrument went through multi-stages and multi-years with thousands of students. A total of 12 editions of the instrument were piloted. The content validity was established through expert panel review; construct validity was established through item analysis and exploratory factor analysis. Internal consistency reliability for the subscales was claimed to be above 0.90. Studies using STAQ reported Cronbach's alpha coefficients for different subscales ranged from 0.33–0.95 (Owen et al., 2008).

Owen et al. (2008) conducted a validation study of the instrument with a sample of 1,754 secondary (Grades 6-8) students. The sample was randomly divided into two subsamples, one for exploratory and another for confirmatory factor analysis. The exploratory factor analysis found 10 interpretable factors, but only five of the factors had a Cronbach's reliability coefficient greater than 0.70. The five factors were called *motivating science class* (6 items), *self-directed effort* (4 items), *family models* (4 items), *science is fun for me* (4 items), and *peer models* (4 items). A confirmatory factor analysis with the above five had a very good model-data-fit. Additional data collected on stability of scores found that stability was higher across high school grades than across middle school grades.

Women in Science Scale (WiSS) (Erb & Smith, 1984)

WiSS is a Likert-scale survey of early adolescent girls' and boys' attitudes toward women in science. WiSS assumes three dimensions of attitude toward women in science: (a) women possess characteristics that enable them to be successful in science careers, (b) women's roles as mothers and wives are compatible with successful science careers, and (c) women and men should have equal opportunities to pursue science careers. Pilot testing with middle school and high school students resulted in elimination of items with poor item qualities. Construct validity was established based on convergent and divergent validities. The final 27-item instrument had an overall alpha reliability of 0.92 and a test-retest (8 week interval) reliability of 0.82.

Owen et al. (2007) conducted a revalidation study of WiSS using a sample of 1,439 middle school students in Texas. A confirmatory factor analysis based on the claimed three dimensions showed strong intercorrelation (correlation coefficients ranged from 0.89 to 0.90) among the three dimensions, suggesting a significant overlap among dimensions within the instrument. After a series of exploratory and confirmatory factor analysis, the authors found that the 27-item original instrument could be shortened into a 14-item instrument with two meaningful dimensions: gender equality (8 items) and sexism (6 items). The correlation between the two dimensions was 0.78. The Cronbach's alpha coefficients for the two dimensions were 0.78 and 0.75.

Attitude Toward Science in School Assessment (ATSSA) (Germann, 1988)

ATSSA measures secondary school students' general attitudes toward science, specifically, how students feel toward science as a subject in school. An initial list of 34 items was created. A panel review resulted in reduction of 10 items and revision of the remaining items. The remaining 24 items were pilot tested with a group of 125 science students in Grades 7 and 8. Principal component factor analysis found that 14 items loaded highly on the first factor, and the remaining items loaded on four other factors. The 14 items were selected to form the ATSSA instrument. This final instrument was subjected to four subsequent validation studies. Cronbach's alpha estimates from the four studies were all greater than 0.94; all 14 items loaded on only one factor with consistent factor loadings in all four studies. Percentages of variance accounted for by this factor were 64.9, 69.8, 67.4, and 59.2. Item-total correlations ranged from 0.61 to 0.89. Student attitude scores on ATSSA from two classes with known different attitudes toward science were found statistically significantly different. There was also a statistically significant correlation between scores of ATSSA and measures of formal logical reasoning and biology achievement tests.

Early Childhood Women in Science Scale (ECWiSS) (Mulkey, 1989)

ECWiSS is a 27-item Likert-type instrument measuring early childhood children's (K-Grade 4) attitudes toward women scientists. Items are given orally, and students are asked to color the line-drawn faces corresponding to *strongly agree, agree, disagree,* and *strongly disagree*. ECWiSS is modeled after WiSS for middle school students, and covers the same three dimensions: (a) women possess characteristics which enable them to be successful in science careers; (b) women's roles as mothers and wives are compatible with successful science career pursuits; and (c) women and men ought to have equal opportunities to prepare for and pursue science careers. The Cronbach's alpha for the entire instrument was 0.90, and the Guttman split-half reliability coefficient was 0.87. Construct validity of the instrument was established through a causal comparative design and a principal component factor analysis. The scale was able to detect statistically significant differences between groups (e.g., gender, grade level, academic ability, and social economic background). Scores on ECWiSS were also statistically significantly correlated with measures obtained from an occupational inventory and teachers' observational ratings. Principal component factor analysis supported the original hypothesized three dimensions.

Attitudes Toward Science Inventory (ATSI) (Gogolin & Swartz, 1992)

ATSI is a 48-item Likert-type instrument measuring both college science majors' and nonmajors' attitudes toward science. It comprises six scales with eight items per scale. The six scales are: perception of the science teacher, anxiety toward science, value of science in society, self-concept in science, enjoyment of science, and motivation in science. Items were based on modification of a previously published instrument. Alpha coefficients for the six scales based on pretest ranged from 0.73 to 0.90; and from 0.77 to 0.88 based on posttest. Item-scale correlation was all above 0.3 with the exception of one item.

Attitude toward Science Questionnaire (ASQ)
(Parkinson, Hendley, Tanner, & Stable, 1998)

ASQ is a 33-item 5-point Likert-scale instrument for measuring 13-14 year-olds' attitudes to science. The development of items started with asking approximately 100 students to write down statements about science and their science lessons. Those statements that matched the intended measurement objectives were then used to create item statements. Half of the statements were phrased positively and the other half negatively. Principal component factor analysis revealed that there were six factors; they are: enjoyment, level of difficulty, importance, reading and writing, practical work in science, and time. The number of items per factor ranged from 3 to 9. The overall Cronbach's alpha coefficient for the final questionnaire was 0.92. A sample of 72 pupils representing those with high, medium and low attitude toward science was interviewed to provide additional evidence of validity for the instrument.

Secondary School Students' Attitude toward Science (Francis & Greer, 1999)

This is a 20-item unidimensional instrument arranged for scoring on a 3-point Likert scale. The 20 items were selected from the original 60 items based on principal component factor analysis. The content validity of the scale was supported by the observation that items recording the largest item-scale correlation were clearly central to the domain of affective science-related attitudes. A statistically significant correlation was found between students' attitude scores on the instrument and their numbers of science-related subjects studied. The alpha coefficients for different grades of students ranged from 0.88 to 0.91.

Attitude Toward Science (Pell & Jarvis, 2001)

This instrument assesses attitudes to science of 5- to 11-year-old children. Items are stated in the 5-point "smiley" face Likert-scale format with only positively worded statements. The instrument includes three main scales: (a) being in school, (b) science experiments, and (c) what science is. Pilot-testing studies helped revise items and scales. Five subscales were derived: (a) liking school, (b) independent investigator, (c) science enthusiast, (d) social context, and (e) difficult science. The alpha reliability coefficients were 0.65, 0.63, 0.74, 0.68, and 0.63. There was a statistically significant correlation among subscales a to d. Items of a to d together (25 items) formed the Science Interest scale with an alpha coefficient of 0.82.

The Attitude Scale (AS) (Kesamang & Taiwo, 2002)

AS measures Botswana junior high school students' attitudes toward science. An initial set of 26 items covering a wide range of areas related to likes and dislikes of science and the importance of science to mankind were created, and an expert-panel review of the items resulted in deletion of 6 items. The 20-item instrument was then pilot tested with 60 Grade 7 students. Principal component factor analysis revealed two factors related to "likes of science" and "dislikes of science." The split-half reliability was found to be 0.75 after the Spearman-Brown adjustment.

Shark Attitude Inventory (SAI) (Thompson & Mintzes, 2002)

SAI contains 39 Likert-type questions asking students to state their agreement by selecting one of *"strongly agree," "slightly agree," "neutral," "slightly disagree."* and *"strongly disagree."* The initial set of 48 questions was created based on modification of propositions in a published instrument on attitudes toward animals. Responses by a sample of non-science majors taking a college introductory biology course were used to refine the instrument. Principal component factor analysis revealed four factors with an eigenvalue equal to or greater than 2. The four factors were labeled as utilitarian/negative, naturalistic, scientific, and moralistic. The Cronbach's alpha for the above four subscales were 0.43, 0.73, 0.65, and 0.36.

Chemistry Attitudes and Experiences Questionnaire (CAEQ)
(Dalgety, Coll, & Jones, 2003).

CAEQ is a survey instrument for first-year chemistry students. It was based on a modified theory of planned behavior that involves the following constructs: attitude toward chemistry, chemistry self-efficacy, and chemistry learning experiences. The attitude construct includes four subscales: attitude toward chemists, attitude toward chemistry knowledge, attitude toward chemistry methods, and attitude toward chemistry values. Initial items (131) for the subscales came from previously published attitude toward science instruments and were reduced to 20 items (5 per subscale) after interviews with chemistry students and faculty. The chemistry self-efficacy construct includes four subscales: learning chemistry theory self-efficacy, applying chemistry theory self-efficacy, learning chemistry skills self-efficacy, and applying chemistry skills efficacy. Initial items (61) for the self-efficacy subscales came from a similar instrument in biology, and 20 items, or 5 per subscale, resulted after interviewing chemistry faculty and students. The learning experiences construct includes seven subscales based on different classes and instructors: lecture learning experiences, tutorial learning experiences, laboratory learning experiences, laboratory books learning experiences, lecturer learning experiences, tutor learning experiences, and demonstrator learning experiences. Initial items (70) were selected from other related instruments, and interviews of faculty and students resulted in 35 items (5 per subscale). The attitude and self-efficacy items were presented in a semantic differential format with two bi-polar adjectives and 7 points in-between. The learning experience items were stated in a Likert-scale format with five categories from *strongly disagree* (1) to *strongly agree* (5).

A pilot study involving 129 first-year chemistry students from one institution in New Zealand was conducted, and principal component factor analysis revealed the same number of factors as the defined subscales. Nineteen students who completed the survey were also interviewed about their perceptions of the survey. Based on the pilot study results, the instrument was finalized for validation with a larger sample from two institutions. The final instrument contains 21 items on attitude toward chemistry, 17 items on self-efficacy, and 31 items on learning experiences. Principal component factor analysis was conducted again to confirm the construct validity of the subscales. The averaged Cronbach's alpha reliability coefficient over all the subscales was .74 at the start of the year ($n = 332$) and 0.84 at the end of the semester ($n = 337$). The concurrent validity was established by findings that chemistry majors had a statistically significantly more positive attitude toward chemistry, higher chemistry self-efficacy, and more positive learning experiences than non-majors at both administrations of the survey, and that student learning experiences had a statistically significant correlation with students' attitude toward chemistry and self-efficacy in chemistry.

Changes in Attitudes about the Relevance of Science (CARS)
(Siegel & Ranney, 2003)

CARS is a 59-item Likert-scale survey of middle and high school students' attitudes toward the relevance of science to everyday life. The 59 items are divided into three equivalent forms with 17 unique items plus 8 common items for all three forms. The formation of three equivalent forms was based on Rasch difficulty estimates of items. Most items fit the Rasch model well. Alpha reliability coefficient for each of the forms was above .8. The results also showed that CARS was sensitive to the effects of innovative science curriculums.

Attitude Toward Chemistry (ATC) (Salta & Tzougraki, 2004)

ATC is a 23-item Likert-scale survey of high school chemistry students' attitudes toward chemistry. It contains four subscales: the difficulty of chemistry courses (6 items), the interest in chemistry courses (9 items), the usefulness of chemistry courses for future careers (3 items), and the importance of chemistry for student life (5 items). Development of the instrument went through three stages taking place in Greece. Stage 1 involved an expert panel review of items to ensure content validity. Pilot testing was used to revise items and study preliminary properties of the instrument. The main study was used to establish construct validity through exploratory factor analysis and reliability through computing Cronbach's alpha coefficients. The four factors explained 47% of total variance. The alpha coefficients for the four subscales were 0.87, 0.89, 0.71, and 0.67 respectively.

Attitude Toward Critical School Science Activity (ATCSSA) and Attitude Toward Progressive School Science Activity (ATPSSA) (Zacharia & Calabrese Barton, 2004)

ATCSSA and ATPSSA are two parallel forms of an instrument for measuring urban middle school students' attitudes toward Progressive School Science (PSS) and Critical School Science (CSS). PSS is represented by current major reform documents such as National Science Education Standards (National Research Council, 1996), while the CSS is represented by such science curriculum emphases as critical science, feminist science, and multicultural science. Each form contains 13 items in both close-ended (i.e., 4-point Likert-scale format) and open-ended formats. The 13 items in each form respond to a scenario reflective of either PSS or CSS. Principal component factor analysis showed that items 9-13 highly loaded on one dominant factor, that is, attitude toward either PSS or CSS. Cronbach's alpha was above .90 for both forms. Interrater reliability for open-ended questions was all above .90. Results showed that some students had a negative attitude toward PSS but a positive attitude toward CSS.

The Colorado Learning Attitude about Science Survey (CLASS)
(Adams, Perkins, Podolefsky, Dubson, Finkelstein, & Wieman, 2006)

CLASS is a 42-item Likert scale measuring high school and college physics students' attitude toward science. Validation involved interviewing both students (34) and physics experts (16), and factor analysis of pilot-testing data. Reliability was established by comparing surveys of two different physics classes in different semesters. Results were very similar for both calculus-based and algebra-based physics classes.

Affective Characteristics Scale (ACS) (Gungor, Eryrilmaz & Fakroglu, 2007)

ACS is a set of 53 items scored on a 5-point Likert scale with each item labeled from 1 (*strongly disagree*) to 5 (*strongly agree*). It measures secondary school physics students' attitude toward science. It includes 10 subscales: importance of physics, personal interest, situational interest, extra curriculum activities, student motivation, achievement motivation, self-efficacy, self-concept, course anxiety, and test anxiety. Initial items came from various published relevant instruments in science and mathematics. Translation from English into Turkish was conducted with the assistance of a language expert. An expert panel review and exploratory factor analysis during the pilot study resulted in the revision and deletion of some initial items. Cronbach's alpha coefficients for the 10 subscales based on the final 53 items ranged from 0.84 to 0.92.

Attitude to Science Measures (ASM) (Kind, Jones, & Barmby, 2007)

ASM assesses secondary school students' attitudes toward science. It has the following subscales: learning science in school, self-concept in science, practical work in science, science outside of school, future participation in science, importance of science, general attitude toward school, and combined interest in science. The instrument adopted a Likert-scale format, with each measure being made up of a series of statements asking students to state their level of agreement to the statements by choosing one response from *"strongly agree," "agree," "neither agree nor disagree," "disagree,"* and *"strongly disagree."* Statements were made to capture various attributes of the attitude object and express different evaluative dimensions.

Reliability analysis and factor analysis were conducted on pilot study data; items that reduced the internal reliability of attitude measures or did not group together with other items were either removed from the measures, or their wording was modified. In the final validation study, the revised questionnaire was given twice to students: 2 weeks before and 2 weeks after a university mobile lab outreach program.

Principle component factor analysis using oblique rotation on seven factors found that the extracted factors did indeed correspond to the seven expected areas of attitudes toward science. However, one item "Scientists have exciting jobs" did not load on any of the factors, and this item was removed from the final instrument. Further principal component factor analysis on items of individual subscales found that each subscale was unidimensional. For all the attitude subscales, the Cronbach's internal reliability coefficient was above 0.7. Correlation between the seven subscale measures ranged from 0.3 to 0.7.

Science Achievement Influences Survey (SAIS) (Odom, Stoddard, & LaNasa, 2007)

SAIS is a 31-item survey to measure middle school students' self-reported attitudes toward science (in a Likert-scale format from *strongly agree* to *strongly disagree*) and frequency of exposure to classroom teacher practices and peer and home support (in a five option rating scale from *Less than once a month* to *More than once a week*). Factor analysis using principal component extraction with varimax rotation identified five factors: attitudes about science (7 items), peer participation (4 items), student-centered teaching practices (7 items), home support (4 items), and teacher-centered teaching practices (4 items). Cronbach alpha coefficients ranged from 0.607 to 0.883 for the above subscales.

Attitude to Science Instrument (ASI) (Shortened Version)
(Caleon & Subramaniam, 2008)

ASI, shortened version, is a 17-item Likert-scale survey of upper elementary school students' attitudes toward science. The questions include three of five subscales from its original instrument with minor modifications in presentation formats (e.g., using all positive statements and smiley faces). The three subscales correspond to enjoyment of science— interest in out-of-school science activities, social implications of science the value students give to science in improving lives, and career preference for science   preference, interest, and enjoyment in science careers. There are six items for the first two subscales and five items for the last subscale. The Flesch-Kincaid readability level of the instrument is 3.9. Cronbach's alpha internal consistency coefficients were 0.77 for enjoyment of science, 0.72 for social implications, 0.87 for career preference, and 0.89 overall. A statistically significant difference was found in enjoyment of science between gifted students and nongifted students, and between above-average students and average achievement students. Similarly, a statistically significant difference was found in both career preference and social implications between gifted students and average students, and between above-average students and average students.

INSTRUMENTS FOR MEASURING STUDENTS' MOTIVATION, INTEREST, AND SELF-EFFICACY

The Scientific Curiosity Inventory (SCI) (Campbell, 1971)

SCI measures junior high school students' curiosity about science. Items correspond to the first three levels of the Krathwohl's affective domain taxonomy, that is, receiving, responding, and valuing. The questions ask students to indicate how far they would go to satisfy their curiosity about a set of content questions related to physics, chemistry, biology, and earth science. Validation of the instrument involved an expert panel review and pilot-testing with a heterogeneous junior high school sample. Items included in the instrument had biserial correlation coefficients from .39 to .69 with a mean value of .54. The adjusted split-half reliability coefficient was .89, and standard error of measurement was 1.66.

Self-Efficacy Instrument (SI) (Baldwin, Ebert-May, & Burns, 1999)

SI is a 23-item rating-scale survey for measuring university nonbiology majors' self-efficacy related to biology. Each item asks students to think about how confident he/she feels in carrying out a given task by selecting from "totally confident," "very confident," "fairly confident," "only a little confident," and "not at all confident." The development of the instrument underwent three phases: developing items, identifying dimensions of the biology self-efficacy, and establishing criterion-related validity. The item development phases involved review of literature, interview of select students, and pilot-testing of the draft instrument. The revised instrument was then pilot tested again with a bigger university non-biology major sample. Principal component factor analysis suggested that there were three dominant factors as expected. Factor 1 related to students' sense of perceived confidence in writing and critiquing his/her biology ideas through laboratory reports as well as using analytical skills to conduct experiments in biology; factor 2 related to perceived confidence in generalizing skills learned from one biology course to other biology/science courses; factor 3 related to students' perceived confidence in his/her ability to apply biological concepts and skills to everyday events. The alpha internal consistency coefficients for the above three scales were 0.88, 0.88 and 0.89. Correlation between scores on the SI and scores on the biology achievement tests was small (0.18 to 0.27), demonstrating good discriminant validity.

Social-Cultural Scale (SCS) (Kesamang & Taiwo, 2002)

SCS measures Botswana junior high school students' Setswana customs and beliefs as they relate to identifiable practices at home, at the lands and at the cattle posts, as well as beliefs about death, rainfall, drought, etc. A total of 30 Likert-scale items were initially constructed. A five-member expert panel reviewed the items, resulting in the removal of 10 items. A pilot study involving 60 Grade 7 students revealed that the instrument had a split-half reliability of 0.86 after the Spearman-Brown adjustment. Principal component factor analysis resulted in six factors.

Cognitive Conflict Levels Test (CCLT)
(G. Lee, Kwon, Park, Kim, Kwon, & Park, 2003)

CCLT is a 12-item classroom survey of high school students' levels of cognitive conflict. Cognitive conflict is defined by four components; they are recognition of contradiction, interest, anxiety, and cognitive reappraisal of situation. There are 3 items for each of the above four components; each item consists of a statement (e.g., the result of the demonstration confuses me) and a five-choice rating scale from 0 (*not at all true*) to 4 (*very true*). A six-expert panel reviewed the items. Development of the instrument went through three pilot-tests, all taking place in South Korea. Pilot-test 1 involved 152 tenth-grade students plus an interview of selected students; pilot-test 2 involved 88 tenth-grade students as well as interview of a few selected students. Items were revised based on content review, item analysis, construct validation, and reliability review. The final pilot-test involved 279 tenth-grade students. All pilot-tests followed the following procedures: (a) assessment of student preconceptions and strength in their beliefs (about 7 minutes), (b) demonstration of an anomalous situation (about 2 minutes), and (c) administration of CCLT (about 4 minutes). Factor analysis showed that there were four dominant factors in student responses to CCLT; the four factors explained over 72% total variance. Correlation between the four subscales ranged from –0.04 to 0.48. Cronbach's alpha internal consistent coefficients for the four subscales ranged from 0.69 to 0.87.

Students' Motivation toward Science Learning (SMTSL)
(Tuan, Chin, & Shieh, 2005)

SMTSL is a 35-item questionnaire measuring secondary school students' motivation to learn science. It contains six subscales: (a) self-efficacy (7 items), (b) active learning strategies (8 items), (c) science learning value (5 items), (d) performance goal (4 items), (e) achievement goal (5 items), and (f) learning environment stimulation (6 items). All items are in a Likert-scale format, with 1 for "strongly disagree", 2 "disagree", 3 "no opinion", 4 "agree", and 5 "strongly agree". Validation took place in Taiwan with a sample size of 1407. Principal component factor analysis found six factors as expected. Cronbach's internal consistency reliability coefficients for the six subscales ranged from 0.7 to 0.91; the alpha for the entire instrument was 0.91. Correlation coefficient among the subscales ranged from 0.09 to 0.51. In addition, students' SMTSL scores were found to be statistically significantly correlated with their attitude toward science scores and with their science achievement scores.

Intrinsic Motivation for Learning Science (IMLS)
(Juriševi, Glažar, Puko, & Devetak, 2007)

The 125-item IMLS questionnaire assesses intrinsic motivation for learning biology (IMLS biology), physics (IMLS physics), and chemistry (IMLS chemistry), as well as general intrinsic motivation for studying (IMLS general learning), and motivations for learning mathematics

(IMLS mathematics) and foreign languages (IMLS foreign language). In the part of the IMLS for chemistry, special attention is directed to the assessment of students' intrinsic motivation for learning chemical concepts on the three levels of chemical representation (i.e., macro, submicro, and symbolic). Each item is stated in a Likert-scale format, with 1 = *strongly disagree*, 2 = *disagree*, 3 = *sometimes disagree/sometimes agree*, 4 = *agree*, and 5 = *strongly agree*. The internal consistency (Cronbach α) of the IMLS was 0.78. The subscales measuring intrinsic motivation for learning different levels of chemical concepts correlated statistically significantly ranging from 0.21 to 0.60 (n = 140). Student intrinsic motivation for learning chemistry was statistically significantly correlated with students' understanding of chemistry concepts (r = 0.30). Statistically significant differences were found between intrinsic motivation for learning chemistry and intrinsic motivation for learning biology and physics; a statistically significant difference was also found between intrinsic motivation for learning chemistry and general intrinsic motivation for learning.

Affective Assessment in Cell Biology (AACB)
(Kitchen, Reeve, Bell, Sudweeks, & Bradshaw, 2007)

AACB is a set of three instruments for assessing three affective variables related to a university cell biology course. The three instruments are: (a) attitude toward college courses that focus on the development of thinking skills versus courses that focus on factual recall, (b) self-efficacy toward understanding basic concepts in cell biology and solving problems that require the interpretation of experimental data, and (c) interest in learning various concepts and skills in cell biology. The attitude instrument contains 10 adjective pairs forming a semantic differential scale. The scale is presented in two sets, one referring to the development of thinking skills, and another to the focus on factual recall. Item-total correlation ranged from 0.63 to 0.79 for items in the analytic set, and from 0.25 to 0.70 for items in the recall set. The overall internal consistency reliability was 0.92 for the analytic skill set and 0.87 for the recall set. Principal component factor analysis revealed that the majority of items loaded on one factor.

The self-efficacy (confidence) instrument assesses students' self-efficacy regarding cell biology based on seven tasks: (a) a graphical figure on conventional coordinates, (b) an electropherogram, (c) a textbook figure, (d) a table with several columns of experimentally derived numbers, (e) a page of text, and (f) and (g) the title pages from two published papers on cellular biology topics. The tasks represent what practicing biologists engage daily in research. Students are asked to rate their confidence on a 5-point scale from 0 *(not confident at all)* to 4 *(extremely confident)* in either reading or comprehending the item (textual excerpt) or drawing conclusions from the data presented in graphs and tables. The item-total correlation was above 0.6 for six items and 0.48 for one item. Internal consistency reliability was 0.87.

The interest instrument contains two sets of 11 items, each measuring interest in cell biology topics and interest in cognitive reasoning skills in cell biology. The item-total correlation coefficients for all items in the interest in topics scale were above 0.45, and the internal consistency reliability was 0.93. Similarly, the item-total correlation coefficients for all items in the interest in cognitive skills scale were above 0.50, and the internal consistency reliability was 0.91.

Sources of Science Self-Efficacy Scale (S^3ES) (Britner, 2008)

S^3ES was adapted from a scale to measure the same construct in mathematics. It consists of four subscales measuring effects of mastery experiences (8 items), vicarious experiences (5 items), social persuasions (8 items), and physiological states (8 items). The physiological state subscale is also called the science anxiety scale. Exploratory factor analysis was conducted to validate the above subscale structure. Items for each of the subscales loaded on one factor. Loadings for mastery experience items ranged from 0.56 to 0.85; vicarious experience items from 0.49 to 0.85; social persuasion items from 0.63 to 0.86; and physiological state items from 0.61 to 0.87. Cronbach's alpha reliability indices for the above subscales were 0.87 for mastery experiences, 0.81 for vicarious experiences, 0.92 for social persuasions, and 0.92 for physiological states.

Conceptions of Learning Science Questionnaire (COLS)
(Lee, Johanson & Tsai, 2008)

COLS is a 31-item survey on high school student conceptions of learning science. Conceptions of learning science were identified from previous phenomenographic studies, and include views of learning science as: (a) memorizing, (b) preparing for test, (c) calculating and practicing tutorial problems, (d) increasing knowledge, (e) applying, (f) understanding, and (g) seeing in a new way. Initially, six to eight items were constructed for each of the above seven categories, and all items followed a Likert scale format with five categories from *strongly agree, agree, no opinion, disagree*, and *strongly disagree*. An expert reviewed the items for content validity. Construct validity was established through both exploratory and confirmatory factor analyses. Categories of *understanding* and *seeing in a new way* were combined after factor analysis. Cronbach's alpha coefficients for the final six subscales were 0.85, 0.91, 0.90, 0.84, and 0.91, and the alpha for the entire instrument was 0.91.

Intellectual Risk Taking, Interest in Science, Creative Self-Efficacy and Perceptions of Teacher Support Survey (Beghetto, 2009)

This 18-item survey measures elementary school (Grades 3-6) students on four constructs: intellectual risk taking, interest in science, creative self-efficacy, and perceptions of teacher support. Each item is rated by students from 1 *(not true)* to 5 *(very true)*. Intellectual risk taking is measured based on students' reports of engaging in intellectually risky learning behaviors (e.g., sharing tentative ideas, asking questions, willingness to try and learn new things) when learning science. Interest in science is measured based on student content-specific feeling-related (e.g., I like science) and value-related (e.g., Science is important to me) responses. Creative self-efficacy is measured based on student beliefs about their ability to generate novel and useful ideas in science and whether they view themselves as having a good imagination in science. Finally, perceptions of teacher support are related to key teacher support aspects identified in the literature. Principal component analysis found that the above four factors explained 49.5% of total variance and items loaded highly on their expected factors. Cronbach's alpha coefficients for the above four scales were 0.80, 0.77, 0.83, and 0.77. Student intellectual risk taking scores were statistically significantly correlated with measures of student science abilities, science interest, and creative self-efficacy in science.

Test for Ethical Sensitivity in Science (TESS) Plus (Fowler, Zeidler, & Sadler, 2009)

TESSPlus is an adapted version of the Test for Ethical Sensitivity in Science (TESS) (Clarkeburn, 2002) with the addition of one more scenario. It assesses high school students' ability to recognize the moral aspects associated with scientific issues. TESSplus consists of two socioscientific scenarios which students read and are asked to list up to five possible questions or issues they would raise before reaching a decision about the scenario. One scenario, taken from the original TESS, describes a situation involving the development of pharmaceutical milk using genetically modified cows (genetic modification scenario). The other scenario describes a situation involving reproductive cloning for infertile parents (reproductive cloning scenario). Scoring of the TESSplus is done by rating each response on a scale of 0 to 3 points based on the degree of moral considerations present (0 being none to 3 being strong moral consideration). Scores from both scenarios are added to provide a measure of moral sensitivity. Two researchers were involved in scoring the TESSplus. Interrater consistency was 97%.

Science Motivation Questionnaire (SMQ)
(Glynn & Koballa, 2006; Glynn, Taasoobshirazi, & Brickman, 2009)

SMQ is a 30-item Likert-scale instrument for measuring students' motivation to learn science in college science courses. It has the following subscales: (a) intrinsically motivated science learning (5 items), (b) extrinsically motivated science learning (5 items), (c) relevance of learning science to personal goals (5 items), (d) responsibility (self-determination) for learning science (5 items), (e) confidence (self-efficacy) in learning science (5 items), and (f) anxiety about science assessment (5 items). The overall Cronbach's alpha was 0.93.

An initial validity study (Glynn & Koballa, 2006) found that the Cronbach's coefficient alpha was 0.93. The SMQ scores were statistically significantly correlated with student college science GPAs and the student belief that science was relevant to one's career. Each item is rated from 1 *(never)* to 5 *(always)*. Out of a total possible maximal score of 150, a score between 30 and 59 is interpreted as "never to rarely" motivated; a score between 60-89 is interpreted as "rarely to sometimes" motivated, a score between 90-119 is interpreted as "sometimes to often" motivated, and a score between 120-150 is interpreted as "often to always" motivated.

A further validation study with non-science majors (Glynn et al., 2009) was also conducted. Principal component factor analysis revealed five factors; they are: intrinsic motivation and personal relevance (10 items), self-efficacy and assessment anxiety (9 items), self-determination (4 items), career motivation (2 items), and grade motivation (5 items). The five factors explained 60% of total variance. Cronbach's coefficient alpha was found to be 0.91. Correlation between SMQ scores and students' college science GPAs, and between SMQ scores and student beliefs on the relevance of science to their careers was statistically significant. Student essays about their motivation to learn science and interviews with 48 students provided additional support to the construct and criterion-related to the instrument.

INSTRUMENTS FOR MEASURING TEACHER AFFECTIVE VARIABLES

Attitude Toward Science (ATS) (Button & Stephens, 1963)

ATS measures preservice elementary teachers' attitudes toward elementary school science. The development of the instrument followed the approach to developing an equal interval Thurston scale. One hundred subjects sorted the 50 statements into 11 groupings from 1 (dislike) to 11 (like). Categories 1-5 were considered unfavorable, 6 neutral, and 7-11 favorable. Q values (distance between the first quartile and the third quartile) were used to select the final 20 items to form the instrument. The final 20 items met the following requirements: (a) low Q values, (b) normal distribution of scale values from 1 through 11, and (c) an equal number of favorable and unfavorable statements. The test-retest reliability coefficient was .93.

An Attitude Inventory (Hoover & Schutz, 1963)

This attitude inventory is a 54-item survey for measuring science teachers' attitudes toward environmental conservation. Each item presents a brief hypothetical situation to which the subject might react on a 5-point Likert scale. Pilot-testing involved 104 science teachers. Cluster analysis found 16 clusters. However, only 3 of 16 clusters had a KR-20 reliability greater than .70. Cluster 1 (18 items) was interpreted as Assistance for the Common Good (KR-20 = .93); cluster 2 (20 items) was interpreted as Regulation for the Common Good (KR-20 = .93); and cluster 3 (16 items) was interpreted as Private Rights versus Conservation (KR-20 = .87).

Beliefs About Nature of Science, Nature of Children, and Role of a Teacher (Good, 1971)

This instrument measures elementary teachers' beliefs about nature of science, nature of children, and the role of a teacher. The initial version was tried with prospective elementary teachers in three quarters as both pre- and posttests; items that showed significant increase from pre- to postcourse were retained. The final version contains 30 items. Each item has five possible responses ranging from (1) *strongly agree* to (5) *strongly disagree*.

Checklist for Assessment of Science Teachers (CAST) (Brown, 1973)

CAST has two forms: the supervisor's perceptions form (CAST: SP), and the pupil's perceptions form (CAST: PP). CAST: SP consists of three subscales: (a) student-teacher relations, (b) classroom activities used by the teacher, and (c) teacher's personal adjustment. CAST: PP consists of only subscales A and B above. Each subscale consists of five questions, and each question has five responses describing various characteristics of the teacher's instructions. Items were selected from the available related instruments at the time. A group of professors and doctoral students in science education rated teachers. Intraclass correlations ranged from .53 to .98 with a mode of .86 for the 15 items. KR-20 was .74 for CAST: PP.

The Science Attitude Scale (SAS) (Shrigley, 1974; Thompson & Shrigley, 1986)

SAS is a five-category Likert-scale instrument for measuring elementary preservice science teachers' attitudes toward science. There are 23 items, 14 positive ones and 9 negative ones. It measures two related attitude domains: (a) attitude toward teaching science, and (b) attitude toward taking science courses. After the publication of the original instrument in 1974, the instrument was revised and revalidated (Thompson & Shrigley, 1986). First, the original 23 items were reviewed by an expert panel of three science educators who recommended that 10 of 23 items be eliminated. The remaining items were also revised and 36 new items were written. The items together related to four subcomponents of the attitude: (a) the comfort-discomfort of teaching science, (b) the handling of science equipment, (c) time required to prepare and teach science, and (d) the basic need American students have for science. The revised instrument was then pilot-tested with 83 preservice elementary teachers. Twenty-two items were retained based on the criteria that items had high item-total correlation, low percent of neutral responses, a skewed distribution among the five choices, and were related to one of four subcomponents. The retained 22 items were given to 226 preservice science teachers. The coefficient alphas for the four subcomponents/subscales ranged from 0.63 to 0.79; intercorrelation between the four subscales ranged from 0.46 to 0.70. Principal component factor analysis found that there were four dominant factors, but the four factors did not correspond to the defined four subcomponents. The first factor contained 8 items, which was interpreted as teacher anticipation or the preparation for the teaching of science. The second factor contained five items and the third factor contained 3 items; factors 2 and 3 were interpreted as comfort-discomfort of teaching science. The fourth factor only had one item about children's curiosity about science. Coefficient alpha based only on the 16 items related to factors 1-3 was 0.88. Correlation between scores on SAS and scores on a metrication attitude scale was 0.34, and the correlation between scores on SAS and scores on a reading attitude scale was 0.08, indicating convergent and divergent validity.

Inquiry Science Teaching Strategies (ISTS) (Lazarowitz & Lee, 1976)

ISTS is a 40-item Likert scale measuring secondary science teachers' attitudes toward inquiry science teaching. Inquiry science teaching involves three areas: classroom teacher-student interaction, laboratory investigations, and textbook uses. Validation of the instrument involved expert panel reviews of items, and pilot-testing with preservice science teachers. Construct validity was established using five groups with various degrees of attitudes toward inquiry teaching and the five groups scored as expected with science experts scoring the highest and ordinary science teachers the lowest. Cronbach's alpha of the instrument based on the above groups ranged from .54 to .85.

Teacher Orientation to Science Instruction (TOTSI)
(Connelly, Finegold, Wahlstrom, & Ben-Peretz, 1977)

TOTSI assesses science teachers' assumptions on the following four dimensions: nature of the learner, nature of scientific knowledge, cultural setting for the curriculum, and nature of the teacher. In addition, the instrument assesses interactions among these factors. TOTSI has 8 subtests, and each subtest has 3 to 8 items. The teacher indicates how well the statements match his or her own positions. Because there may be a difference between what a teacher actually does in class and what a teacher would like to do in class, every response has two columns: column A relates to actual classroom situation and column B relates to desired classroom situation. The instrument was field-tested with science teachers. Reliability coefficients ranged from .21 to .79 for various sets of items.

Moore Assessment Profile (MAP) (Moore, 1977)

MAP is a 117-item science teacher needs assessment. Each item is followed by a continuum from 1 to 4, representing "no need," "little need," "moderate need," and "much need." Space is available for teachers to list additional needs. Validation involved panel review of items, and pilot-testing with elementary, middle and high school science teachers. The reliability based on Hoyt's analysis of variance was .986. Factor analysis indicated that there were 13 main factors accounting for 73% of the total variance.

Science Teaching Efficacy Beliefs Instrument (STEBI) (Riggs & Enochs, 1990)

STEBI measures elementary science teachers' self-efficacy related to teaching science. It contains two scales: the personal science teaching efficacy belief scale, and the science teaching outcome expectancy scale. Items are presented in a Likert-scale format with choices from *strongly agree* to *strongly disagree*. Initial items were reviewed by an expert panel. A preliminary study with 71 practicing elementary teachers resulted in further revisions of items and refinement of the instrument. The main study involved 331 subjects. Cronbach's alpha for the personal science teaching efficacy belief scale was 0.91, and 0.77 for the science teaching outcome expectancy scale. Principal component factor analysis showed that there were only two factors with an eigenvalue greater than one, supporting the hypothesized two scales of the instrument. Teachers' scores on the two scales were also found statistically significantly correlated with a list of criterion variables such as years of teaching, use of activity-based science instruction, and so on.

Context Beliefs about Teaching Science (CBATS)
(Lumpe, Haney, & Czerniak, 2000)

   CBATS is a 26-item survey of science teachers' context beliefs. Each item asks teachers to state their degree of agreement in a Liket-scale format with the stated factor to enable them to be an effective teacher—the enabling subscale, and to indicate how likely each stated factor will occur in their schools by choosing one from "very likely," "somewhat likely," "neither," "somewhat unlikely," and "very unlikely"—the likelihood subscale. Three groups of teachers were involved in the development. Interviewing 130 science teachers generated a pool of items for creating the initial instrument. The initial instrument was pilot-tested with a sample of 71 teachers. Based on the item and test analysis of pilot-testing data, the instrument was revised and then given to a larger sample of science teachers. Factor analysis suggested that there were two dominant factors accounting for 23.9% variance. Science teachers' CBATS scores were found to be modestly correlated with their outcome expectancy scores $(r = 0.34, p = 0.000)$ and with science teaching capability beliefs $(r = 0.19, p = 0.002)$. In addition, CBATS scores were statistically significantly correlated with years of teaching, number of science methods courses taken, number of science teaching strategies used, and minutes spent on teaching science. Science teachers demonstrated statistically significant higher enabling beliefs than likelihood beliefs. The alpha for the enabling subscale was 0.86, for the likelihood subscale 0.85, and for the entire instrument 0.85.

Self-Efficacy Beliefs about Equitable Science Teaching and Learning (SEBEST)
(Ritter, Boone, & Rubba, 2001)

   SEBEST assesses preservice elementary science teachers' personal self-efficacy and outcome expectancy beliefs with regard to teaching and learning science in an equitable manner when working with diverse learners. A seven-step plan was followed to develop the instrument. Step 1 involved the definition of the construct and content to be measured; a content matrix consisting of three dimensions, that is, positive/negative x personal self-efficacy/outcome expectancy x ethnicity/language minorities/gender/ socioeconomic, was developed. Step 2 involved item preparation; 195 Likert-type items were developed. Step 3 involved review of draft items by 10 graduate students in science education. Step 4 involved five experts who reviewed the content validity of the revised items; 48 items were retained to form the draft instrument. Step 5 involved the first try-out of the draft instrument with 226 preservice elementary science teachers. Step 6 involved formulation of the instrument based on item and factor analysis. Principal component factor analysis identified four significant factors. Eleven items loaded on factor 1 that was identified as personal self-efficacy associated with socioeconomic status, gender and ethnicity. Ten items loaded on factor 2 that was identified as outcome efficacy with language minorities, socioeconomic status, gender and ethnicity. Six items loaded on factor 3 that was identified as personal self-efficacy associated with language minorities; and eight items loaded on factor 4 that was identified as outcome expectancy across all content contexts. Internal consistency reliability coefficients for the four subscales ranged from 0.72 to 0.82. The reliability coefficient for the entire instrument was 0.87. Step 7 was a further study of reliability with different samples. Alpha coefficients were consistently high. Finally, Rasch rating scale modeling was applied to the data to provide additional evidence for the construct validity of the instrument.

Attitudes toward Teaching of Environmental Risk (ATER) (Zint, 2002)

ATER is a 14-item instrument for measuring science teachers' attitudes toward teaching environmental risks. The items are related to three theories about attitude: theory of reasoned action, theory of planned behavior, and theory of trying. Each item has seven response options described as *extremely, quite, slightly, neither, slightly, quite,* and *extremely.* Validation involved a mail-survey of over two thousand teachers with an adjusted return rate of 80%. Construct validity was established by confirmatory factor analysis. Composite reliability based on weighted factor loadings was reported to be high (over .90 for three major subscales).

The Attitudes and Beliefs about the Nature and the Teaching of Mathematics and Science (McGinnis, Kramer, Shama, Graeber, Parker, & Watanabe, 2002)

This instrument measures preservice science teachers' attitudes and beliefs about the nature and the teaching of math and science. Most items are from the available related instruments at the time. All items are in the Likert-scale format. Phase 1 development involved expert reviews of draft items. Two additional phases of pilot-testing resulted in the final 37-item version of the instrument. Factor analysis revealed 5 main factors. Alpha reliability coefficients ranged from .60 to .81 for the above five factors. Results showed that preservice teachers who participated in reformed courses improved significantly toward the intended direction on their attitudes and beliefs about the nature and the teaching of mathematics and science.

Teacher Perceptions and Practices Regarding the Use of the History of Science in Their Classrooms (Wang & Marsh, 2002)

This survey measures elementary and secondary science teachers' values and practices of integrating history of science into science teaching. The survey covers three aspects regarding history of science: (a) conceptual understanding, (b) procedural understanding, and (c) contextual understanding. Thirteen items are included, with 4 on conceptual understanding, 3 on procedural understanding, and 6 on contextual understanding. The response to each item is from two 5-point scales, one is in the Likert scale (i.e., from *strongly disagree* to *strongly agree*) on values of integrating history of science, and another is a rating scale (i.e., from *rarely occurred* to *occurred frequently*) on practices of integrating history of science. Cronbach's alpha for the perceptions scale was .904, and alpha for the practice scale was .949.

Attitude to Science Education (ASE) (Pell & Jarvis, 2003)

ASE is a 49-item Likert scale survey of primary teachers' attitudes toward science teaching. It measures two main constructs: attitude toward science teaching and attitude toward professional preparation for science teaching. Initial questions (58) came from previously published instruments to make them appropriate for primary teachers in England and Wales. Eighteen teachers were involved in a pilot study to finalize the instrument containing 52 items. The main study involved 58 teachers. The pilot study and main study samples were pooled into one sample for the final validation study. Thirty-three items were related to effective science teaching in the classroom. Principal component factor analysis revealed three major factors forming three subscales: investigative, pupil-centered science pertaining to the value teachers put on encouraging pupil initiative, interest and wonder; classroom management pertaining to value given to systematic, structured approaches to the learning within the classroom; and general scientific method pertaining to views about the natural philosophy underlying an empirical, pupil-participative science. Cronbach's alpha coefficients for the above three subscales were 0.89, 0.83, and 0.83.

Nineteen items were related to preparation and professional aims. Principal component factor analysis revealed three major factors forming three subscales: in-service improvement pertaining to teachers' attitude toward the worth of in-service education with an emphasis on appropriate use of human and physical resources; theoretically grounded science teaching pertaining to the extent teachers feel they should operate from a child-centered constructivist process; and testing pertaining to attitude toward a formative approach to assessment. Cronbach's alpha coefficients for the above three subscales were 0.86, 0.86, and 0.65. Combining items for the above two constructs by excluding three items formed the composite scale called "Attitude to Science Teaching." The Cronbach's alpha for this composite scale was 0.94.

Biology Teachers' Attitude toward and Use of Indiana's Evolution Standards (Donnelly & Boone, 2007)

This instrument measures biology teachers' attitudes toward standard and evolution in particular. The instrument includes 24 items related to four subscales: US (teacher use of standards, 8 items), AS (teacher attitude toward standards, 7 items), UES (teacher use of evolution standards, 7 items), and ETP (teachers' evolution teaching practices, 5 items). Its development followed an iterative process guided by Rasch modeling. Initial items were developed based on hypotheses, and Rasch modeling was used to test the hypotheses. The initial draft form (Form A) was revised by modifying/deleting/adding items based on reviews of selected science teachers and university science educators, and on fit statistics and person-item maps produced by Rasch modeling. Data for Rasch modeling came from a stratified random sample of biology teachers in Indiana. Item reliability coefficients based on item separation indices for the revised form (Form B) were 0.98 (US), 0.97 (AS), 0.90 (UES), and 0.98 (ETP). The construct validity was claimed based on person-item map and its agreement with researchers' hypotheses.

Biotechnology Attitude Questionnaire (BAQ) (Prokop, Leskova, & Kubiatlo, & Diran, 2007)

BAQ is a 17-item Likert-scale survey to measure university preservice science teachers' attitudes toward biotechnologies. Questions for the instrument came from various previously published instruments. The content validity of the instrument was established through review by three experts in the fields of genetics and biology education who were asked whether the items were relevant to the goal of the questionnaire. BAQ had a reliability (Cronbach's alpha) of 0.76. A statistically significant correlation was found between students' biotechnology knowledge and their attitude toward biology technology.

Commentary

A large number of measurement instruments are available; they measure a variety of affective variables related to teachers and students. One major consideration when choosing a measurement instrument to use is the appropriateness of the defined construct. Because affective variables are diverse, and different theories may define affective variables quite differently, the applicability of the theory that was used to define the measured construct to the intended uses must be critically evaluated. Take attitude as an example. We can see from the above instruments that the instruments measure a wide variety of attitudes, reflecting diverse theoretical frameworks related to attitude. The diversity in theoretical frameworks requires that an attitude instrument has a clearly defined construct of attitude. This is an issue of construct validity. Unfortunately, many of the instruments have an unclear definition of attitude, thus the construct validity is questionable. This limitation in attitude instruments has been pointed out in many previous reviews of attitudinal scales. For example, Germann (1988) concluded that, in many of the instruments, "First, the construct of attitude has been vague, inconsistent, and ambiguous. Second, research has been conducted without a theoretical model of the relationship of attitude with other variables" (p. 689). One consensus emerging from the literature is that there is no such thing as a general attitude toward science; instead, attitude is quite domain and context specific. For example, attitude toward science and attitude toward chemistry may be quite different (Salta & Tzougraki, 2004); attitude toward the importance of science, attitude toward science careers, and attitude toward science curriculums may also be quite different from each other (Menis, 1989).

Examination of the literature has shown that the validity of the above instruments varies greatly. Researchers have raised questions about validity of many instruments. For example, based on a review of 56 instruments on attitudes toward science, Munby (1983b) concluded that most of the instruments lack construct validity. Laforgia (1988) claimed that many attitude instruments have inadequate criterion-related validity. Doran, Lawrenz and Helgeson (1994) concluded that "ambiguity of terms and quality of instruments are two serious problems facing those interested in assessing attitudes to science" (p. 428). Blalock et al. (2008) conducted a comprehensive review of 66 measurement instruments published in peer-reviewed journals from 1935 to 2005; only 20 of the instruments were directly related to attitude toward science. They used a scoring rubric to rate every measurement instrument in terms of the theoretical background, reliability, validity, dimensionality and development/usage with higher weights given for reliability, validity and dimensionality. Scores for the 20 attitudes toward science instruments ranged from 3 to 22 out of a total of possible 28 points, with the highest score (22) for Attitude Toward Science in School Assessment (Germann, 1988). They expressed a number of methodological concerns with the published attitude instruments including absence of reliability and validity evidence, overall poor quality of validation studies, a nearly universal disregard for missing data, and a dominance of instrument validation in a single study. Many of the instruments rely heavily on content and face validity established by expert panel reviews while ignoring other types of evidence. Given the above, any instrument should be chosen with a critical eye. Also, continuing validating the chosen instrument based on new data should always be conducted.

It is common for attitude measurement instruments to adopt the Likert scale. Besides the potential issue with fakability (i.e., responses may not be truthful) (Laforgia, 1988), one serious issue associated with the Likert scale is obtaining a total scale score by adding individual item scores. Values such as 1-5 assigned to five choices of a statement do not have the same origin and interval unit because they are not on a ratio or interval scale. Also, some items are easier to endorse, while others more difficult to endorse. The consequence of the above is that individual item scores cannot be meaningfully added into a total score. This should make sense if we consider that individual items represent different levels of attitude, and a same value such as 2 can mean quite different things on different items. Consider "I am happy to attend the science class" and "I want to major in science at university." Choosing "agree" to the above two statements, thus receiving a same score of 4, would mean very different levels of attitude toward science. Adding two 4s together does not make logical sense. In order to address this issue, different ways of analyzing Likert scale data than using total scores should be adopted. For example, responses to different items in an attitude scale may be represented by a profile, and the difference in profiles between different groups or between two time points can be meaningfully compared. Chi-square or nonparametric statistics, instead of parametric inferential statistics (e.g., t test) may be applied for statistical testing. One best way currently available is to use Rasch modeling to convert raw scores into latent scores so that respondents' attitudes will be measured on a latent attitude scale. Some of the measurement instruments (e.g., Donnelly & Boone, 2007; Siegel & Ranney, 2003) have been developed using Rasch modeling. Alternatives to the Likert scale should also be considered. Examples of such alternatives are the Thurston scale (1925), Guttman scale (1944), semantic differential (Osgood, Suci, & Tannenbaum, 1971), and checklist.

As for measurement instruments for teachers, it is important to make a differentiation between teacher beliefs and teacher practices (Connelly et al., 1977; Wang & Marsh, 2002). This distinction is very important because the two are not necessarily always the same. Understanding the discrepancy between teachers' beliefs and practices can inform ongoing science education reforms so that best practices promoted in university classrooms are actually implemented in K-12 classrooms. This issue also points to the critical importance of assessing actual teaching practices and their direct impact on student learning.

DEVELOPING INSTRUMENTS FOR MEASURING AFFECTIVE VARIABLES

Identify the Primary Purpose(s) for Which the Measurement Results Will Be Used

The need for measuring affective variables comes from various demands. Many affective outcomes are part of national and state science curriculum standards, and measurement of these affective learning outcomes is an important part of program evaluation. For example, in the National Assessment of Educational Progress (NAEP) science assessment, the student background questionnaire typically includes a scale for measuring students' attitudes toward science. Information from this measurement can help science education policy making at the national level. Similarly, affective learning outcomes are an important part of a teacher education program, thus measurement of teacher affective learning outcomes may be a part of the teacher education program evaluation. Because the measurement of affective variables primarily relies on self-reports, measurement of affective learning outcomes for accountability purposes may not be appropriate.

In addition, because cognitive, affective, and psychomotor domains are closely related, measurement of affective variables related to both students and teachers is important for monitoring science teaching and learning processes. Research on science teaching and learning may require examination of the relationship between cognitive, affective and psychomotor variables, and measurement of affective variables can help study the quantitative relationships among various cognitive, affective, and psychomotor variables.

Define the Construct to Be Measured

Affective variables are vast and diverse, it is critically important to clearly define the construct to be measured. Although it is possible to measure more than one construct in one measurement administration, essentially each measurement instrument should measure one and only one construct. In this way, each measurement instrument defines one scale and each measure is based on only one scale.

Identifying and defining the construct to measure must be consistent with theories. Different theoretical orientations suggest different variables related to the construct. For example, motivation from a behavioral orientation would focus on such variables as rewards, benefits, peer pressures, and so on; while a social-cultural orientation toward motivation would focus on such variables as peer interaction, cultural values, societal norms, historical evolution, and environmental settings. Because of the contextualized nature of affective variables, when defining the affective construct, it is important to consider the construct's relevance to specific science content domains, nature of the target students (e.g., elementary, secondary and university science students) and teachers (e.g., preservice and inservice, or elementary and secondary science teachers), and its relations with other cognitive, affective and psychomotor variables. For example, attitudes toward science may be differentiated as attitude toward school science as taught in the school, attitude toward science as it is involved in everyday life, attitude toward science as it is considered as a future career, etc. Whatever theory is used to define the construct to measure, keep in mind that developing measurement instrument is not to validate the theory; on the contrary, the theory needs to be assumed in order to guide the development process of the measurement instrument.

One basic assumption of measurement is the difference in quantity of the defined construct among subjects. Any defined construct must imply a hierarchy of subjects' performances on the construct. For example, if the defined construct is secondary students' attitude toward science, then it is assumed by this construct that there are different levels of attitude toward science among secondary students, and this difference can be quantified on a unidimensional linear scale.

Identify Behaviors That Represent the Construct

Once the construct is defined, specific subjects' behaviors related to the defined construct should then be identified. Because the defined construct implies a linear scale, the specific behaviors should form a clear hierarchy or progression. For example, interest in school science may be

Conducting extra readings and projects beyond homework

Completing homework

Actively seeking opportunities to participate in science activities

Participating in science activities when invited

Making efforts to attend science class when there is conflict

Attending science class

Knowing that learning science is compulsory

Figure 4.2.   A hierarchy of student behaviors related to interest in school science. Higher behaviors represent higher interest in school science.

defined by a collection of student behaviors from attending to science class on time, active participation in science activities, and making efforts to complete science assignments, and so on. These student behaviors can be hypothesized to form a progression according to their interest in school science. Figure 4.2 shows a sample hierarchy of behaviors that represent the interest in school science.

Prepare a Test Specification

Once behaviors that define the affective construct are identified, the next step in development of the measurement instrument is to specify how many items will be developed and what behavior each of the items will measure. A two-dimensional specification table is commonly used for this purpose. In the specification table, specific behaviors are labeled on one axis, and types of items are labeled on the other axis. The cell values are number of items for specified behaviors. For example, a specification table for measuring interest in school science is as follows (Table 4.1).

In the above example, the instrument for measuring student interest in school science will consist of 35 items, with five items for each of the seven identified behavior types. Also, there will be two types of questions, Likert scale and rating scale. Of course, a measurement instrument may use only one item format, such as Likert-scale type questions. The guidelines suggested in chapter 3 for deciding test length are also applicable here when developing a test specification for measurement of an affective construct.

**Table 4.1.   A Test Specification
for Measurement of Interest in School Science**

	Likert-Scale Type Questions	Rating Scale
Conducting extra-science readings and activities beyond homework	0	5
Completing homework	0	5
Actively participating in science activities	5	0
Participating in science activities when asked	0	5
Making efforts to attend science classes	5	0
Attending science classes	0	5
Science is compulsory	5	0

Construct an Initial Pool of Items

Many item formats are available for measuring affective variables, depending on the construct to be measured. Most commonly used item types are Likert-scale, rating scale, semantic differential, and checklist or inventory.

Likert Scale

Likert-scale questions are attributable to Rensis Likert who first invented this question type to construct an attitude scale (Likert, 1932). A typical Likert-scale type question contains a statement followed by a list of five-category choices from *strongly agree* (SA), *agree* (A), *undecided* (U), *disagree* (D), and *strongly disagree* (SD). The respondent selects one of the five categories as his/her agreement to the statement. Guidelines for constructing Likert-scale items are available in chapter 1.

Rating Scale

Rating scale questions are very similar to Likert-scale questions. Both contain a statement and a set of hierarchical categories. Subjects respond to both rating scale and Likert-scale questions by choosing one of the categories. However, one difference between rating scale questions and Likert-scale questions is how categories are phrased. Compare the following two statements:

Statement 1:   School science is exciting
                    SA   A   U   D   SD

Statement 2:   School science is exciting
Always Most times Sometimes Occasionally Never

Statement 1 expresses a value judgment about school science, and respondents will decide to what degree they will agree or disagree with the judgment. Statement 1 is typical for Likert-scale questions. Statement 2 presents a phenomenon—school science is exciting, and respondents will decide how to respond by indicating the frequency of the phenomenon. Further, rating scale categories can be any descriptions that represent a quantitatively or qualitatively different hierarchy (e.g., 1, 2, 3, 4, 5; or excellent, very good, good, fine, and bad), while Likert-scale categories are different degrees of agreement (e.g., SA, A, U, D, SD). Because of the above differences, rating scale questions are more appropriate for measuring constructs related to behaviors, while Likert-scale questions are more appropriate for measuring constructs related to values and judgments.

Semantic Differential

Semantic differential was first proposed by Osgood and colleagues (Osgood, Suci, & Tannenbaum, 1971). It is intended to probe both cognitive and affective aspects of a construct. A construct is assumed to have three dimensions of meanings: evaluation (e.g., good-bad), potency (e.g., strong-weak), and activity (e.g., fast-slow). Evaluation pertains to feeling or value associated with the construct; potency pertains to the usefulness of the construct; and activity pertains to the dynamic nature of the construct. Each dimension typically consists of 3-15 bipolar adjectives. Scores on each of the dimensions are then averaged, and the three averaged scores are used to describe a respondent's cognitive and affective meanings assigned to the construct. The three dimensions together define a semantic space of the construct.

The following is an example of a semantic differential for school science:

What Does School Science Mean to You?

For each of the following bipolar pairs of adjectives, decide your agreement to each of the bipolar adjectives in relation to "School Science" by placing a ✓ mark on a dash. The closer the dash to an adjective, the more agreement you have on the adjective.

School Science is

Good	__	__	__	__	__	__	__	Bad
Positive	__	__	__	__	__	__	__	Negative
Valuable	__	__	__	__	__	__	__	Little use
Useful	__	__	__	__	__	__	__	Useless

Powerful	—	—	—	—	—	—	—	Powerless
Helpful	—	—	—	—	—	—	—	Helpless
Fun	—	—	—	—	—	—	—	Boring
Busy	—	—	—	—	—	—	—	Light
Engaged	—	—	—	—	—	—	—	Inattentive

When writing semantic differential items, it is important to keep three dimensions in mind and try to write items accordingly. As the case with any other item type, more items than specified in the specification table need to be created to give room for item deletions and revisions after pilot-testing.

Inventory/Checklist

Inventory or checklist questions contain a set of descriptive scenarios or facts; respondents are asked to check if they apply to them or not. Choices are typically binary; i.e., they are either Yes or No. Inventory and checklist are more appropriate for measuring affective variables closely related to behaviors.

Here is a set of sample inventory or checklist items that measure science teachers' awareness of professional development activities.

Example: For each of the following activities, please circle *Yes* if you think it is beneficial for your professional development related to teaching, and *No* if you think it is not beneficial for your professional development related to teaching.

Attending workshops offered by the school district	Yes	No
Attending the annual state science teacher conference	Yes	No
Reading popular science magazines	Yes	No
Reading newspapers	Yes	No
Reading science education research journals	Yes	No

In the above example, selecting *Yes* to an activity indicates a teacher's awareness of the potential of the activity for professional development.

Item Review and Try-Out

After a pool of items has been created, it is necessary to have items reviewed by a panel of experts consisting of both content experts and methodologists. The panelists should be briefed on the purpose of the measurement and the construct to be measured. Test specification may also be presented to the panelists to facilitate their review. Specific questions pertaining to the item content accuracy, language clarity, and alignment with the intended construct may also be prepared to help panelist review items.

After items have been reviewed by the panel and necessary revisions have been made to the items, the items should then be tried out by a small number of respondents. The respondents will not only respond to the items, but also state their impressions or comments on the clarity of the items. Interviews with a few respondents may also be helpful.

Field-Test

The resulting items from the previous development steps will then go for a field-testing. The sample chosen for the field testing should represent the intended population, particularly in the range of the construct to be measured. For example, if the construct is attitude toward school science, then the variation in attitude toward school science among the respondents in the sample should be expected to be similar to that of the population. Sample size should also be adequate. For rating scales including the Likert scale, Linacre (2004) suggests that at least 10 observations per category in the item should be used. For example, for an attitude survey using Likert-scale questions that contain five categories from *"strongly agree"* to *"strongly disagree,"* the minimal sample size should be 50 (10 × 5). A large sample size, such as 25 to 50 observations per category, can help maintain the stability of item parameter estimates during Rasch modeling.

Conduct Rasch Modeling

Statistical properties of items will then be studied using the pilot-testing data. As usual, a variety of fit statistics should be reviewed. During Rasch modeling, particular attention should be paid to the item category structure, because questions used for measuring affective variables typically involve more than two categories. Item category structure refers to the hierarchical progression among the categories. For Likert-scale questions, item categories are degrees of agreement from *"strongly agree"* to *"strongly disagree"*; for rating scale questions, item categories are various levels of ratings assigned to an aspect; for semantic differential items, item categories are the steps between two bi-polar adjectives; and for inventory or checklist questions, item categories are two incidents representing yes or no. Categories should clearly form a progression. Figure

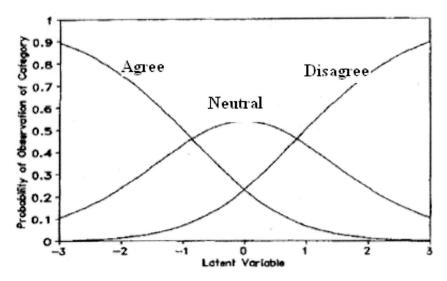

Figure 4.3. Expected category structure for a 3-category Likert-scale question (adapted from Linacre, 2004, p. 264). Each category has its own peak in its characteristic curve.

4.3 shows an ideal category structure for a 3-category Likert-scale question.

In Figure 4.3, the three categories (agree, neutral, and disagree) clearly form a progression. As a respondent's latent trait (e.g., attitude) increases, which is indicated by the increase in value on the x-axis, the respondent is becoming less and less likely to be in favor of the construct. Although the three categories overlap to some degree, each of them has its own unique zone of most probable trait level. Specifically, when a respondent's latent trait level (e.g., attitude) is smaller than −1, the respondent is most likely to be in favor, that is, agree, with the construct; when a respondent's latent trait level is between −1 and +1, the respondent is most likely to be neutral on the construct; and when the respondent's latent trait level is greater than +1, the respondent is most likely to be in disfavor, that is, disagree, of the construct. Ideally, step difficulties should increase by at least 1.4 logits but less than 5 logits between two adjacent categories (Linacre, 2004).

Considering a different category structure as shown in Figure 4.4, there are three categories contained in each of the questions, but only two categories have their unique zones of responses; category "neutral" is subsumed by the above two categories. In this case, the three categories do

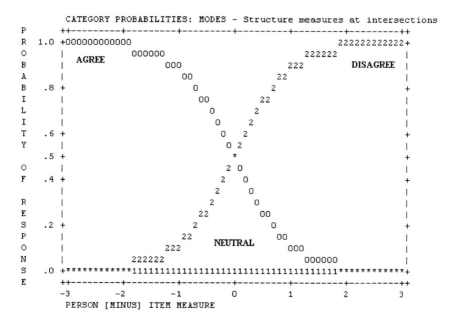

Figure 4.4.   A sample inappropriate category structure for a Likert-scale question. Category "neutral" is subsumed by the other two categories; category "neutral" has no distinct characteristic curve.

not form a clear progression. We could remove category "neutral" and make the item a binary one, that is, agree or disagree.

Figure 4.5 shows the empirical category structure for a Likert scale of university engineering students' attitude toward nanotechnology. In the Likert-scale questions, there are 5 categories from *Strongly Agree* (5), *Agree* (4), *Neutral* (3), *Disagree* (2), and *Strongly Disagree* (1). However, the category structure graph shows only 4 categories; category 5 is missing. This indicates that no respondent chose category 5 (Strongly Agree). In this case, although categories 1 to 4 form a clear progression, category 5 is not needed, thus should be removed from the items.

Design and Conduct Validity and Reliability Studies

Validity Study

Evidence for the validity of the measurement instruments may be established in terms of test content, response processes, internal structure, external structure, and consequences. Examination of test content may involve review of the definition of the affective construct to be mea-

```
CATEGORY PROBABILITIES: MODES - Structure measures at intersections

P      ++------+------+------+------+------+------+------+------++
R  1.0 +                                                          +
O      |                                                          |
B      |                                                          |
A      |11                                                     444|
B   .8 +  11                                                 44   +
I      |    11                                             44     |
L      |      11                                         44       |
I      |       1                                        4         |
T   .6 +        11        22222222                      4         +
Y      |          1    22           22        3333333  44         |
 .5 +          122            22  33        33 4               +
O      |          221              22  33         33 4            |
F   .4 +         2    11            *3              *3            +
|      |    22      1         3     33 22         4  33           |
R      |       22       11       2      44      33      3         |
E      |     2           1    33      2   4        33           |
S   .2 +  222             1*3          2244       333          +
P      |22               33 11          422          33 |
O      |               333       111    444     22          3|
N      |       333333         44***11         222222          |
S   .0 +***********444444444444444    1111111111111111**********+
E      ++------+------+------+------+------+------+------+------++
-4       -3      -2      -1       0       1       2       3       4
                       PERSON [MINUS] ITEM MEASURE
```

Figure 4.5. Category structure for a Likert scale on attitude toward nanotechnology. Although each category (i.e., 1, 2, 3, and 4) has its own distinct characteristic curve, category 5 is not shown in the graph, because none selected the response (i.e., strongly agree) for any item.

sured and how the test items cover the entire range of variation of the construct. Important questions to ask are: (a) Is the definition based on commonly accepted theories? (b) Is the defined construct clearly affective, that is, involving feeling, judgment, or values? (c) Is there an underlying linear progression for the construct? And (d) How do the test items represent the variation of specific behaviors indicating the construct? Answers to the above questions should be based on the stated theoretical framework and the test specification. A negative answer to any of the questions will call the measurement validity into question.

Response processes may be examined by reviewing examinees' response patterns. In addition, qualitative studies of item functioning during item try-out, and observation, interview, and artifacts of respondents about the measurement instruments can also enhance claims about the validity of the measurement instrument in terms of response processes.

Internal structure of the measurement instrument may be examined in a number of ways. In addition to reviews of various item-fit statistics and item category structure discussed earlier, the Wright map and dimensionality map can provide additional evidence to support the claim for the construct validity. Figure 4.6 shows the Wright map for a 7-item Likert scale measuring university engineering students' attitude toward nanotechnology. The seven items are:

	SA (5)	A (4)	U (3)	D (2)	SD (1)
1. All engineering students should know about nanotechnology					
2. More funding should be invested in developing nanotechnology					
3. Nanotechnology can stimulate economic growth					
4. All engineering majors should take nanotechnology courses					
5. Nanotechnology courses should be offered in high school					
6. Nanotechnology is critical for national defense					
7. Nanotechnology can solve important social problems					

Although item fit statistics showed adequate fit between data and the rating scale Rasch model, the range of item difficulties and person abilities shown in Figure 4.6 indicates a few noticeable gaps. For example, the difference in difficulty or endorsability between item 1 (Q1) and item 3 (Q3) is almost 1 logit, and there are very few students whose attitudes fall within this range. Thus the measurement instrument will not be able to differentiate students within this range. Also, we see that the range of item difficulty is not large enough to cover the student attitude range, because at both ends of the attitude continuum, there are no items to measure students. This Wright map suggests that the construct validity of the measurement instrument needs to be improved.

Figure 4.7 shows the dimensionality map of the nanotechnology sale. It shows that only items 2, 3, and 7 fall along one dimension, and the other four items do not conform with the same dimension because their residuals correlate highly with one potential additional construct. In fact, the Rasch measures explained only 43% of the total variance in observations, leaving 57% unexplained. This lack of unidimensionality further calls the construct validity of the instrument into question.

External structure can be examined by conducting correlation studies between examinees' Rasch scale scores and their measures of other variables. One important consideration is obviously the selection of the criterion variable for the correlation study. Finally, for consequence-related validation, because results from affective measurement are typically not

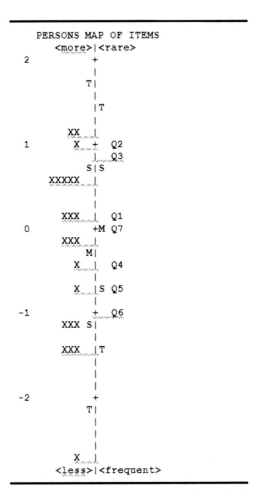

Figure 4.6.   Wright map for the measurement instrument of university engineer students' attitude toward nanotechnology. The difficulty range of items does not match the ability range of students, and there are noticeable gaps in the distribution of items.

used for important decision making such as accountability, a decision procedure related validity is thus of less importance for affective measurement validation.

Reliability Study

Reliability evidence of affective measurement may be established through the review of reliability of item and subject measures, and review

```
Variance explained by measures      =     5.3    43.1%
Unexplained variance (total)        =     7.0    56.9%
Unexpl var explained by 1st factor  =     2.3    18.7%
```

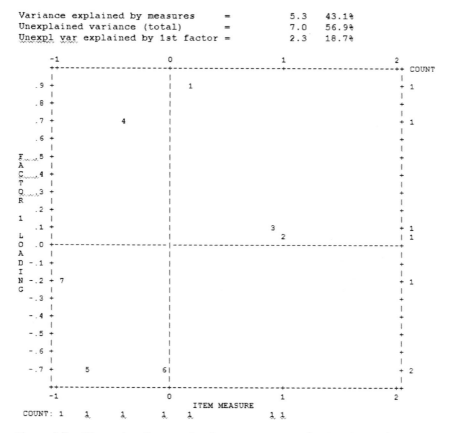

Figure 4.7.   Dimensionality map for the measurement of university engineer students' attitude toward nanotechnology. Items 1, 4, 5, and 6 have loadings beyond ±0.4, suggesting multidimensionality.

of the reliability of the instrument as a whole. After item and person parameters are calibrated, standard errors of measurements for each item and person should be reviewed. Person separation index and its equivalent Cronbach's alpha should be reviewed for their adequacy of reliability for person measures as a whole.

Develop Guidelines for Use of the Instrument

As with any other measurement instrument, appropriate documentation should be available to facilitate users to appropriately use the mea-

**Table 4.2.   Raw Score to Rasch Scale Score Conversion Table
for the Nanotechnology Attitude Scale**

SCORE	MEASURE	S.E.	SCORE	MEASURE	S.E.	SCORE	MEASURE	S.E.
7	-5.22E	18.70	15	42.47	5.80	23	68.40	6.06
8	7.98	10.81	16	45.77	5.70	24	72.28	6.42
9	16.66	8.24	17	48.98	5.63	25	76.76	7.01
10	22.55	7.22	18	52.13	5.59	26	82.38	8.09
11	27.35	6.67	19	55.25	5.59	27	90.85	10.73
12	31.57	6.33	20	58.38	5.61	28	103.94E	18.66
13	35.42	6.10	21	61.57	5.69			
14	39.03	5.93	22	64.88	5.83			

surement instrument. Documentation should include the construct definition, test specification, scoring, validity and reliability evidence, and score reporting and interpretation. In order to help users to convert raw scores into Rasch scale scores, a raw score to Rasch scale score conversion table should be included. Table 4.2 is a Winsteps output table for the engineering students' attitude toward nanotechnology instrument described earlier. It gives the logit equivalent score for each of the possible raw scores ranging from 7 to 28. As noted earlier, although each question has five categories, only four of five categories were functional, because no one selected *strongly agree* (SA) to any of the questions. This explains why the total possible raw score in the table is 28. The logit scale scores are set with a mean of 50 and a standard deviation of 10.

CHAPTER SUMMARY

The affective domain includes various variables related to interests, attitudes, valuing, appreciation, and adjusting; it is closely related to the cognitive and psychomotor domains. One influential conceptualization of affective variables is the taxonomy of affective education objectives (Krathwohl, Bloom, & Masia, 1964). This taxonomy perceives affective variables as a continuum from external influences to internal driving forces. This continuum is also hierarchical, that is, a higher category subsumes all its lower categories. The Krathworhl's affective taxonomy includes the following five levels or categories: receiving, responding, valuing, organization, and characterization. Each level also contains a few subcategories. Interest is primarily related to categories of receiving, responding, and valuing; attitude is primarily related to categories of valuing and organization.

Specifically in science education, various definitions of attitude are available. Attitude contains three dimensions: feeling, cognition, and behavior. No matter what attitude is to be measured, it is important to note that attitude cannot be separated from its context and the underlying body of influences that determine its real significance. Motivation is another affective construct commonly studied in science education. Although there is no universally-agreed upon definition of motivation, motivation relates to one's desire to act or not to act. Motivation is also contextualized, such as motivation to learn science, motivation to teach science, motivation to implement a new science curriculum, to name a few.

There is a large collection of measurement instruments of affective variables in science education; some are for students and others for teachers. The validity and reliability of these instruments varies greatly. In particular, the construct validity of many instruments may be questioned because our understanding of the constructs have changed over the years. Continuously validating and expanding the variety of evidence for validity and reliability claims of current instruments is necessary. Another issue in using current measurement instruments is associated with the ordinal nature of raw total scores. It is common for attitude measurement instruments to adopt a Likert scale. One serious issue associated with the Likert scale is the use of a total score by adding individual item scores. Values such as 1-5 assigned to five choices of a statement do not have the same origin and interval unit because they are not on a ratio or interval scale. The consequence of being non-interval or ratio is that we can not meaningfully add individual item scores into a total score. Also, different items may have different degrees of endorsability. Rasch scale scores address the above issues.

Developing measurement instruments for affective variables based on Rasch modeling starts with a clear definition of the affective construct to be measured. The defined construct must be consistent with an accepted theory. The construct should also suggest a hierarchy of subjects' behaviors along the construct. Affective measurement instruments typically use question formats of the Likert scale, a rating scale, semantic differential, and checklist/inventory. Rasch modeling can help identify best category structure of items, and establish evidence for the validity and reliability of the measurement instrument.

EXERCISES

1. Read Blalock et al.'s (2008) review of attitude toward science instruments. Apply the validity and reliability standards described

in chapter 1 to evaluate the appropriateness of their scoring rubric used to evaluate the measurement instruments, is the rubric reasonable? How would you revise, if you deem necessary?

2. The development of the instrument, Changes in Attitudes About the Relevance of Science (CARS) (Siegel & Ranney, 2003), was based on Rasch modeling. Read the article carefully and critique the adequacy of the application of Rasch modeling in the development of the instrument. Based on your critique, summarize the instrument's strengths and weakness and recommend appropriate uses of the instrument.

3. Suppose that you are going to develop a measurement instrument on high school students' attitude toward biotechnology careers. Based on your best knowledge of biotechnology careers, complete the following initial steps in developing the measurement instrument: (a) define the construct, (b) identify behaviors that represent the defined construct, and (c) write a few sample items for the measurement instrument.

REFERENCES

Adams, W. K., Perkins, K. K., Podolefsky, N. S., Dubson, M., Finkelstein, N. D., & Wieman, C. E. (2006). New instrument for measuring student beliefs about physics and learning physics: The Colorado Learning Attitudes about Science Survey. *Physical Review Special Topic— Physics Education Research, 2*, 010101.

American Association for the Advancement of Science. (1993). *Benchmarks for science literacy*. New York, NY: Oxford University Press.

Baldwin, J. A., Ebert-May, D., & Burns, D. J. (1999). The development of a college biology self-efficacy instrument for nonmajors. *Science Education, 83*, 397-408.

Beghetto, R. A. (2009). Correlates of intellectual risk taking in elementary school science. *Journal of Research in Science Teaching, 46*(2), 210-223.

Blalock, C. L., Lichtenstein, M. J., Owen, S. V., Pruski, L. A., Marshall, C. E., & Toepperwein, M. A. (2008). In pursuit of validity: A comprehensive review of science attitude instruments 1935-2005. *International Journal of Science Education, 30*(7), 961-977.

Britner, S. L. (2008). Motivation in high school science students: A comparison of gender differences in life, physical, and earth science classes. *Journal of Research in Science Teaching, 45*(8), 955-970.

Brown, W. R. (1973). Checklist for assessment of science teachers and its use in a science preservice teacher education project. *Journal of Research in Science Teaching, 10*(3), 243-249.

Button, W. H., & Stephens, L. (1963). Measuring attitudes toward science. *School Science and Mathematics, 63*, 43-49.

Caleon, I., & Subramaniam, R. (2008). Attitudes towards science of intellectually gifted and mainstream upper primary students in Singapore. *Journal of Research in Science Teaching, 45*(8), 940-954.

Campbell, J. R. (1971). Cognitive and affective process development and its relation to a teacher's interaction ratio. *Journal of Research in Science Teaching, 8*(4), 317-323.

Clarkeburn, H. (2002). A test for ethical sensitivity in science. *Journal of Moral Education, 31,* 439-453.

Connelly, F. M., Finegold, M., Wahlstrom, M. W., & Ben-Peretz, M. (1977). TOTSI matches teacher to curriculum. *Science Teacher, 44*(2), 24-26.

Dalgety, J., Coll, R. K., & Jones, A. (2003). Development of chemistry attitudes and experiences questionnaire (CAEQ). *Journal of Research in Science Teaching, 40*(7), 649-668.

Donnelly, L. A., & Boone, W. J. (2007). Biology teachers' attitudes toward and use of Indiana's evolution standards. *Journal of Research in Science Teaching, 44*(2), 236-257.

Doran, R., Lawrenz, F., & Helgeson, S. (1994). Research on assessment in science. In D. Gabel (Ed.), *Handbook of research on science teaching and learning* (pp. 388-442). New York, NY: Macmillan.

Eagly, A. H. (1992). Uneven progress: Social psychology and the study of attitudes. *Journal of Personality and Social Psychology, 63,* 693-710.

Erb, T. O., & Smith, W. S. (1984). Validation of the attitude toward women in science scale for early adolescents. *Journal of Research in Science Teaching, 21,* 391-397.

Fowler, S. R., Zeidler, D. L., & Sadler, T. D. (2009). Moral sensitivity in the context of socioscientific issues in high school science students. *International Journal of Science Education, 31*(2), 279-296

Francis, L. J., & Geer, J. E. (1999). Measuring attitudes toward science among secondary school students: The affective domain. *Research in Science & Technology Education, 17,* 219-226.

Fraser, B. J. (1978). Development of a test of science-related attitudes. *Science Education, 62,* 509-515.

Gardner, P. L. (1975). Attitudes to science. *Studies in Science Education, 2,* 1-41.

Germann, P. J. (1988). Development of the attitude toward science in school assessment and its use to investigate the relationship between science achievement and attitude toward science in school. *Journal of Research in Science Teaching, 25,* 689-703.

Glynn, S. M., Kobbala, T. R., Jr. (2006). Motivation to learn in college science. In J. Mintzes & W. H. Leonard (Eds.), *Handbook of college science teaching* (pp. 25-32). Arlington, VA: National Science Teachers Association Press.

Glynn, S., Taasoobshirazi, G., & Brickman, P. (2009). Science motivation questionnaire: Construct validation with nonscience majors. *Journal of Research in Science Teaching, 46*(2), 127-146.

Gogolin, L., & Swartz, F. (1992). A quantitative and qualitative inquiry into the attitudes toward science of nonscience college majors. *Journal of Research in Science Teaching, 29,* 487-504.

Good, R. G. (1971). Study of the effects of a 'student-structured' laboratory approach to elementary science education methods courses: Affective domain. *Journal of Research in Science Teaching, 8*(3), 255-262.

Gungor, A., Eryrilmaz, A., & Fakroglu, T. (2007). The relationship of freshmen's physics achievement and their related affective characteristics. *Journal of Research in Science Teaching, 44*(8), 1036-1056.

Guttman, L. (1944). A basis for scaling qualitative data. *American Sociological Review, 9*, 139-150.

Hopkins, K. D. (1998). Educational and psychological measurement and evaluation (8th edition). Needham Height, MA: Allyn & Bacon.

Hoover, K. H., & Schutz, R. E. (1963). Development of a measure of conservation attitudes. *Science Education, 47*(1), 63-68.

Jones, M. G., & Carter, G. (2007). Science teacher attitudes and beliefs. In S. K. Abell & N. G. Lederman (Eds.), *Handbook of research on science education* (pp. 1067-1104). New York, NY: Routledge.

Juriševi, M., Glažar, S. A., Puko, C. R., & Devetak, I. (2007). Intrinsic motivation of preservice primary school teachers for learning chemistry in relation to their academic achievement. *International Journal of Science Education, 30*(1), 87-107.

Kesamang, M. E. E., & Taiwo, A. A. (2002). The correlates of the socio-cultural background of Botswana junior secondary school students with their attitudes towards and achievements in science. *International Journal of Science Education, 24*(9), 919-940.

Kind, P., Jones, K., & Barmby, P. (2007). Developing attitudes towards science measures. *International Journal of Science Education, 29*(7), 871- 893.

Kitchen, E., Reeve, S., Bell, J., Sudweeks, R. R., & Bradshaw, W. S. (2007). The development and application of affective assessment in an upper-level cell biology course. *Journal of Research in Science Teaching, 44*(8), 1057-1087.

Koballa, T. R., & Glynn, S. M. (2007). Attitudinal and motivational constructs in science learning. In S. K. Abell & N. G. Lederman (Eds.), *Handbook of research on science education* (pp. 75-102). New York, NY: Routledge.

Krathwohl, D. R., Bloom, B. S., & Masia, B. B. (1964). *Taxonomy of educational objectives: Handbook 2 affective domain*. New York, NY: Longman.

Laforgia, J. (1988). The affective domain related to science education and its evaluation. *Science Education, 72*, 407–421.

Lazarowitz, R., & Lee, A. E. (1976). Measuring inquiry attitudes of secondary science teachers. *Journal of Research in Science Teaching, 13*(5), 455-460.

Lee, G., Kwon, J., Park, S. -S., Kim, J. -W., Kwon, H. -G., & Park, H. -K. (2003). Development of an instrument for measuring cognitive conflict in secondary-level science classes. *Journal of Research in Science Teaching, 40*(6), 585-603.

Lee, M. -H., Johanson, R. E., & Tsai, C. -C. (2008). Exploring Taiwanese high school students' conceptions of and approaches to learning science through a structural equation modeling analysis. *Science Education, 92*(2), 191-220.

Lichtenstein, M. J., Owen, S., Blalock, C., Liu, Y., Ramirez, K. A., Pruski, L. A., et al. (2008). Psychometric reevaluation of the scientific attitude inventory-revised (SAI-II). *Journal of Research in Science Teaching, 45*(5), 600-616.

Likert, R. (1932). A technique for the measurement of attitudes. *Achieves of Psychology, 22,* 5-53.

Linacre, J. M. (2004). Optimizing rating scale category effectiveness. In E. V. Smith, Jr., & R. M. Smith (Eds.), *Introduction to Rasch measurement* (pp. 258-278). Maple Grove, MN: JAP Press.

Liu, X. (2009). Standardized measurement instruments in science education. In M. -W. Roth & K. Tobin (eds.), *The world of science education: Handbook of research in North America* (pp. 649-677). Rotterdam, The Netherlands: Sense.

Lumpe, A., Haney, J., & Czerniak, C. (2000). Assessing teachers' beliefs about their science teaching context. *Journal of Research in Science Teaching, 37,* 275-292.

Menis, J. (1989). Attitudes towards school, chemistry and science among upper secondary chemistry students in the United States. *Research in Science and Technological Education, 7,* 183–190.

McGinnis, J. R., Kramer, S., Shama, G., Graeber, A. O., Parker, C. A., & Watanabe, T. (2002). *Journal of Research in Science Teaching, 39*(8), 713-737.

Moore, K. D. (1977). Development and validation of a science teacher needs-assessment profile. *Journal of Research in Science Teaching, 14*(2), 145-149.

Moore, R. W., & Foy, R. L. H. (1997). The scientific attitude inventory: A revision (SAI-II). *Journal of Research in Science Teaching, 34,* 327-336.

Moore, R. W., & Sutman, F. X. (1970). The development, field test and validation of an inventory of scientific attitudes. *Journal of Research in Science Teaching, 7*(2), 85-94.

Mulkey, L. (1989). Validation of early childhood attitudes toward women in science scale (ECWiSS): A pilot administration. *Journal of Research in Science Teaching, 26,* 737-753.

Munby, H. (1983a). Thirty studies involving the "scientific attitude inventory": What confidence can we have in this instrument? *Journal of Research in Science Teaching, 20,* 141-162.

Munby, H. (1983b). *An investigation into the measurement of attitudes in science education.* Columbus, OH: ERIC Science, Mathematics and Environmental Education Clearinghouse, Center for Science and Mathematics Education, Ohio State University.

Munby, H. (1997). Issues of validity in science attitude measurement. *Journal of Research in Science Teaching, 34*(4), 337–341.

National Research Council. (1996). *National science education standards.* Washington, DC: National Academic press.

Odom, A., Stoddard, E. R., & LaNasa, S. M. (2007). Teacher practices and middle-school science achievements. *International Journal of Science Education, 29*(11), 1329-1346.

Osborne, J., Simon, S., & Collins, S. (2003). Attitude towards science: A review of the literature and its implications. *International Journal of Science Education, 25*(9), 1049-1079.

Osgood, C. E., Suci, G. J., & Tannenbaum, P. H. (1971). *The measurement of meaning.* Chicago, IL: University of Illinois Press.

Owen, S. V., Toepperwein, M. A., Pruski, L. A., Blalock, C. L., Liu, Y., Marshall, C. E., et al. (2007). Psychometric reevaluation of the women in science scale (WiSS). *Journal of Research in Science Teaching, 44*(10), 1461-1478.

Owen, S. V., Toepperwein, M. A., Marshall, C. E., Lichtenstein, M. J., Blalock, C. L., Liu, Y., et al. (2008). Finding pearls: Psychometric reevaluation of Simpson-Troost Attitude Questionnaire (STAQ). *Science Education, 92*(6), 1076-1095.

Parkinson, J., Hendley, D., Tanner, H., & Stables, A. (1998). Pupils' attitudes to science in key stage 3 of the national curriculum: A study of pupils in South Wales. *Research in Science and Technological Education, 16*, 165-177.

Pell, T., & Jarvis, T. (2001). Developing attitude to science scales for use with children of ages five to eleven years. *International Journal of Science Education, 23*, 847-862.

Pell, A., & Jarvis, T. (2003). Developing attitude to science education scales for use with primary teachers. *International Journal of Science Education, 25*(10), 1273-1295.

Prokop, P., Leskova, A., Kubiatlo, M., & Diran, C. (2007). Slovakian students' knowledge of and attitudes toward biotechnology. *International Journal of Science Education, 29*(7), 895-907.

Riggs, I. M., & Enochs, L. E. (1990). Toward the development of an elementary teacher's science teaching efficacy belief instrument. *Science Education, 74*, 625-637.

Ritter, J. M., Boone, W. J., & Rubba, P. A. (2001). Development of an instrument to assess prospective elementary teacher self-efficacy beliefs about equitable science teaching and learning (SEBEST). *Journal of Science Teacher Education, 12*, 175-198.

Russell, J., & Hollander, S. (1975). A biology attitude sale. *American Biology Teacher, 37*(5), 270-273.

Salta, K., & Tzougraki, C. (2004). Attitudes toward chemistry among 11th grade students in high schools in Greece. *Science Education, 88*(4), 535-547.

Shrigley, R. (1974). The attitude of preservice elementary teachers toward science. *School Science and Mathematics, 74*, 243-250.

Siegel, M. A., & Ranney, M. A. (2003). Developing the changes in attitude about the relevance of science (CARS) questionnaire and assessing two high school science classes. *Journal of Research in Science Teaching, 40*(8), 757-775.

Skinner, R., & Barcikowski, R. S. (1973). Measuring specific interest in biological, physical, and earth sciences in intermediate grade levels. *Journal of Research in Science Teaching, 10*(2), 153-158.

Schwirian, P. M. (1968). On measuring attitudes toward science. *Science Education, 52*, 172-179.

Simpson, R. D., Koballa, T. R., Oliver, J. S., & Crawley, F. (1994). Research on the affective dimension of science learning. In D. Gable (Ed.), *Handbook of research on science teaching and learning* (pp. 211-234). New York, NY: Macmillan.

Simpson, R. D., & Troost, K. M. (1982). Influences on commitment to learning of science among adolescent students. *Science Education, 66*(5), 763-781.

Thompson, T. L, & Mintzes, J. J. (2002). Cognitive structure and the affective domain: On knowing and feeling in biology. *International Journal of Science Education, 24*(6), 645-660.

Thompson, C. L., & Shrigley, R.(1986). What research says: Revising the science attitude scale. *School Science and Mathematics, 86*, 331-343.

Thurston, L. L. (1925). A method of scaling psychological and educational tests. *Journal of Educational Psychology, 16*, 433-451.

Tuan, H. -L., Chin, C. -C., & Shieh, S. -H. (2005). The development of a questionnaire to measure students' motivation towards science learning. *International Journal of Science Education, 27*(6), 639-654.

Wang, H. A., & Marsh, D. D. (2002). Science instruction with a humanistic twist: Teachers' perception and practice in using the history of science in their classrooms. *Science & Education, 11*, 169-189.

Weigel, R., & Weigel, J. (1978). Environmental concern: The development of a measure. *Environment and Behavior, 10*(1), 3-15.

Zacharia, Z., & Calabrese Barton, A. C. (2004). Urban middle-school students' attitudes toward a defined science. *Science Education, 88*(2), 197-222.

Zint, M. (2002). Comparing three attitude-behavior theories for predicting science teachers' intentions. *Journal of Research in science Teaching, 39*(9), 819-844.

Zusho, A., Pintrich, P. R., & Coppola, B. (2003). Skill and will: The role of motivation and cognition in the learning of college chemistry. *International Journal of Science Education, 25*(9), 1081-1094.

USING AND DEVELOPING INSTRUMENTS FOR MEASURING SCIENCE INQUIRY

This chapter is about science inquiry. Science inquiry is concerned with both content of learning and an approach to teaching and learning; it is an important domain of measurement in science education. This chapter will first review various theoretical frameworks about science inquiry. It will then introduce standardized instruments for measuring science inquiry. Finally, this chapter will describe the process for developing new instruments for measuring science inquiry using the Rasch modeling approach.

WHAT IS SCIENCE INQUIRY?

Science inquiry is a comprehensive construct for organizing science curriculum, instruction, and teacher professional development. Accordingly, science inquiry can be conceptualized in three ways—as curriculum content, as epistemology, and as pedagogy (R. D. Anderson, 2007). Science inquiry as content for science learning, a way of knowing, and an approach to science teaching has been around for almost a century, dating back to Dewey's scientific methods in the 1910s, to Schwab's invitations to science enquiry during 1960s, and to hands-on based science

Using and Developing Measurement Instruments in Science Education:
A Rasch Modeling Approach, pp. 165–203

learning promoted in National Science Foundation-funded science curriculums in the 1960s and 1970s (National Research Council [NRC], 2000). Science inquiry as content requires students as well as teachers to demonstrate the ability to conduct science inquiry.

Science inquiry involves posing meaningful questions, designing appropriate procedures to collect data necessary for answering the questions, and analyzing and interpreting data in order to answer the research questions. The *National Science Education Standards* (NRC, 1996) state that:

> *Scientific inquiry* [italics added] refers to the diverse ways in which scientists study the natural world and propose explanations based on the evidence derived from their work. Inquiry also refers to the activities of students in which they develop knowledge and understanding of scientific ideas, as well as an understanding of how scientists study the natural world. (NRC, 1996, p. 23)

Although inquiry does not take place in a step-by-step fashion, there are essential aspects common to all inquiry activities. These aspects are: hands-on skills pertaining to data collection and analysis, reasoning skills in relating data to theories, and the ability to perform inquiry tasks. Examples of hands-on manipulative skills commonly expected in science curriculums are (Liu, 2009a, pp. 85-86):

Elementary and Middle School Science:

- use hand lens to view objects
- use stopwatch to measure time
- use ruler (metric) to measure length
- use balances and spring scales to weigh objects
- use thermometers to measure temperature (C°, F°)
- use measuring cups to measure volumes of liquids
- use graduated cylinders to measure volumes of liquids

High School Biology:

- count the growth of microorganism
- determine the size of a microscopic object, using a compound microscope
- dissect a frog or a worm
- geminate seeds
- make a serial dilution
- manipulate a compound microscope to view microscopic objects

- prepare a wet mount slide
- sketch an organism
- slice a tissue for microscope examination
- sterilize instruments
- take a pulse
- use appropriate staining techniques
- use paper chromatography and electrophoresis to separate chemicals

High School Chemistry:

- boil liquid in beakers and test tubes
- conduct an acid-base titration
- cut, bend and polish glass
- dilute strong acids
- pour liquid from a reagent bottle
- prepare solutions of a given concentration
- separate mixtures by filtration
- smell a chemical
- transfer powders and crystals from reagent bottles
- weigh chemicals using an analytic balance

High School Earth Science

- analyze soils
- classify rocks
- classify fossils
- determine the volume of a regular- and an irregular-shaped solid
- grow crystals
- locate the epicenter of an earthquake
- measure weather variables (e.g., barometer, anemometer, etc.)
- orient a map with a compass
- plot the sun's path
- test the physical properties of minerals
- use a stereoscope to view objects

High School Physics

- connect electrical devices in parallel and series circuits
- determine the focal length of mirrors and lenses

- determine the electrical conductivity of a material using a simple circuit
- determine the speed and acceleration of a moving object
- locate images in mirrors
- solder electrical connections
- use electric meters

Besides manipulative skills listed above, "inquiry is in part a state of mind—that of inquisitiveness" (NRC, 2000, p. xii). These *thinking-oriented inquiry skills* relate to generating testable hypotheses, designing controlled experimentation, making accurate observation, analyzing and interpreting data, and making valid conclusions. Lunetta and Tamir (1979) have identified the following thinking-oriented inquiry skills:

Planning and Designing

- Formulates a question or defines a problem to be investigated
- Predicts experimental result
- Formulates hypothesis to be tested
- Designs observation or measurement procedure
- Designs experiment

Performance

- Carries out qualitative observation
- Carries out quantitative observation or measurement
- Records results, describes observation
- Performs numeric calculation
- Explains or makes a decision about experimental technique
- Works according to own design

Analysis and Interpretation

- Transforms result into standard form (other than graphs)
- Graphs data
- Determines qualitative relationship
- Determines quantitative relationship
- Determines accuracy of experimental data
- Defines or discusses limitations and/or assumptions that underlie the experiment

- Formulates or proposes a generalization or model
- Explains a relationship
- Formulates new questions or defines problem based upon the result of investigation

Application

- Predicts, based upon result of this investigation
- Formulates hypothesis based upon results of this investigation
- Applies experimental techniques to new problem or variable

Specific inquiry skills described above focus on individual actions involved in science inquiry. Although they are essential, additional complex processes are necessary. Science inquiry is essentially an integrated practice that involves generating and evaluating scientific evidence and explanations. Generating and evaluating scientific evidence and explanations encompasses the knowledge and skills used for building and refining models and explanations, designing and analyzing empirical investigations and observations, and constructing and defending arguments with empirical evidence (NRC, 2007). The sociocultural context is also essential in science inquiry activities. Accordingly, science inquiry involves a range of activities that involve cognitive, affective and psychomotor domains. The above integrated practices may be generally called scientific reasoning. Research in cognitive sciences and science education over the past few decades has shown that school children develop their scientific reasoning with age, but this development is significantly enhanced by their prior knowledge, experience, and instruction (NRC, 2007). That is, scientific reasoning is intimately intertwined with conceptual knowledge of the natural phenomena under investigation.

Besides the ability to demonstrate science inquiry described above, the National Science Education Standards also expect students to demonstrate understanding about science inquiry (NRC, 1996). *Understanding about science inquiry* relates to "how and why scientific knowledge changes in response to new evidence, logical analysis, and modified explanations debated within a community of scientists" (NRC, 2000, p. 21). Examples of understanding about science inquiry are:

- Different kinds of questions suggest different kinds of scientific investigation;
- Current scientific knowledge and understanding guide scientific investigation;

- Technology used to gather data enhances accuracy and allows scientists to analyze and quantify results of investigations; and
- Scientific investigations emphasize evidence, have logically consistent arguments, and use scientific principles, models, and theories.

Related to understanding science inquiry is understanding the nature of science. Because science inquiry is an essential component of science, understanding science inquiry is an essential component of understanding the nature of science. *Nature of science* (NOS) refers to the epistemology of science or science as a way of knowing, including "the values and assumptions inherent to science, scientific knowledge, and/or the development of scientific knowledge" (Lederman, 1992, 2007), or in brief, the epistemology of science as distinct from science process and content (Lederman, Wade, & Bell, 1998). According to Lederman (2007), important understandings of NOS relevant to K-12 include the distinction between observation and inference, the distinction between scientific laws and theories, the roles of both observation and human imagination and creativity in knowledge construction, the theory-laden nature of scientific knowledge, the cultural context of scientific enterprise, and the tentative nature of scientific knowledge. Similarly, Osborne, Collins, Ratcliffe, Miller, and Duschl (2003) identified the following aspects of NOS by consensus of representatives of the "science expert community" that should be taught in schools: scientific method and critical testing, creativity, historical development of scientific knowledge, science and questioning, diversity of scientific thinking, analysis and interpretation of data, science and certainty, hypothesis and prediction, and cooperation and collaboration. Thus, while understanding inquiry is concerned with the nature of science inquiry processes, understanding about NOS is concerned with both the processes and products of science inquiry—scientific knowledge. The two constructs are different but overlap significantly.

Science inquiry as related to teaching and learning requires that teachers understand the nature and process of developing scientific knowledge as inquiry, and conduct science teaching through science inquiry. The *National Science Education Standards*, Teaching Standard A, states that teachers of science plan an inquiry-based science program for their students (NRC, 1996). Essential features of inquiry science teaching and learning include:

- Learners are engaged by scientifically oriented questions;
- Learners give priority to evidence, which allows them to develop and evaluate explanations that address scientifically oriented questions;
- Learners formulate explanations from evidence to address scientifically oriented questions;

- Learners evaluate their explanations in light of alternative explanations, particularly those reflecting scientific understanding;
- Learners communicate and justify their proposed explanations. (NRC, 2000, p. 25)

Based on the above conceptualizations of science inquiry, measurement of science inquiry may include three areas: measurement of students' inquiry abilities, measurement of understanding science inquiry, and measurement of science teachers' understanding and practices of inquiry science teaching. The first area includes measurement of specific inquiry skills and integrated inquiry performances. The second area involves measurement of student understanding processes and products of science inquiry. The last area involves measurement of the ways science teachers conceptualize, plan, teach and evaluate student science learning.

Although this chapter focuses on science inquiry, it is important to note that there are other constructs used in the science education literature that are closely related to science inquiry. For example, the National Research Council's recent report, *Taking Science to School* (NRC, 2007), conceptualizes student proficiency in science to contain four strands: (a) know, use, and interpret scientific explanations of the natural world, (b) generate and evaluate scientific evidence and explanations, (c) understand the nature and development of scientific knowledge, and (d) participate productively in scientific practices and discourse. Strands *b* and *c* are closely related to science inquiry abilities and an understanding of science inquiry discussed above. Given that there are diverse theoretical orientations in science education research, when using and developing instruments for measuring any construct including science inquiry, it is critically important to situate the construct within a particular theoretical framework and define it accordingly. All definitions of construct have a theoretical orientation, and thus not applicable universally, regardless of the assessment purpose and context.

INSTRUMENTS FOR MEASURING SCIENCE INQUIRY

A variety of standardized measurement instruments related to science inquiry are available in science education. Liu (2009b) has reviewed standardized measurements developed by researchers in North America and published in refereed journals over the past 50 years (pp. 650-654). The following summative descriptions expand Liu's review by including instruments developed outside North America and most recently published instruments. The majority of the instruments have been developed based on CTT. They are for various intended uses and based on different theoretical frameworks of science inquiry. Please note, the following descriptions of the instruments are for readers' information only; whether or not a science education researcher will choose an instrument for a particular research question requires a critical review of the instrument by the researcher, which is beyond the scope of this book.

Instruments for Measuring Specific inquiry Skills

Evaluating Laboratory Work in High School Biology (Robinson, 1969)

This performance assessment contains 15 items organized in two groups: identifying objectives and placing objects into designated groups. The test measures high school biology students' lab performances in four areas: measuring, identifying, selecting, and computing. Students rotate around the stations to perform the tasks. Point-biserial correlation for the items ranged from .29 to .68. Correlation between scores on this test and that on a 63-item multiple choice achievement test was .33. Reliability coefficient was .63.

The Inquiry Skill Measure (ISM) (Nelson & Abraham, 1973)

This test measures upper elementary school students' inquiry skills. The test employs a sealed box with a number of different colored sticks protruding from it. The child examines the outside of the box using all of five senses in order to tell as much about the outside of the box as possible. This portion of the test is to obtain a measure of students' ability to observe. The child is then asked what is likely to be inside the box based upon observations. This procedure provides a measure of the child's ability to draw inferences. For each inference made, the child is asked to give the reason, and to describe how to verify the inference without opening the box. The child's ability to classify is measured by presenting nine transparent vials of varying sizes containing different amounts of different colored liquids. The child tries to group the vials using different criteria. Validation of the instrument involved expert panel review and pilot-testing. Factor analysis showed that four factors were present: verifying, inferring, classifying, and frequency. The equivalent form reliability coefficients ranged from .441 to .707.

Science Process Skills Test (SPST) (Molitor & George, 1976)

SPST measures upper elementary, that is, grades 4-6, school students' science process skills. It has 20 multiple-choice items, 10 for each of the following two process skills: (a) the ability to make an inference, and (b) the ability to verify. Instrument validation involved review of items by an expert panel, and pilot-testing which involved comparison between student responses and their provided reasons. Students who had studied the *Science: A Process Approach* curriculum for four years scored significantly higher than students who had not studied the curriculum. KR-20 for the inference scale ranged from .54 to .59 from Grade 4 to Grade 6, and for the verification scale ranged from .72 to .84 from Grade 4 to Grade 6.

Test of Enquiry Skills (TOES) (Fraser, 1980)

   TOES measures nine separate enquiry skills that fall into three major groups: (a) using reference materials such as dictionaries, encyclopedias, library card indexes, book indices, and tables of contents, (b) interpreting and processing information such as reading various scales, calculating averages, percentages and proportions, interpreting charts and tables, using graphical materials, and (c) critical-thinking-in-science skills such as comprehension of science reading materials, design of experimental procedures in science, and the ability to draw valid conclusions and generalizations from data. Each skill forms one scale. Items in TOES are of the multiple-choice format with five alternatives per item. Items are also content-free, that is, they measure general intellectual skills which transcend all science contents.

   Development of TOES proceeded in a number of identifiable stages. The first stage was a comprehensive review of the science education literature. The second stage was development of a large pool of items to measure the nine enquiry skills. The third stage involved the scrutiny of the initial pool of items by an expert panel of 15 people. The fourth stage involved pilot-testing the instrument. The fifth stage involved the assembling and pilot-testing a second version of TOES. The sixth and last stage was the assembling and administration of the final version of TOES to 1158 students from Grades 7-10. KR-20 coefficients for the nine scales ranged from 0.57 to 0.83 for the Grade 7 sample, from 0.57 to 0.83 for the Grade 8 sample, from 0.53 to 0.77 for the Grade 9 sample, and from 0.50 to 0.75 for the Grade 10 sample. The test-retest reliability ranged from 0.65 to 0.82. Standard error of measures ranged from 1.1 to 1.5. Intercorrelations among the nine scales ranged from 0.30 to 0.56, providing evidence for the discriminant validity.

Test of Integrated Process Skills (TIPS) (Dillashaw & Okey, 1980)

   TIPS is a multiple-choice question test for measuring 7th-10th grade students' process skills associated with planning, conducting, and interpreting results from investigations. Questions are related to independent variables, dependent variables, controlled variables, hypotheses, experimental designs, graphing of data, and pattern of relationships. Validation involved expert panel review of items and field test with students of diverse backgrounds. The alpha internal consistency reliability was .89.

Practical Test Assessment Inventory (PTAI)
(Tamir, Nussinovitz, & Friedler, 1982)

PTAI is a categorization and scoring system to grade student practical performances. It was validated by three science educators who read 100 papers and classified questions and answers into categories. Interrater reliability was checked by three raters who assessed independently the same 40 tests by assigning marks to each response. PTAI classifies student performances into the following 21 categories: (a) formulating problems, (b) formulating hypotheses, (c) identifying dependent variable, (d) identifying independent variable, (e) designing control, (f) the fitness of the experiment to the tested problem or hypothesis, (g) completeness of experimental design, (h) understanding the role of the control in experiment, (i) making and reporting measurements, (j) determining and preparing adequate dilutions, (k) making observations with a microscope, (l) describing observations, (m) making graphs, (n) making tables, (o) interpreting observed data, (p) drawing conclusions, (q) explaining research findings, (r) examining results critically, (s) analyzing knowledge, (t) understanding and interpreting data presented in a graph, and (u) suggesting ideas and ways to continue the investigation.

Instruments for Measuring Cognitive and Metacognitive Reasoning

A Test of Science Comprehension (TSC) (C. H. Nelson & Mason, 1963)

TSC is a 60-item test of Grades 4-6 students' critical thinking skills. Items are in blocks, with each block centering around the interpretation of a situation, the application of scientific principles or theory in accounting for what has happened, and analysis of the situation as a basis for arriving at a solution to the problem. Validation of the instrument involved classes that explicitly taught critical thinking and classes that did not. Students took both pre- and posttests. The gains were statistically significant for classes that had received explicit instruction. Reliability coefficients ranged from .63 to .76 on the pretest and from .72 to .82 on the posttests for different classes.

X-35 Test of Problem Solving (TPS, Forms A and B) (Butts, 1964)

TPS assesses secondary school students' ways of knowing in terms of hypothesis formation, experimental design, independent and dependent variables, and hypothesis verification. It has only two problems and each problem has three parts: Part I presenting a problem, Part II presenting data, and Part III presenting solutions. Professors of child psychology and science education reviewed the problems and scoring guides. The overall agreement between the investigator's evaluation and the experts' was .75. The correlation between students' scores on the two problems was .54.

Cognitive Preference Test: High School Chemistry (Marks, 1967)

This test contains 100 items. Each item has four options corresponding to four cognitive preferences: memory or recall of chemical facts, practical application, critical questioning of information, and identification of a fundamental principle. The 100 items are divided equally into four subtests, one for each cognitive style. The mean biserial correlations of items for the four cognitive preference subtests ranged from 0.44 to .82, and Cronbach's alphas ranged from 0.28 to .70 for different student samples.

The Classification-Seriation Test (CST) (Bridgeham, 1969)

CST measures third-grade students on two Piagetian constructs, classification and seriation. The assessment tasks involve students in classifying various geometric shapes that are made of plywood, and painted into one of seven colors. There are seven items on hierarchical classification and four on multiplicative classification; there are also three items on seriation. The correlation between the hierarchical and additive classification test scores was .31, and the correlation between the seriation test scores and classification test scores was $\leq .35$.

The Mathematical Skill Test (MAST) in Chemistry (Denny, 1971)

MAST measures mathematical skills identified in popular chemistry texts from 1960-1970. Examples of math skills are logarithm, percentage, manipulation of one-variable equations, and interpreting x, y graphs. Items were reviewed by experts as being essential. Pilot-testing was conducted to ensure appropriate item discrimination and difficulty. Three levels of math skills were tested; level I had 14 items, level II 32 items, and level III 14 items. Correlation between MAST scores and the American Chemical Society's (ACS) chemistry test was .633, and between MAST scores and ACS chemistry calculation subtest was .823 ($df = 200, p = .01$). KR-20 was .963, with a standard error of .78.

Test for Formal Reasoning (TFR) (Lawson, 1978)

TFR is a 15-item test for assessing Grades 8-12 students' concrete and formal operational reasoning. Each item involves a demonstration using some physical materials and/or apparatus, and student responses in writing on test booklets. Students respond by checking the box next to the best answer and explaining why they choose the answer. Most items were based on interview tasks used by Piaget and his associates. Face validity was established by a panel who were Piagetian research experts. The concurrent validity based on correlation between student test scores and scores on two Piagetian interview tasks was found to be .76 ($p < .001$). Factor analysis of combined test scores and interview scores showed that all the test items and interview tasks loaded on the same factors (i.e., formal reasoning, early formal reasoning, and concrete reasoning). KR-20 was .78.

Piagetian Task Instrument (PTI) (Walker, Hendrix, & Mertens, 1979)

PTI measures university students' formal operational thinking. The six problems are based on the published tasks Piaget and his colleagues used. Adaptations were made to make them as a paper-and-pencil test. Construct validity was determined by comparing the interview results and the written responses. Validation of the instruments also involved students responding to the problems both verbally and in writing. There was no statistically significant correlation between student ages and their test scores. A biology genetic course was found to increase students' scores from 72% correct to 91%.

A Scientific Creativity Structure Model (SCSM) (Hu & Adey, 2002)

SCSM is an open-ended, paper-and-pencil test consisting of seven tasks to be completed within 60 minutes, or one class period. It measures secondary school students' scientific creativity. Scientific creativity is defined "as a kind of intellectual trait or ability producing or potentially producing a certain product that is original and has social or personal value, designed with a certain purpose in mind, using given information" (p. 392). It involves three dimensions: process (i.e., imagination and thinking), trait (i.e., fluency, flexibility, and originality), and product (i.e., technical product, science knowledge, science phenomena, and science problems). An initial set of 48 items, two for each of the 24 cells of the three dimensions' interaction, were developed. Fifty science education researchers and teachers in China reviewed the items and found 9 to be appropriate for measuring secondary school students' creativity. The 9 items were then tried out by sixty 13-year-old girls in London, which resulted in the deletion of 2 more items. The final instrument consists of 7 items, with a scoring rubric for each.

Field testing of the instrument took place with 160 students from year 7 to year 10 (ages 12, 13, and 15) in a suburban school in England. Item discrimination was found to be high, ranging from 0.654–0.892. Cronbach's alpha internal consistency coefficient was found to be 0.893. Inter-rater reliability measured by correlation coefficients between two sets of scores was found to be between 0.793–0.916 for the 7 items. Face validity was established by 35 science education researchers and teachers in China and England who stated that the items were measuring creativity. The construct validity was established by principal component factor analysis which found only one dominant factor. Significant difference in creativity was found between year 7 students and year 8 students, and between year 8 students and year 10 students. Also, significant difference in creativity was found between high-ability students and low-ability students.

Well-Structured Problem-Solving Process Inventory (WPSPI) and Ill-Structured Problem-Solving Process Inventory (IPSPI) (Shin, Jonassen, & McGee, 2003)

WPSPI and IPSPI are a 2-item essay question instrument measuring high school students' problem-solving skills in the context of astronomy. Students may use any resources including computers to solve the problems. Validation of the instruments involved extensive expert review of the content, pilot-testing and scoring based on data from both expert problem solvers and novice problem solvers. Students who took the reformed astronomy course designed specifically for improving problem-solving abilities scored significantly higher than those who did not take the course. Interrater reliability was .83.

Metacognition Baseline Questionnaire (MBQ) (Anderson & Nashon, 2007)

MBQ is a 53-item Likert-scale survey of students' self-reported engagement in metacognition learning situations within both formal and informal learning settings. Metacognition is conceptualized to consist of six dimensions: awareness, control, evaluation planning, monitoring, and self-efficacy. Each item asks students to self-assess their degrees of agreement with propositions related to the above six dimensions by selecting *always or almost always true of me* (5), *frequently true of me* (4), *half of the time true of me* (3), *sometimes true of me* (2), and *only rarely true of me* (1). The items were derived from a wide consultation of experienced high school teachers and research partners. Extensive review of items by teachers and science education researchers resulted in deletions and revisions of initial items. The instrument was then pilot-tested with 40 Grade 11 students. The Cronbach's alpha coefficients for the six dimensions were: 0.798 (control), 0.717 (monitoring), 0.671 (awareness), 0.765 (evaluation), 0.842 (planning), and 0.894 (self-efficacy).

Self-Efficacy and Metacognition Learning Inventory–Science (SEMLI-S)
(Thomas, Anderson, & Nashon, 2008)

SEMLI-S is a 30-item rating scale survey of high school students' meta-cognitive science learning orientations. Meta-cognitive science learning orientations are based on students' self-perceptions of elements of their meta-cognition, self-efficacy and science learning processes. An extensive literature review on meta-cognition, self-regulation and constructivist science learning processes helped generate an initial list of 72 items. An iterative factor analysis and Rasch modeling resulted in reduction of the items into the final set of 30 items. The 30 items are related to the following five subscales: (a) constructivist connectivity (7 items), (b) monitoring, evaluation and planning (9 items), (c) science learning self-efficacy (6 items), (d) learning risks awareness (5 items), and (e) control of concentration (3 items). The Rasch fit statistics for the above 30 items indicated a good model-data-fit. Cronbach's alpha coefficients for the above five subscales were 0.84, 0.84, 0.85, 0.77, and 0.68. Correlation coefficients among the subscales ranged from 0.29 to 0.58. The instrument is available in both English and Chinese.

Approaches to Learning Science Questionnaire (ALS)
(Lee, Johanson & Tsai, 2008)

ALS is a 24-item survey on high school students' approaches to learning. ALS questions were adapted from a similar published instrument to make them science-specific. Approaches to learning were conceptualized as a hierarchical construct with two elements: motivation and strategy. ALS includes four subscales; they are deep motive, deep strategy, surface motive, and surface strategy. Initially, each subscale had six to nine items presented as bipolar always/never statements on a five-point scale. An expert reviewed the initial items to ensure its content validity. Both exploratory and confirmatory factor analyses were conducted to establish the construct validity. Cronbach's alpha coefficients for the four subscales were 0.90, 0.89, 0.84, and 0.84, and the alpha for the entire instrument was 0.89.

Instrument for Measuring Understanding About Science Inquiry and Nature of Science

Given the considerable overlap between understanding about science inquiry and understanding about NOS, and there is no separate chapter on using measurement instrument for understanding of NOS, this section includes instruments for measuring both constructs.

Nature of Science Scale (NOSS) (Kimball, 1967)

NOSS is a 29-item Likert-scale survey of university students' and science teachers' conceptions of science. Nature of science was defined by eight assertions such as "the fundamental driving force in science is curiosity concerning the physical universe." Development of the instrument involved expert reviews of the initial items, and pilot-testing with university science and nonscience majors. Items included in the final version had few neutral responses by students, discriminated in favor of science majors, and presented a logical progression either from agreeing to disagreeing or from disagreeing to agreeing. The split-half reliability was .72. Philosophy students scored significantly better than those in other fields including science education. Science teachers did not score significantly different from practicing scientists.

Nature of Science Test (NOST) (Billeh & Hasan, 1975)

NOST is a 60-item multiple-choice test assessing students' understanding of the nature of science in the following aspects (a) assumptions of science (8 items), products of science (22 items), processes of science (25 items), and ethics of science (5 items). The test consists of two types of items. The first type measures the individual's knowledge of assumptions and processes of science, and the characteristics of scientific knowledge; the second type presents situations which require the individual to make judgments in view of his/her understanding of nature of science. The validation took place in Jordan. The content validity of the instrument was established by a panel of 25 scientists, science educators, and science supervisors. Correlation of NOST scores with general GPA was 0.58, and with mathematics GPA was 0.60. The instrument was also found to discriminate significantly between comparable groups of secondary school students majoring in science and arts. The split-half reliability for different sample of students ranged from 0.58 to 0.82.

Conceptions of Scientific Theories Test (COST) (Cothan & Smith, 1981)

COST is a 40-item Likert-scale instrument measuring preservice elementary teachers' conceptions of science. The items are presented in five contexts: Bohr's theory of the atom, Darwin's theory of evolution, Oparin's theory of abiogenesis, theory of plate tectonics, and a nontheoretical context. Items selected through pilot-testing had high item-subscale correlation. Results showed that elementary teachers scored significantly differently than university chemistry major and philosophy students. Standard error of measurement for the instrument was .3.

Views on Science–Technology–Society (VOSTS) (Aikenhead & Ryan, 1992)

VOSTS assesses high school students' viewpoints of science and its relations to technology and society. It contains 114 items. There is no need to administer 114 items entirely; users can select the most appropriate items to form a survey. Each item presents an extreme viewpoint about science that students have to determine how strongly they agree or disagree with the viewpoint. Underneath each statement is a list of positions about that statement. The student is asked to read each and to select which statement seems to fit their own position. The development of the instrument began with thousands of Grade 12 students writing a paragraph about their views of science, technology and society. Common themes were identified from student writings as "student positions." To determine how well these VOSTS "student positions" fit with the students' true beliefs, further interviews were conducted. Strictly speaking, VOSTS is not an instrument ready to use; no scoring schemes were provided. VOSTS items can be used to develop specific measurement instruments.

Views About Sciences Survey (VASS) (Halloun & Hestenes, 1996, 1998)

VASS contains 30 items probing high school and college students' personal beliefs about the nature of science and learning science in specific science disciplines. There is one scale in each of physics, chemistry and biology. Beliefs about science involve three scientific dimensions: structure, methodology and validity. Beliefs about learning science involve three cognitive dimensions: learnability, reflective thinking, and personal relevance. Each dimension is framed by pairs of contrasting views that are primarily held by scientists/experts and novices. When responding to an item, the student chooses from an eight-point scale representing a continuum from the two contrasting views. Expert reviews and interview with students validated the items.

Views of Nature of Science Questionnaire Form B and Form C (VNOS-Form B and VNOS-Form C) (Lederman, Abd-El-Khalick, Bell, & Schwartz, 2002)

VNOS is a constructed-response question survey of preservice and inservice science teachers' views about the nature of science. It is administered in a controlled condition with no time limit (but typically taking about 1.5 hours). After the survey, a sample of respondents (e.g., 10%) is interviewed. VNOS assesses the following aspects of the nature of science: scientific knowledge is tentative; empirical; theory-laden; partly the product of human inference; imagination and creativity; and socially and culturally embedded. Three additional important aspects are the distinction between observation and inference, the lack of a universal recipelike method for doing science, and the functions of and relationships between scientific theories and laws. VNOS-B contains 7 items, and VNOS-C contains 10 items; both are the results of many rounds of interviews and analyses in addition to expert panel reviews. According to Lederman (2007), there is a shorter version, VNOS-D, producing almost identical results in a much shorter time frame (i.e., less than one hour), and another version, VNOS-E, has been specifically developed for younger age students (K-3) or those who can not read or write. Responses to the survey and interview questions were then analyzed qualitatively, including coding for different levels of understanding and constructing different profiles of understanding.

Thinking About Science Instrument (TSI) (Cobern & Loving, 2002)

TSI is a 35-item Likert scale survey of preservice elementary teachers' views about science. It covers the following aspect of science: epistemology, science and the economy, science and the environment, public regulation of science, science and public health, science and religion, science and aesthetics, science race and gender, and science for all. Items were validated by a group of experts, and verified by reviews of a small group of elementary teachers. The alpha for the entire instrument was .82, and alphas for the subscales ranged from 0.41 to 0.80. Survey results showed that elementary teachers had different views on different aspects of science, but overall viewed science positively.

Scientific Epistemological Views (SEVs) (Tsai & Liu, 2005)

SEVs include the following dimensions:

1. The role of social negotiation (SN): The development of science relies on communications and negotiations among scientists.

2. The inventive and creative nature of science (IC): Scientific reality is invented rather than discovered.

3. The theory-laden exploration (TL): Scientists' personal assumptions, values, and research agendas influence the scientific explorations they conduct.

4. The cultural impacts (CU): Scientific knowledge is culture-dependent.

5. The changing and tentative nature of scientific knowledge (CT): Scientific knowledge is always changing and its status is tentative.

Questions for SEVs were based on previous interview studies with students. They are presented in a 5-point Likert-scale format. Validation took place in Taiwan with 613 high school students. Initially, 35 items were developed, but only 19 retained based on principal component factor analysis. The SN subscale contains 6 items with an alpha of 0.71; the IC subscale contains 4 items with an alpha of 0.60; the TL subscale contains 3 items with an alpha of 0.68; the CU subscale contains 3 items with an alpha of 0.71; and the CT subscale contains 3 items with an alpha of 0.60. The alpha for the entire instrument was 0.67. Correlation among the five subscales ranged from 0.09 to 0.27. Four students from each of three different levels of understanding of scientific epistemology based on SEVs scores were interviewed to further study the construct validity.

Views on Science and Education Questionnaire (VOSE) (Chen, 2006)

VOSE is a written survey of university students' and preservice science teachers' conceptions of the nature of science (NOS) and their related teaching attitude. Conceptions of NOS is differentiated as views on what NOS is (actual), and views on what NOS ought to be (ought). VOSE is in both Chinese and English. It has 15 questions, each followed by several items representing different philosophical positions and asking respondents to rate on a five-point scale their degrees of agreement. Altogether, there are 85 items. Items are based on previously published both qualitative and quantitative surveys, particularly VOSTS and VNOS. The development of VOSE went through three stages. The first stage involved a comprehensive literature review and a pilot study to collect college students' NOS views and attitudes. Results of the first stage helped determine the content and format of the questionnaire. The second stage involved actual item development, pilot testing, and a review of the items by a panel consisting of six experts. The initial draft instrument contained 102 items organized around 19 questions. Interviews of seven students also helped develop the items. The third stage was the actual field testing for establishing evidence for validity and reliability. Field testing took place at two research universities in Taiwan. The clarity of the instrument was checked again through interviews after the field testing.

VOSE focuses on seven aspects of NOS relevant to K-12 science education, they are: tentativeness of scientific knowledge, nature of observation, scientific methods, hypotheses, laws, and theories, imagination, validation of scientific knowledge, and objectivity and subjectivity in science. The Cronbach's alpha coefficients for the above aspects/subscales ranged from 0.34 to 0.81. The attitudes toward teaching the NOS issues contain the following aspects/subscales: tentativeness, nature of observations, scientific methods, theories and laws, and subjectivity and objectivity; the Cronbach's alpha coefficients for the above subscales ranged from 0.59 to 0.81. Test-retest reliability was 0.82.

Instruments for Measuring Science Teachers' Inquiry Conceptions and Practices

Reformed Teaching Observation Protocol (RTOP)
(Admson et al., 2003)

RTOP is a rating scale for measuring science teachers' degrees of incorporating effective science teaching practices promoted in current reform documents. It has 25 statements related to the following aspects: (a) lesson design and implementation, (b) propositional knowledge, (c) procedural knowledge, (d) classroom culture, and (e) student-instructor relationships. Each aspect has five statements, and each statement is scored from 0 through 4, with 0 being *"never occurred"* and 4 being *"very descriptive."* Written observations and comments are also recorded to substantiate ratings. Strong and positive correlations have been found between the degree of reformed teaching practices measured by RTOP and student achievements at the college level.

Survey of Instructional and Assessment Strategies (SIAS)
(Walczyk & Ramsey, 2003)

SIAS is a 51-item survey on college faculty's teaching practices. Among the 51 items, 6 items are directly related to planning for instruction, 15 to delivery of instruction, and 7 to assessment of learning. Each of the above items is responded by faculty on a rating scale from Always to Never. Experienced college instructors reviewed the items and judged them to be valid. Principal component factor analysis found that the subscale on planning contained two main factors, the subscale on delivery contained four main factors, and the subscale on assessment contained two factors. Point-biserial correlation between participation in NSF math and science education reform projects and SIAS scores suggested that SIAS discriminated well. The alphas for the above three subscales were .67, .56, and .71.

Science Lesson Plan Analysis Instrument (SLPAI)
(Jacobs, Martin, & Otieno, 2008)

SLPAI is a 20-item rating scale of science teachers' lesson plans. The 20 items are grouped into the following categories: (a) alignment with endorsed practices (2 items), (b) lesson design and implementation—cognitive and metacognitive issues (7 items), (c) lesson design and implementation—sociocultural and affective issues (6 items), and (d) portrayal and use of the practices of science (5 items). Each item is rated as *exemplary* (2 points), *making progress* (1 point), and *needs improvement* (0 point). A weight from 1 to 3 is also assigned to an item. A total weighted score, standardized as a percentage, is derived as the measure of a lesson plan. Development of the items were based on some published lesson plan evaluation and science class observation instruments, and informed by current reform documents and research syntheses. Validation of the instrument was conducted through comparing the results with that obtained from two other instruments, one based on teacher self-reporting (The Standards-Based Teaching Practices Questionnaire, SBTPQ), and another based on classroom observation (the Reformed Teaching Observation Protocol, RTOP). Agreement was found between conclusions made based on SLPAI and on SBTPQ. However, no consistent statistically significant correlations in scores between relevant SLPAI and RTOP items were found, likely due to the fact that the lessons evaluated using SLPAI were not the same lessons taught and evaluated using RTOP. Interrater agreement between two developers of the instrument was 96%, and between one developer of the instrument and another new researcher was 89%.

Commentary

A number of measurement instruments related to various aspects of science inquiry are available. Selecting an instrument to use should first clearly define the construct related to the science inquiry to be measured. This definition will then guide the selection of an available instrument to use. In most situations, a perfect match between the defined construct and the construct measured by an instrument is unlikely. One approach to using current measurement instruments is to modify a best available instrument and collect data to further validate it. Even if there is a good match between the defined construct and the measured construct of an instrument, continuing to validate the instrument is still necessary because the sample involved in the original validation study may not represent the sample in your study.

Many of current NOS instruments adopt a Likert-scale or rating scale that is often accompanied by some kind of scoring (such as scores 1 to 5 for "*strongly agree*" to "*strongly disagree*"). Two potential problems are associated with this practice. One problem, as Aikenhead (1973) pointed out, is the ambiguity of total scores: What does a total score on an instrument mean and what does a difference between two students or between two tests means in terms of student understanding of the nature of science? Many instruments do not have a clear scale to facilitate qualitative interpretation. Another potential problem is bias or privilege assigned to a particular version of the nature of science. This problem is pointed out by Lederman et al. (1998) in their review of measurement instruments of nature of science. Because there is no universally agreed-upon version of nature of science, any selected response or close-ended response question format, such as the Likert scale, is likely to force students to think in terms of one version of nature of science, and it remains unclear exactly what are students' true understandings of the nature of science. In order to address the above two problems, VOSTS adopts the no-scoring approach and VNOS adopts the interview and open-ended response question format. As Lederman et al. (1998) pointed out, a forced response format like a Likert scale can still play a role in assessing a specific version of nature of science, but a more comprehensive and accurate assessment of students' and teachers' understandings of nature of science may require a combination of both quantitative and qualitative methods.

DEVELOPING INSTRUMENTS FOR MEASURING SCIENCE INQUIRY

Identify the Primary Purpose(s)
for Which the Test Scores Will Be Used

The first step in developing an instrument for measuring inquiry is to consider the uses of scores derived from the instrument. There are various reasons for which we need to measure science inquiry. Given that science inquiry is one of the key science learning standards in national and state science content standards, it is necessary to measure student mastery of science inquiry during the instructional processes as formative assessment and at the end of instructional processes as summative assessment. Assessing teachers' practices of inquiry science teaching and understanding of science inquiry may also be necessary for development and evaluation of effective preservice and inservice teacher education programs. Different intended uses of test scores will have implications on the process and technical quality requirements of the measurement instrument development.

Define the Construct to Be Measured

Science inquiry includes many constructs; different constructs may have quite different theoretical underpinnings and content domains. For example, an inquiry ability on formulating a hypothesis is very different than an inquiry ability to conduct a collaborative scientific investigation. Similarly, understanding science inquiry is fundamentally different in both theoretical frameworks and content from conducting science inquiry. Thus, it is very important to clearly define the science inquiry construct and its content domains.

One requirement of the construct is its linearity. That is, the construct should imply a linear progression along which various levels of performance on inquiry may be differentiated. This unidimensional progression is assumed to underlie both subjects' inquiry performances and items' difficulties; it will guide the subsequent development of the measurement instrument. The linearity of the construct should not simply be assumed; it should be derived from a commonly accepted theory or theories. Clearly stating the theory or theories is necessary and important for the subsequent development stages.

When defining the science inquiry construct, it is important to keep in mind that science inquiry is both context and content dependent (Wong & Hodson, 2008). Researchers have pointed out that general science inquiry abilities and understanding of science inquiry applicable to all science content domains and contexts are neither real nor informative for improving science teaching and learning (Elby & Hammer, 2001; Rudolph, 2000). "There is no single set of NOS elements, static with time and fitting all disciplines and contexts" (Wong & Hodson, 2008, p. 123). Thus, when defining the construct of science inquiry to measure, it is very important to situate the construct in a specific science context (e.g., everyday, industrial, research laboratory) and identify subject performances and behaviors that are related to specific science content. For example, understanding of nature of observation may be situated within an everyday context and be related to specific topics of chemistry, physics, or biology. Similarly, the ability to perform science inquiry may be situated in a school laboratory setting and be related to one of the school science subjects.

Identify Behaviors That Represent the Construct

Once the construct has been defined, the specific behaviors that describe different levels of subjects' performance on the construct should then be identified. These behaviors are related to specific science contents and contexts. For example, if the construct is on secondary school students' conceptions of science and technology, then the behaviors that represent the construct may include the following:

1. Define science and technology;
2. Recognize similarities and differences between science and technology;
3. Explain how science and technology interact with each other;
4. Analyze how science and technology are involved in society;
5. Appreciate the historical and sociocultural dimensions of science and technology.

The above behaviors are related to science subjects taught in secondary schools and represent different levels of subjects' conceptions of science and technology; they are derived from a defined construct of conceptions of science and technology. Once these behaviors are identified, they will then be used to develop a test specification.

Prepare a Set of Test Specifications

The most important consideration in developing a test specification is the number of questions. The number of questions should be determined by the defined construct and its content domain, specifically the range of variation of performances or behaviors within the target population. There should be questions for every possible level of performance, and the difficulty range of test items should well cover the range of the performances. Based on the above considerations, there will be no fixed number of items for all measurement instruments; different constructs and target populations require different number of items. However the general rule that the more items in a measurement instrument, the more reliable the measurement scores are, is still applicable. Measurement instruments should also strive for efficiency—achieving maximum reliability using the least number of items.

Construct an Initial Pool of Items

Depending on the context and content domain of the construct to be measured, items can be in various formats and media such as paper-and-pencil tests using multiple-choice and constructed response questions, performance assessment using objects and materials, observation using a checklist, paper-and-pencil Likert-scale questions asking subjects to agree or disagree, to name a few.

Measuring Laboratory Skills

Although laboratory skills in using tools may be assessed using paper-and-pencil test questions, the most effective assessment of using tools involves observation of students performing the skills. In order to observe student mastery of laboratory tools during labs, a systematic plan must be in place. An observation plan can be a checklist or a rating scale. A sample rating scale for a laboratory skill assessment on using a microscope is presented below.

A Rating Scale for Using a Microscope

Name_____ Date_____

Lab Skills	Developing	Mastery	Proficient
1. Carry a microscope with two hands	_____	_____	_____
2. Clean up microscope lenses	_____	_____	_____
3. Identify parts of a microscope	_____	_____	_____
4. Prepare a microscope slide	_____	_____	_____
5. Mount a slide on the microscope stage	_____	_____	_____
6. Set the microscope light control	_____	_____	_____
7. Focus the view using coarse and fine adjustments	_____	_____	_____

Paper-and-pencil tests using multiple-choice and constructed response questions may also be used to assess laboratory skills involving reasoning. For example, the instrument Test of Integrated Process Skills (TIPS) (Dillashaw & Okey, 1980) is a multiple-choice question test for measuring 7th-10th grade students' laboratory skills associated with planning, conducting, and interpreting results from investigations. Questions are related to independent variables, dependent variables, controlled variables, hypotheses, experimental designs, graphing data, and pattern of relationships. Table 5.1 shows some sample questions from TIPS.

Measuring Integrated Science Inquiry Performances

Integrated science inquiry performances are best measured by performance assessment. Performance assessment is a hands-on test that requires students to perform a task by carrying out a scientific procedure,

Table 5.1.   Sample TIPS Questions

Assessment Objective	*Sample Item*
A. Given a description of an investigation, identify the independent, dependent, and controlled variables and the hypothesis being tested	Sarah wanted to find out if temperature has an effect of the growth of bread mold. She grew the mold in nine containers containing the same amount and type of nutrients. Three containers were kept at 0° C, three were kept at 90° C, and three were kept at room temperature (about 27° C). The containers were examined and the growth of the bread mold was recorded at the end of four days. The dependent or responding variable is: 1. growth of bread mold 2. amount of nutrients in each container 3. temperature of the containers 4. number of containers at each temperature.
B. Given a description of an investigation, identify how the variables are operationally defined	The superintendent is concerned about the accidents in schools. He makes the hypothesis that safety advertising will reduce school accidents. He decides to test the hypothesis in four middle schools. Each school will use a different number of safety posters to see if the number of accidents are reduced. Each school nurse will keep a record of students that come to the office because of an accident. How is safety advertising measured in this study? 1. number of accidents reported to the nurse 2. number of middle schools involved 3. number of safety posters in each school 4. number of accidents in the school
C. Given a problem with a dependent variable specified, identify variables which may affect it	Sue wants to find out what might affect the length of bean seedlings. She places a bean wrapped in moist tissue paper in each of ten identical test tubes. She puts five tubes in a rack in a sunny window. She puts the other five tubes on a rack in a dark refrigerator. She measures the lengths of the bean seedlings in each group after each week. Which of the following variables might affect the length of the bean seedlings? 1. temperature and moisture 2. moisture and length of test tubes 3. light and temperature 4. light and amount of time

(Table continues on next page)

Table 5.1. (Continued)

Assessment Objective	Sample Item
D. Given a problem with dependent variables specified and a list of possible independent variables, identify a testable hypothesis	A student has been playing with a water rocket. He can change the amount of water in the rocket and the angle at which he releases the rocket. He can also change the weight of the rocket by adding sand in the nose cone. He wants to see what might affect the height to which the rocket will rise. Which of the following is a hypothesis he could test?

1. Rockets with warm water will rise higher than rockets with cold water
2. Rockets with four tail fins will rise higher than rockets with two tail fins
3. Rockets with pointed nose cones will rise higher than rockets with rounded nose cones
4. Rockets with more water will rise higher than rockets with less water.

Assessment Objective	Sample Item
E. Given a verbally described variable, select a suitable operational definition for it	The effect of exercise on pulse rate is studied by a science class. Students do different numbers of jumping jacks and then measure their pulse rates. One group does jumping jacks for one minute. A second group does these for 2 minutes. A third group jumps for three minutes. A fourth group does not jump. How would you measure the pulse rate in this study?

1. by counting the number of jumping jacks for one minute
2. by counting the number of heart beats in one minute
3. by counting the number of jumping jacks done by each group
4. by counting the number of exercises for each group

Assessment Objective	Sample Item
F. Given a problem with dependent variable specified, identify a testable hypothesis	Some chickens lay an egg almost every day. Other chickens produce few eggs. A study is planned to examine factors that might affect the number of eggs produced by chickens. Which of the following is NOT a suitable hypothesis for the study?

1. More eggs are produced by chickens that receive more hours of light
2. The more eggs produced by chickens the more weight they lose
3. The larger the cage for chickens the more eggs they will produce
4. The more proteins there are in the feed the more eggs produced

conducting a scientific investigation, or producing a useful product. Performance assessment usually takes place as an investigation, which can be both structured investigation and open-ended or extended investigation.

Performance assessment in the forms of investigations and extended investigations consists of three components: performance task, response format, and scoring rubric (Brown & Shavelson, 1996). Liu (2009a, pp. 74-76) provides an elaboration of the above three components. Specifically, a performance task should be around a problem and meet the following requirements:

1. The problem invites students to solve a problem or conduct an investigation. The problem can be well-structured or ill-structured. Well-structured problems have all elements of the problem and a known solution. The procedures required to solve the problem are also routine and predicable. On the other hand, ill-structured problems do not necessary have all elements of the problem presented. More importantly, ill-structured problems may posses multiple solutions, solution paths, or no solutions at all. Because ill-structured problems are open-ended, personal judgment is constantly needed in the process of solving the problem. Well-structured problems are more appropriate for short investigations, and ill-structured problems are more appropriate for extended investigations.

2. The problem requires the use of concrete materials. This requirement is to differentiate performance assessment tasks from paper-and-pencil based problems. Performance tasks must involve hands-on operations.

3. Provide a concrete contextualization of the problem or investigation. Context makes the problem authentic. Performance assessment tasks approximate real-world problems, thus presenting the problem in a meaningful context is important.

Once a performance task is defined, the next component is to decide on the response format. The response format is to gather evidence of student performance for scoring. The response format must meet the following requirements: (a) provides opportunities for students to record processes and solutions; (b) prompts students for specific information; (c) allows students to decide how to summarize findings, and (d) asks students to justify solutions.

The last component of performance assessment is a scoring scheme or rubric. A rubric is a continuum along which different levels of competence in performing a task are differentiated. Given a task, there is always a variation in student performances; some are more novicelike while others more expertlike. The rubric must capture the "right" answer and reasonableness of procedures. It should also provide students useful feedback plus numerical scores. Given the number of students to be scored, the scoring rubric should also be easy and quick to use.

Here is a sample performance assessment with its scoring rubric for assessing students' integrated inquiry performance involving energy transfer and conservation for eighth-grade students.

Task: Working in groups of three, you will design a simple machine system to lift a 20-gram weight by 1 meter. You will use the materials provided in the materials box. You will have a total of 4 weeks to complete this task. Class time will be provided to complete the task. After you have completed the task, you will write a report describing the process you followed (including changes in your plans), identifying what forms of energy are involved, and how different forms of energy are transferred in your final design.

Materials: omitted

Scoring Rubric:

Level	Quantitative Reflection (QR)	Design Capacity (DC)	Relational Thinking (RT)	Design Consistency and Success (DCS)	Score
Energy conservation	The heat energy generated by pulley accounts for the imperfect efficiency	Task + four types of simple machines	Characteristics (nature of energy such as state or property of matter)	Plans changed systematically and task completed successfully	4
Energy degradation	The efficiency can never be 100%	Task + three types of simple machines	Evidence (energy loss during transformation due to friction)	Plans changed systematically and task completed unsuccessfully	3
Energy transfer	Quantitative relationships among three or more variables	Task + two types of simple machines	Leads-to (sequential energy transformation)	Plans change irregularly and task completed unsuccessfully	2
Energy does work	Quantitative relationships between two variables	Task + one simple machine	Type-of or kind-of (e.g., energy types, sources, etc.)	Plans changed irregularly and task not completed	1
Energy as activity	Listing pulley, weight, incline plane etc. separately/no connection between them	Task + confused	No explicit discussion of the nature of energy	No attempt to complete the task	0

Measuring Understanding About Science Inquiry

Various item formats are available for measuring understanding science inquiry. The most commonly used item format remains paper-and-pencil multiple-choice questions (e.g., Chen, 2006). Open-ended questions followed by in-depth interview are also viable (e.g., Lederman et al., 2002). The following question is from VOSTS (Aikenhead & Ryan, 1992):

Item 10411 Science and technology are closely related to each other:

Your position, basically: (please read from A to H, and then choose one)

They are closely related to each other

A. because science is the basis of all technological advances; though it is hard to see how technology could aid science.
B. because scientific research leads to practical applications in technology, and technological developments increase the ability to do scientific research.
C. because although they are different, they are linked so closely that it's hard to tell them apart.
D. because technology is the basis of all scientific advances, though it's hard to see how science could aid technology.
E. science and technology are more or less the same thing.
F. I don't understand
G. I don't know enough about this subject to make a choice.
H. none of these choices fits my basic viewpoint.

Item Review

Items should be reviewed for content validity. This is typically accomplished by an expert panel. "Experts" for the panel should be selected based on their demonstrated expertise instead of assumed expertise. For example, if the items are intended to measure understanding about science inquiry, science teachers may not necessarily be considered experts because research has shown repeatedly that many science teachers do not possess an adequate understanding of the nature of science. Practicing scientists may not have the highest level of understanding of nature of science either. Besides content validity, items may also be reviewed by assessment experts on the appropriateness of item formats and scoring. Item bias in terms of cultures, gender, and socioeconomic status should also be reviewed and avoided.

Item Tryout and Field Test

Items should also be tried with a small number of selected subjects before field-testing. This can be in the form of interviewing or think-aloud. Item try-out can help expose problems and issues with the items so that necessary revisions may be made before they go to field-testing. Item try-out can also provide an opportunity to understand the process of measurement in order to better plan for field-testing.

After items have been tried out and necessary revisions have been made, the draft instrument can now go through a field-testing. The sample for the field-testing should be representative of the intended population. Representativeness of the sample does not necessarily have to be achieved by random sampling—a major challenge in most science education research situations. One important consideration of representativeness is the range of performance variations in the target population. Thus, field-testing samples may be conveniently selected based on the variation in subject performances that matches the variation of subject performances in the target population.

Conduct Rasch modeling

Data collected from field-testing will then be submitted to Rasch modeling, and review of model-data-fit will then begin. When performance assessment is used to measure student science inquiry performances, it is common that more than one rater will score each student's performance. In Rasch modeling, the many-facet Rasch model is applicable to this situation. In many-facet Rasch modeling, raters are considered to be one additional facet, in addition to the two facets, that is, students and items, in a typical multiple-choice test situation. When including raters as one additional facet, each rater's degree of severity in scoring is estimated as a measure placed on the same scale as item difficulty and subject ability measures. This way, we can directly compare a rater's bias or scoring severity against item difficulties and subject abilities.

Table 5.2 presents the fit statistics obtained for the middle school performance assessment task on energy transfer described earlier based on Many-facet Rasch modeling.

Like item analysis for developing other types of measurement instruments, various statistics related to items based on Rasch modeling outputs should be reviewed. In particular, item fit statistics, point-biserial correlation, misfitting responses, and category structures should be reviewed. From Table 5.2, we see that the fit statistics suggest that all three items seem to have a good fit with the model. As for the two raters/judges, judge 1 is less severe than judge 2 in scoring; the difference between the two judges' severity measures is 0.34. Statistical testing for the difference by considering their standard errors of measures suggested that the difference was statistically insignificant. Thus, there was overall a good inter-

**Table 5.2.   Fit Statistics for Items on a
Middle School Performance Assessment on Energy Transfer**

Item	Measure	SE	INFIT MNSQ	INFIT ZSTD	OUTFIT MNSQ	OUTFIT ZSTD
Capacity	−5.59	0.36	0.9	0.0	1.0	0.0
Qualitative	2.19	0.32	0.6	−1.0	0.3	−2.0
Quantitative	3.40	0.34	0.6	−2.0	0.7	−1.0
Judge 1	−0.17	0.24	0.7	−1.0	0.8	−1.0
Judge 2	0.17	0.25	0.6	−1.0	0.6	−2.0

Source: Liu and Collard (2005).

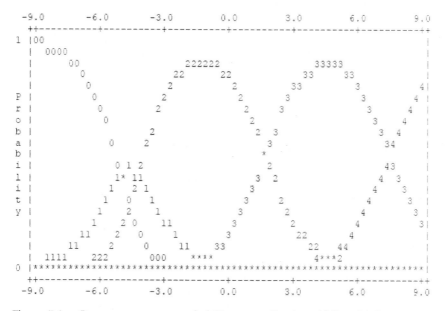

Figure 5.1.   Category structure probability curves for the middle school energy transfer performance assessment. Although categories 0, 2, 3, and 4 have distinct characteristic curves, category 1 does not possess a distinct characteristic curve.

rater agreement. The two judges' fit statistics are also within the acceptable ranges, thus the judges' scoring performances fit the Rasch model well.

Figure 5.1 shows the scoring category functions for five levels of performance specified in the scoring rubric for the same middle school performance assessment. Only categories 0, 2, 3, and 4 are distinct, that is, having their own peaks, suggesting that category 1 is not distinct and may be combined with either category 0 or category 2. In the performance assessment on energy transfer, categories correspond to different stages of energy concept development. Category 0 is about energy responsible for work; category 1 is about energy sources and forms; category 2 is about energy transfer; category 3 is about energy degradation; and category 4 is about energy conservation.

Figure 5.2 shows the Wright map for the performance assessment on energy transfer based on the same middle school group of students.

In Figure 5.2, measures are in logit; two raters are labeled judge 1 and judge 2; students are marked by x; *trait* corresponds to the three aspects specified in the scoring rubric and is considered as *item*; finally *stage* is the category in the scoring rubric corresponding to different stages of energy concept development. We can see from Figure 5.2 that the two judges' severity degrees are very close and at about the average of students' ability levels, thus the two judges are unlikely to be biased against most students. This Wright map also shows that *ql* and *qt* are above most students' ability levels, and there is a need for more items at the average level of most students' abilities.

Design and Conduct Validity and Reliability Studies

Rasch modeling provides various ways to establish evidence related to validity. First and foremost, the entire measurement development process is guided by the theory of science inquiry on the construct, and the Rasch modeling is a tool to test the agreement between data and the progression. If there is an overall good model-data-fit based on item fit statistics, then there is evidence for construct validity. Construct validity can also be demonstrated by examining the interaction between persons and items. A good match in range of measures between persons and items, and an even distribution of items along the construct demonstrates construct validity. Construct validity can further be demonstrated by examining the dimensionality of the items. If the factor analysis of residuals shows no additional dominant factors, then there is evidence for the construct validity, as the instrument is unidimensional.

The above validation processes primarily address validity related to internal structure of the measurement instrument; additional validity studies may also be conducted to establish other validity related evidence. For example, if it is known that understanding about science inquiry should be statistically significantly correlated with students' science achievement, then a criterion-related validation may be conducted to

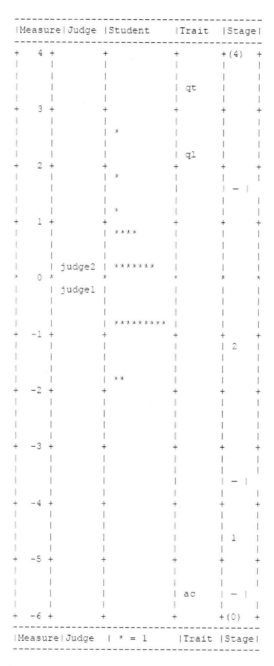

Figure 5.2. Wright map for the middle school energy transfer performance assessment. Two judges showed similar severity in scoring; different traits possess different difficulties.

establish the prediction validity—external structure. Similarly, if there is another valid and reliable instrument available, administering the available instrument to the same sample may be conducted to establish concurrent validity, that is, external structure, of the measurement instrument under development. Validity evidence related to the test content, response processes, and consequences may also be established following such procedures as expert item review, think-aloud of respondents when answering items, and examination of impacts of Rasch score uses.

Rasch modeling provides a variety of ways to examine the reliability of the instrument. First, item and person standard errors of measurement provide an indication on the precision of item and person measures. Lower standard errors of measurement relative to the item and person measures are desirable. Second, the person separation index and its Cronbach's alpha equivalent provide an indication of how the items are internally spread along the construct and are able to differentiate subjects. The higher the separation index and the alpha, the more reliable the instrument. Third, for measurement instruments that involve more than one rater, many-facet Rasch modeling also provides information on interrater reliability. The difficulty estimates for different raters should be statistically insignificant.

Develop Guidelines for Use of the Instrument

After the instrument has been finalized through cycles of revisions and field-testing, and the validity and reliability of the instrument have been established, the instrument is ready for dissemination and adoption by others. Detailed documentation should then be developed to facilitate users' administration of the instrument. The documentation should clearly state the intended uses of the test scores, the construct measured and the correspondent domains of performance and behaviors. The documentation should also include the procedures for administering the instrument, scoring responses, and reporting measures of subjects. Information on the validity and reliability of the instrument should also be provided in the documentation.

CHAPTER SUMMARY

Science inquiry is a comprehensive construct for organizing science curriculum, instruction, and teacher professional development. Science inquiry can be conceptualized as content for science learning, a way of knowing, and an approach to science teaching. Although inquiry does not take place in a step-by-step fashion, there are essential aspects common to all inquiry activities. These aspects are: hands-on skills pertaining to data collection and analysis, reasoning skills in relating data to theories, and abilities to perform inquiry tasks. Science inquiry is essentially an integrated practice that involves generating and evaluating scientific evidence and explanations. Generating and evaluating scientific evidence and explanations encompasses the knowledge and skills used for building and refining models and explanations, designing and analyzing empirical investigations and observations, and constructing and defending arguments with empirical evidence. The sociocultural context is also essential in the above inquiry activities.

Besides the ability to demonstrate science inquiry described above, the *National Science Education Standards* also expect students to demonstrate understanding about science inquiry. Understanding about science inquiry relates to how and why scientific knowledge changes in response to new evidence, logical analysis, and modified explanations debated within a community of scientists. Related to understanding about science inquiry is understanding about the nature of science. Because science inquiry is an essential component of science, understanding about science inquiry is an essential component of understanding about the nature of science. In addition, science inquiry as teaching and learning, requires that teachers understand the nature and process of students' developing scientific knowledge as inquiry, and conduct science teaching through science inquiry.

Many measurement instruments are available for science inquiry. These instruments use a variety of questions formats, including multiple-choice, true-false, rating scale, Likert scale, checklist or inventory, and performance assessment. When selecting a measurement instrument to use, one most important consideration is the validity of the construct the instrument is intended to measure. Theories about science inquiry have changed considerably over the years. As the result, many theories that underlie the constructs of previous instruments may be outdated, which makes the construct validity of those instruments questionable. Consideration should also focus on other types of evidence of validity and reliability for the instruments. Even if a measurement instrument developed in the past is reported to be valid and reliable, it is still necessary to further validate the instrument because the targeted subject population (e.g., students, teachers) may have changed considerably.

Developing measurement instruments for science inquiry follows a systematic process. This process starts with identifying a valid and commonly accepted theory about science inquiry. Based on the theory, the intended construct of measurement is defined and the subject behaviors corresponding to different levels of performance on the construct are identified. The measurement instrument development process continues with the development of a test specification, item constructions, item review, item try-out and field testing. Data collected from field-testing are then submitted to Rasch modeling. If more than one rater is involved in scoring, a many-facet Rasch model is applied. Review of fit statistics, the Wright map, dimensionality map, as well as separation indices and alpha reliability should be conducted according to established conventions. Using Rasch modeling to develop measurement instruments helps establish evidence for the instrument's validity and reliability.

EXERCISES

1. There are at least three approaches to developing measurement instruments on understanding of the nature of science. One approach is using selected response question formats such as the Likert scale questions; another approach is using a nonscoring items such as that in VOSTS; and the third approach is using open-ended questions such as items in VNOS. Compare the above three approaches, discuss the pros and cons of each of the approaches to measuring understanding of the nature of science.

2. One important characteristic of inquiry science teaching is authentic science investigation activities. Suppose that you are interested in developing a measurement instrument to measure the degree of authenticity of science investigation activities performed by students. Please complete the following initial steps of developing such an instrument: (a) define the construct of authenticity, (b) identify student behaviors that represent different degrees of authenticity, and (c) write five sample items corresponding to five different levels of authenticity.

3. The development of Self-Efficacy and Metacognition Learning Inventory–Science (SEMLI-S) (Thomas, Anderson, & Nashon, 2008) was based on Rasch modeling. Read the report to critique the adequacy of application of Rasch modeling in the development of the measurement instrument.

4. Hands-on performance tasks are claimed to be one of best ways to measure student science inquiry abilities. Develop a plan to conduct validity and reliability studies for the development of a measurement instrument that is based on hands-on performance tasks.

REFERENCES

Admson, S. L., Banks, D., Burtch, M., Cox, F., Judson, E., Turley, J. B., et al. (2003). Reformed undergraduate instruction and its subsequent impact on secondary school teaching practice and student achievement. *Journal of Research in Science Teaching, 40*(10), 939-957.

Aikenhead, G. (1973). The measurement of high school students' knowledge about science and scientists. *Science Education, 57*(4), 539-549.

Aikenhead, G. S., & Ryan, A. G. (1992). The development of a new instrument: Views on science–technology–society (VOSTS). *Science Education, 76,* 477-491.

Anderson, R. D. (2007). Inquiry as an organizing theme for science curricula. In S. K. Abell & N. G. Lederman (Eds.), *Handbook of research on science education* (pp. 807-830). New York, NY: Routledge.

Anderson, D., & Nashon, S. (2007). Predators of knowledge construction: Interpreting students' metacognition in an amusement park physics program. *Science Education, 91*(2), 298-320.

Billeh, V. Y., & Hasan, O. E. (1975). Factors influencing teachers' gain in understanding the nature of science. *Journal of research in Science Teaching, 12*(3), 209-219.

Bridgham, R. G. (1969). Classification, serration, and the learning of electrostatics. *Journal of Research in Science Teaching, 6,* 118-127.

Brown, J. H., & Shavelson, R. J. (1996). *Assessing hands-on science: A teacher's guide to performance assessment*: Thousand Oaks, CA: Corwin Press.

Butts, D. P. (1964). The evaluation of problem solving in science. *Journal of Research in Science Teaching, 2,* 116-122.

Chen, S. (2006). Development of an instrument to assess views on nature of science and attitudes toward teaching science. *Science Education, 90*(5), 803-819.

Cobern, W. W., & Loving, C. C. (2002). Investigation of preservice elementary teachers' thinking about science. *Journal of Research in science Teaching, 39*(10), 1016-1031.

Cothan, J., & Smith, E. (1981). Development and validation of the conceptions of scientific theories test. *Journal of Research in Science Teaching, 18*(5), 387-396.

Denny, R. T. (1971). The mathematical skill test (MAST) in chemistry. *Journal of Chemical Education, 48*(12), 845-646.

Dillashaw, F. G., & Okey, J. R. (1980). Test of the integrated science process skills for secondary science students. *Science Education, 64*(5), 601-608.

Elby, A., & Hammer, D. (2001). On the substance of a sophisticated epistemology. *Science Education, 85*(5), 554-567.

Fraser, B. J. (1980). Development and validation of a test of enquiry skills. *Journal of Research in Science Teaching, 17,* 7-16.

Halloun, I., & Hestenes, D. (1996, March). *Views about sciences survey: VASS.* Paper presented at the annual meeting of the National Association for Research in science Teaching, St. Louise, MO.

Halloun, I., & Hestenes, D. (1998). Interpreting VASS dimensions and profiles for physics students. *Science & Education, 7,* 533-577.

Hu, W., & Adey, P. (2002). A scientific creativity test for secondary school students. *International Journal of Science Education, 24*(4), 389-403.

Jacobs, C. L., Martin, S. N., & Otieno, T. C. (2008). A science lesson plan analysis instrument for formative and summative program evaluation of a teacher education program. *Science Education, 92*(6), 1096-1126.

Kimball, M. E. (1967). Understanding of the nature of science: A comparison of scientists and science teachers. *Journal of Research in Science Teaching, 5,* 110-120.

Lawson, A. E. (1978). The development and validation of a classroom test for formal reasoning. *Journal of Research in Science Teaching, 15*(1), 11-24.

Lederman, N. G. (1992). Students' and teachers' conceptions of the nature of science: A review of the research. *Journal of Research in Science Teaching, 29*(4), 331-359.

Lederman, N. G. (2007). Nature of science: Past, present, and future. In S. K. Abell & N. G. Lederman (Eds.), *Handbook of research on science education* (pp. 831-879). New York, NY: Routledge.

Lederman, N. G., Abd-El-Khalick, F., Bell, R. L., & Schwartz, R. S. (2002). Views of nature of science questionnaire: Toward valid and meaningful assessment of learners' conceptions of nature of science. *Journal of Research in Science Teaching, 39*(6), 497-521.

Lederman, N. G., Wade, P. D., & Bell, R. L. (1998). Assessing understanding of the nature of science: A historical perspective. In W. McComas (Ed.), *The nature of science and science education: Rationales and strategies* (pp. 331-350). Dordrecht, The Netherlands: Kluwer Academic.

Lee, M. -H., Johanson, R. E., & Tsai, C. -C. (2008). Exploring Taiwanese high school students' conceptions of and approaches to learning science through a structural equation modeling analysis. *Science Education, 92*(2), 191-220.

Liu, X. (2009a). *Essentials of science classroom assessment.* Thousands, CA: Sage.

Liu, X. (2009b). Standardized measurement instruments in science education. In M. -W. Roth & K. Tobin (Eds.), *The world of science education: Handbook of research in North America* (pp. 649-677). Rotterdam, The Netherlands: Sense.

Liu, X., & Collard, S. (2005). Using Rasch model to validate stages of understanding the energy concept. *Journal of Applied Measurement, 6*(2), 224-241.

Lunetta, V. N., & Tamir, P. (1979). Matching lab activities with teaching goals. *The Science Teacher, 46*(5), 22–24.

Marks, R. L. (1967). CBA high school chemistry and concept formation. *Journal of Chemical Education, 44*(8), 471-474.

Molitor, L. L., & George, K. D. (1976). Development of a test for science process skills. *Journal of Research in Science Teaching, 13*(5), 405-412.

National Research Council. (1996). *National science education standards.* Washington, DC: National Academy Press.

National Research Council. (2000). *Inquiry and the national science education standards: A guide for teaching and learning.* Washington, DC: National Academic Press.

National Research Council. (2007). *Taking science to school: Learning and teaching science in grades K-8.* Washington, DC: The National Academic Press.

Nelson, M., & Abraham, E. C. (1973). Inquiry skill measures. *Journal of Research in Science Teaching, 10*(4), 291-297.

Nelson, C. H., & Mason, J. M. (1963). A test of science comprehension for upper elementary grades. *Science Education, 47*(4), 319-330.

Osborne, J., Collins, S., Ratcliffe, M., Millar, R., & Duschl, R. (2003). What "ideas-about-science" should be taught in school science? A Delphi study of the expert community. *Journal of Research in Science Teaching, 40*(7), 692-720.

Robinson, J. T. (1969). Evaluating laboratory work in high school biology. *American Biology Teacher, 31*(4), 236-240.

Rudolph, J. L. (2000). Reconsidering the "nature of science" as a curriculum component. *Journal of Curriculum Studies, 32*(3), 403-419.

Shin, N., Jonassen, D. H., & McGee, S. (2003). Predictors of well-structured and ill-structured problem solving in an astronomy simulation. *Journal of Research in Science Teaching, 40*(1), 6-33.

Tamir, P., Nussinovitz, R., & Friedler, Y. (1982). The design and use of practical tests assessment inventory. *Journal of Biological Education, 16*(1), 42-50.

Thomas, G., Anderson, D., & Nashon, S. (2008). Development of an instrument designed to investigate elements of science students' metacognition, self-efficacy and learning processes: The SEMLI-S. *International Journal of Science Education, 30*(13), 1701-1724.

Tsai, C. -C., & Liu, S. -Y. (2005). Developing a multi-dimensional instrument for assessing students' epistemological views toward science. *International Journal of Science Education, 27*(13), 1621-1638.

Walczyk, J. J., & Ramsey, L. L. (2003). Use of learner-centered instruction in college science and mathematics classrooms. *Journal of Research in Science Teaching, 40*(6), 566-584.

Walker, R., Hendrix, J. R., & Mertens, T. R. (1979). Written Piagetian task instrument: Its development and use. *Science Education, 63*(2), 211-220.

Wong, S. L., & Hodson, D. (2008). From the horse's mouth: What scientists say about scientific investigation and scientific knowledge. *Science Education, 93*(1), 109-130.

CHAPTER 6

USING AND DEVELOPING INSTRUMENTS FOR MEASURING LEARNING PROGRESSION

This chapter is concerned with learning progression. Learning progression is an emerging field of research in science education; it is gaining attention rapidly. For example, The *Canadian Journal of Science, Mathematics, and Technology Education* devoted an entire issue (volume 4, number 1, 2004) to the topic of learning progression of children's long-term science concept development. Most recently, the *Journal of Research in Science Teaching* devoted its entire issue 6 of volume 46 (2009) to learning progressions in science. With growing recognition of the importance of studying learning progression in science, learning progression is becoming an important measurement domain. This chapter will first review current theoretical frameworks about learning progression. It will then introduce standardized instruments for measuring learning progression. Finally, this chapter will describe the process for developing new instruments for measuring learning progression using the Rasch modeling approach.

Using and Developing Measurement Instruments in Science Education:
A Rasch Modeling Approach, pp. 205–234
Copyright © 2010 by Information Age Publishing

WHAT IS LEARNING PROGRESSION IN SCIENCE?

One key difference between school science learning and informal science learning is the organization of content. School science learning is characterized by a long-term systematic organization of content so that student learning is progressive. National and state science content standards are examples of systematic organization of content to ensure that learning takes place progressively over time across grades. The progressive nature of school science learning requires us to assess student learning over a long time span, often across multiple grades. This type of assessment is important not only to ensure that students have reached certain levels of learning proficiency or standards at a given time, but also to provide information about trajectories of student learning in order to inform ongoing teaching and learning. In order to meet this requirement, it is necessary to develop measurement instruments for assessing learning progression.

Learning progression can be defined as "descriptions of the successively more sophisticated ways of thinking about a topic that can follow one another as children learn about and investigate a topic over a broad span of time" (National Research Council [NRC], 2007, p. 219). Expanding the four key characteristics of learning progression identified by the above National Research Council Committee on Science Learning, a learning progression is characterized by the following six features:

1. *It is domain-specific.* Learning progression must pertain to science content instead of general reasoning or performance skills. This is in contrast to the cognitive development (e.g., logico-mathematical reasoning) in cognitive psychology. Given that only broad topics may be continuously elaborated and learned over time, learning progression should pertain to big ideas in science. For example, the *Benchmarks for Science Literacy* (American Association for the Advancement of Science [AAAS], 1993) has identified systems, models, constancy and change, and scale to be unifying themes in science. Thus, a learning progression on understanding of systems may take place from elementary to high school with different types of systems learned at different grade levels. The *National Science Education Standards* (NRC, 1996) has identified the following unifying concepts and processes in science: systems, order and organization; evidence, models and explanation; change, constancy and measurement; evolution and equilibrium; and form and function. Major ideas in science are related to essential questions (Wiggins & McTighe, 2001), and core ideas (NRC, 2007). If a topic is too specific, such as the Newton's second law of motion, there is not

enough variation in content and cognitive reasoning for a sequence of learning to take place over multiple grades with increasing complexity.

2. *It is interdisciplinary.* Learning progression involves topics of more than one science discipline. Typically, K-12 science content is organized around life science, physical science, and earth and space science. A learning progression may apply to both life science and physical science, or to all major science disciplines. In addition to the major science disciplines, a learning progression may also involve other aspects of science, such as science inquiry, technology, and history and nature of science. The National Research Council Committee on Science Teaching and Learning (NRC, 2007) has conceptualized science proficiency to include four interrelated strands: (a) knowing, using, and interpreting scientific explanations of the natural world; (b) generating and evaluating scientific evidence and explanation; (c) understanding the nature and development of scientific knowledge; and (d) participating productively in scientific practices and discourse. A learning progression involves all of these strands.

3. *It describes different levels of competence.* A learning progression should map out a hierarchy of student learning outcomes from least competent to most competent. This hierarchy is also called a learning trajectory. A learning trajectory starts with what students typically know and can do without formal school science learning; this starting point represents the level of competence students typically develop in informal settings before formal science learning takes place. A learning trajectory ends with what is expected of students as the result of systematic science learning over a period of time. National and state curriculum standards typically describe what is expected of students by the end of a certain grade. However, what is specified in the standards is not necessarily the end point of a learning trajectory, because standards usually specify only a minimal competence. The highest level of a learning trajectory should be a desired level of learning competence, although it may not be achievable by all students. Between the starting and desired levels in the learning trajectory, there can be multiple interim levels of competence. No matter how many interim levels a learning progression contains, the levels must be distinct from each other, that is, qualitatively different and are in increasing sophistication.

4. *It is organized around core ideas.* Specific facts or theories cannot form learning progression, because they may be mastered at once.

Core ideas are conceptual themes and topics that involve a large number of specific facts, theories, reasoning skills, and so on. There is an internal structure among this large number of facts, theories, and reasoning skills according to scientific principles; there is also a psychological structure among this large number of facts, theories, and reasoning skills according to how students learn. Because of these structures, core ideas need to be continuously learned and developed over multiple years. Examples of core ideas are matter, energy, evolution, and so on.

5. *It is multidimensional.* A learning progression is not a fixed linear sequence; instead it may contain multiple paths toward the same ending point. In other words, a learning progression is not the same as a series of lessons or learning units for students to complete. Specific lessons and units need to be designed according to distinct characteristics of students and the learning environment within the framework of a learning progression. An identical learning progression can thus be realized by different learning pathways.

6. *It is curriculum sensitive.* A learning progression should capture the effects of different types of curriculum and instruction.

There are many ways to realize learning progression in curriculum and instruction. One way is to use a spiral curriculum to organize content (Bruner, 1960). According to Bruner, each discipline consists of a few central ideas that form the structure of the discipline. These structures vary in complexity, and cannot be introduced to students completely at once. As the result, it is necessary to teach the central ideas in a progressive way from lower grades through higher grades. A spiral curriculum has the organization of content around central ideas so that they are continually learned in a progressively complex form. Such an organization helps ensure the continuity, integration, articulation, and balance of the curriculum (AAAS, 2001a). Continuity of the curriculum means that major ideas and skills are continuously practiced and developed; integration of curriculum means that all types of knowledge and experiences are connected and unified at a higher level; articulation of curriculum means that various aspects of the curriculum are interrelated; and finally balance of curriculum means that appropriate weights are given to each related basic ideas of central topics.

As an example of learning progression, Catley, Lehrer, and Reiser (2005) have developed a learning progression on evolution for K-8. They conceptualize that evolution accounts for life's diversity at all levels—its variation at genetic, habitat, and species levels. The core concepts involved for a complete understanding of evolution are:

1. *Diversity:* Biodiversity occurs at three levels—diversity of species, diversity within species and among individuals, and diversity of habitats. Species are the units of evolutionary change. The genetic diversity is the engine of evolution; and habitat is the agent of natural selection.

2. *Structure-Function:* Structures perform functions that allow individuals to survive. Structure-function relations are the cornerstone of adaptation.

3. *Ecology/Interrelationships:* Living things populate a particular habitat and are embedded within a complex system. Changes in a habitat affect the functioning of the ecology and the chance for individual organisms to survive and replicate.

4. *Variation:* Random variation results from genetic recombination and genetic mutation; directed variation or natural selection results mostly from habitat variables. The interplay between random and directed variation is the foundation of life's diversity.

5. *Change:* Change occurs at different scales of time and organization.

6. *Geologic Processes:* Geologic processes are related to past environments and the life history of the planet.

7. *Forms of argument:* Model-based reasoning and historic interpretation are primary forms of argument for development of the evaluation theory.

8. *Mathematical tools:* Mathematical tools such as measurement, data creation, distribution, Venn diagrams, and cladograms are critical in representing evolutionary processes

Based on the above core concepts, Catley et al. (2005) propose the following learning progression on evolution by grade span:

Grades K-2

- *Diversity:* Diversity may exist in attribute/character, and can be understood by comparative analysis;
- *Structure-Function:* Attributes often serve specific functions;
- *Ecology:* There are relationships between habitat and the kinds of organisms that live there;
- *Variation:* There are individual differences among everyday "kinds" of life;
- *Change:* Individual organisms change over the course of their life span;

- *Geologic Record:* Fossils are artifacts of some of the processes that created them;
- *Forms of Argument:* Argumentation may take place by using models and comparative analysis;
- *Mathematical Tools:* Measure, Venn diagram, arithmetic (difference) are used to study evolution.

Grades 3-5

- *Diversity:* Diversity is understood by classification and comparative analysis;
- *Structure-Function:* Characters often serve specific functions;
- *Ecology:* There is a relationship between qualities of the environment and characters of the organism;
- *Variation:* There is both within and between species variation;
- *Change:* Individual change helps with survival;
- *Geologic Record:* There are a wide range of fossils;
- *Forms of Argument:* Argumentation may take place using models and comparative analysis;
- *Mathematics Tools:* Measures, Venn diagram, arithmetic (ratios) are used to study evolution.

Grades 6-8

- *Diversity:* Diversity is a result of mechanisms involving change, variation, and ecology;
- *Structure-Function:* External and internal structures help organisms survive and reproduce;
- *Ecology:* What affects one species may affect others in the system;
- *Variation:* Organisms that are of the same species can also be different from one another;
- *Change:* Change occurs continuously at both the individual and population levels;
- *Forms of Argument:* Argumentation may take place using models and comparative analysis;
- *Mathematics Tools:* distribution and cladograms are used to study evolution.

We can see from the above description, learning progression on evolution is multidimensional, around a big idea and domain-specific, because it involves a number of core concepts or dimensions including diversity, structure and function, ecology and interrelation, variation, change, and geological processes. The learning progression is also interdisciplinary, because the above core concepts involve the domains of biology, geology, and chemistry; mathematical tools and logical reasoning are also part of the learning progression. The learning progression also contains a hierarchy of competency levels, organized by three grade spans—Grades K-2, Grades 3-5, and Grades 6-8. The above learning progression can be realized by spiral curriculums, because the core concepts are learned continuously with increased complexity. However, this learning progression does not prescribe how specific lessons and units should be designed, although different curriculums may have different effects on students' learning pathways along the learning progression.

The AAAS Atlases (AAAS, 2001b, 2007) visually present learning progression in a set of strand maps. Each map relates to one major theme in the Benchmarks for Science Literacy (AAAS, 1993); it contains a few core strands that define the theme. Within each map, benchmarks of science literacy related to each strand are mapped vertically from Grades K-12. Connections between benchmarks among different strands within the same map and in strands of other maps are made using arrows. In this way, each map presents a hierarchical web of science benchmarks demonstrating how conceptual understanding of a major theme may progress from lower grades to higher grades. For example, the map on the theme of weather and climate includes four strands: temperature and winds, water cycle, atmosphere, and climate change. For the strand temperature and winds, students in grades K-2 are expected to understand that the sun warms the land, air and water. At Grades 3-5, students are expected to understand that a warmer object can warm a cooler one by contact or at a distance. At Grades 6-8, students are expected to understand that light and other electromagnetic waves can warm objects, and how much an object's temperature increases depends on how intense the light striking its surface is, how long the light shines on the object, and how much of the light is absorbed. At Grades 9-12, students are expected to understand that, because the earth turns daily on an axis that is tilted relative to the plane of the earth's yearly orbit around the sun, sunlight falls more intensely on different parts of the earth during the years, and the difference in intensity of sunlight and the resulting warming of the earth's surface produces the seasonal variations in temperature. The above major understandings are connected to that of other strands in a complex way. Thus, the learning progression on weather and climate is indeed multidimensional, domain-specific, interdisciplinary, and requires continuous and progressive development of competencies.

INSTRUMENTS FOR MEASURING
STUDENT LEARNING PROGRESSION

Because learning progression is a relatively new research area in science education, very few standard instruments are currently available for measuring learning progression. This section introduces three measurement instruments related to learning progression. Although they are for different intended uses and are based on different theoretical frameworks of learning progression, one common element among the three instruments is that Rasch modeling was used to developing them. Please note, the following descriptions of the instruments are for readers' information only; whether or not a science education researcher will choose an instrument for a particular research question requires a critical review of the instrument by the researcher, which is beyond the scope of this book.

The Berkeley Evaluation and Assessment Research (BEAR) Assessment System (Wilson & Sloane, 2000)

The BEAR assessment system is a curriculum embedded assessment to measure students' learning progression during a course. Unlike conventional standardized measurement instruments, the BEAR assessment system uses regular teaching and learning activities as assessment tasks distributed at various points during a course to assess students' learning progression. Although the assessment tasks are not standardized, the scoring is standardized by using a common categorization system (e.g., 4 for above the standard, 3 for meeting the standard, 2 for meeting some aspects of the standard, 1 for meeting one aspect of the standard, and 0 for meeting none aspect of the standard) for all assessment tasks. Further, estimation of students' learning progression based on various assessment tasks is also standardized using a common measurement scale obtained from multidimensional Rasch scaling. Thus, the BEAR assessment system can produce both individual and group student learning trajectories toward a defined learning goal—the learning standard. Teachers and students can use the assessment information to plan appropriate teaching and learning activities according to the learning trajectories, making the BEAR assessment system a formative assessment.

The BEAR assessment system has been implemented in various curriculums such as IEY (Issues, Evidence and You developed at the UC Berkeley's Lawrence Hall of Science). The validity of the BEAR assessment system has been argued from an approach called assessment net which is composed of (a) a framework for describing and reporting the level of student performance along achievement continua, (b) the gathering of information through the use of diverse indicators based on observational practices that are consistent both with the educational variables to be measured and with the context in which that measurement is taken place, and (c) a measurement model that provides the opportunity for appropriate forms of quality control. Evidence of validity for the BEAR assessment system comes from a variety of sources. The construct validity is claimed by developing assessment tasks and scoring rubrics as well as scaling learning progression along a hypothesized learning progression. The instructional validity is claimed by the match between instruction and assessment and teacher management and responsibility to conduct the assessment and interpret the assessment results. The criterion validity is demonstrated by comparing classes implementing the assessment system with classes not implementing the assessment system. The effect size for implementing the assessment system was found to be from 0.22 to 0.75. The reliability of the assessment system was primarily established by multidimensional Rasch modeling with reliability coefficients for different progress variables ranging from 0.65 to .90. Attention has also been given to fairness and absence of bias of the assessment system.

Progression of Understanding Matter (PUM) (Liu, 2007)

PUM is a paper-and-pencil test assessing Grades 3 to 12 students' knowledge and understanding of matter. It consists of both multiple-choice and constructed response questions. It has three forms: Elementary (Grades 3-6), middle school (7-9), and high school (10-12). The three forms are linked by common items. There are 20 questions in the elementary form, 29 in the middle school form and 29 in the high school form. The questions are from publicly released items from TIMSS, NAEP, and the New York state regents exams. One common scale was constructed for all three forms through Rasch scaling so that students' knowledge and understanding at different grades can be directly compared. The validation process follows the Rasch approach to constructing measures. Validity is claimed by adequate model-data-fit, the Wright map and unidimensionality, and reliability is claimed by person and item separation indices (person separation index was 1.94 or alpha equivalent of .79; item separation index was 9.68 or alpha equivalent of .99).

ChemQuery Assessment System (Claesgens, Scalise, Wilson, & Stacy, 2009)

The ChemQuery is a criterion-referenced assessment system to measure the paths of student understanding in chemistry. It includes assessment questions, a scoring rubric, item exemplars, a framework to describe the paths of student understanding that emerge, and criterion referenced analysis using item response theory (IRT) to map student progress.

Understanding of chemistry is called chemistry perspectives and is conceptualized to consist of three "big ideas" or constructs: matter, change and energy. Each construct requires students continuously develop understanding about it; thus each construct is a progress variable. Each progress variable is defined by five hierarchical levels of understanding with increasing complexity: (a) level 1—notions (e.g., what do we know about matter?), (b) level 2—recognition (e.g., how do chemists describe matter?), (c) level 3—formulation (e.g., how can we think about interactions between atoms?), (d) level 4—construction (e.g., how can we understand composition, structure, properties, and amounts?), (e) level 5—generation (e.g., what new experiments can we design to gain a deeper understanding of matter?). All questions are open-ended constructed response questions, and scored by a rubric. Each rubric describes specific student responses for each of the above performance levels.

Validation of the instrument followed an iterative process and was based on Rasch modeling. The iterative process involves:

1. Using a well-balanced expert group and paying attention to the research literature in the area to be measured to propose some "big ideas" and general outlines for an assessment framework;

2. On the basis of the current framework ideas, examine the curriculum to determine appropriate topic areas and contexts to consider for measuring developing conceptual understanding of progress variables;

3. Explore item-type possibilities and scoring approaches with curriculum developers, content experts, instructors, and project participants, and develop sets of items and rubrics;

4. Test items on a small informant population of students;

5. Collect feedback on items during an item paneling and scoring review session, and attempt to develop a body of exemplars, or examples of student work, at each level of scoring;

6. Qualitatively analyze the results of scoring;

7. Refine scoring rubrics and engage in or adjust approaches to rater training for the larger body of data collection to come;

8. Collect and analyze a larger set of diverse student data through both qualitative and quantitative approaches that can be analyzed with the use of measurement models;

9. Use the results of this larger data collection to refine the framework, improve items, evaluate and update the scoring approaches, and assess the appropriate use of measurement models;

10. Repeat the process using the updated approaches, and iteratively engage in further rounds of student data collection.

Examination of item fit statistics and the Wright map shows a good model-data-fit. The expected *a posteriori* estimation based upon plausible values (EAP/PV) was .85 for the matter progress variable and .83 for the change variable, with person separation reliability estimated at .82 and .80, respectively. Difference in Rasch scale scores and their correspondent levels of understanding between high school and university students were found to be significant. ChemQuery may be used for both formative and summative assessment.

DEVELOPING INSTRUMENTS
FOR MEASURING LEARNING PROGRESSION

Identify the Primary Purpose(s)
for Which the Test Scores Will Be Used

Assessment of learning progression can be conducted for either formative or summative evaluation, or both. A formative use of test scores of learning progression assessment is to inform teachers in planning ongoing instruction and for students to reflect on the ongoing progress toward learning goals. This type of learning progression assessment typically takes place during a course of study. An example of such uses is the BEAR assessment system. On the other hand, a summative use of learning progression is to identify the level of student achievement on a defined learning progression. This type of learning progression assessment typically takes place at multiple grade levels. An example of such uses is the PUM. Formative uses of learning progression assessment require that data collection takes place at multiple time points over a time span such as a course, while summative uses of learning progression assessment require data collection to be conducted only once—at the end of a learning cycle. Of course, assessment of learning progression may be used for both formative and summative purposes. In this last scenario, test scores of learning progression assessment at the end of a learning cycle are used for summative purposes, while test scores of learning progression assessment before the end of a learning cycle are used for formative purposes.

Define the Construct to Be Measured

One key task in defining the domain of assessment of a learning progression is to decide on the construct to be assessed. Constructs for learning progression assessment should be unifying themes or big ideas. For example, the BEAR assessment system applied to the IEY curriculum units identifies five IEY progress variables as its measurement constructs. The five progress variables are defined as follows:

1. *Understanding concepts (UC):* Understanding scientific concepts (e.g., properties and interactions of materials, energy or thresholds) to apply the relevant scientific concepts to the solution of problems.

2. *Designing and conducting investigations (DCI):* Designing a scientific experiment, carrying through a complete scientific investigation, performing laboratory procedures to collect data, recording and organizing data, and analyzing and interpreting results of an experiment.

3. *Evidence and tradeoffs (ET):* Identifying objective scientific evidence as well as evaluating the advantages and disadvantages of different possible solutions to a problem based on the variable evidence.

4. *Communicating scientific information (CM):* Organizing and presenting results in a way that is free of technical errors and effectively communicates with the chosen audience.

5. *Group interaction (GI):* Developing skills in working with teammates to complete a task (such as lab experiment) and in sharing the work of the activity.

As can be seen in the BEAR assessment system example, the constructs defined for learning progression assessment are broad and comprehensive; they need to be continuously developed over a long-term period. There can be more than one construct to be measured within a measurement instrument; but for each defined construct, there must be only one dimension of competence that describes the progression of the subjects' performance and the increasing demand of measurement items.

Identify Behaviors That Represent the Construct

Once the construct is defined, then it is necessary to identify subject behaviors or performances that represent the construct. This collection of behaviors defines the domain of assessment. Behaviors should involve both content and reasoning skills. For example, for the core concept or idea of diversity which can be a construct of measurement, it may have the following behaviors for Grades 6-8 according to Cateley et al. (2005):

- *Develop* attributes;
- *Identify* attributes/characters and use them to *classify* an organism;
- *Predict* an attribute given the presence of another attribute;
- *Determine* similarities and differences at the individual species level;
- *Compare and Contrast* species;
- *Construct, revise, present/defend, and critique* explanations of the contrasts observed;
- *Identify* characters which only evolved once and support large radiations of species, that is, metamorphosis;
- *Distinguish* between characters that evolved independently on several occasions (convergent evolution), and those that appeared only once in the history of life;
- *Explain* that convergent evolution is driven by local ecological requirements and does not typically lead to large radiations of species.

The above behaviors are defined by both content and reasoning skills. Since a learning progression describes hierarchical levels of students' performances, it is possible to define students' performances along a continuum from a lower level to a higher level. For example, the above behaviors related to understanding of diversity in living things may be represented in Table 6.1.

Table 6.1.   Student Behaviors of Diversity of Living Things

Student Behaviors	Performance Level
• *Identify* characters which only evolved once and support large radiations of species that is, metamorphosis. • *Distinguish* between characters that evolved independently on several occasions (convergent evolution), and those that appeared only once in the history of life. • *Explain* that convergent evolution is driven by local ecological requirements and does not typically lead to large radiations of species.	3 (Competent)
• *Identify* attributes/characters and use them to *classify* an organism. • *Predict* an attribute given the presence of another attribute. • *Compare and Contrast* species. • *Construct, revise, present/defend, and critique* explanations of the contrasts observed.	2 (Developing)
• *Develop* attributes. • *Determine* similarities and differences at the individual species level.	1 (Basic)

The above identified student behaviors form a hierarchy, similar to a scoring rubric. However, one key difference between the above-defined hierarchical student behaviors and a scoring rubric for an assessment task is that hierarchical student behaviors are not specific to any one assessment task; they apply to all assessment tasks to be developed in the next step.

Prepare a Set of Test Specifications

Depending on the intended uses of learning progression measurement discussed earlier, a test specification based on intended student performances of measurement may take different formats. Taking the above core concept of diversity in living things as an example once again, a sample test specification for the summative use of learning progression assessment to be used by three grade levels is in Table 6.2.

In the above test specification, three forms of the test will be developed, with each form worth 30 points. In addition to the 30 points unique for each form, there will also be 10 additional points of test items from

Table 6.2. Test Specification With Values for Assessment of Learning Progression of Diversity in Living Things

Grade Span	Student Behaviors	Weight	Linking Points
Grade 6	• *Identify* characters which only evolved once and support large radiations of species, that is, metamorphosis. • *Distinguish* between characters that evolved independently on several occasions (convergent evolution), and those that appeared only once in the history of life. • *Explain* that convergent evolution is driven by local ecological requirements and does not typically lead to large radiations of species.	30 points	10 points
Grade 7	• *Identify* attributes/characters and use them to *classify* an organism. • *Predict* an attribute given the presence of another attribute. • *Compare and Contrast* species. • *Construct, revise, present/defend, and critique* explanations of the contrasts observed.	30 points	
Grade 8	• *Develop* attributes. • *Determine* similarities and differences at the individual species level.	30 points	

**Table 6.3. Test of Specification With Values for the
Three Forms of Assessment Instrument for
Learning Progression of Diversity in Living Things**

Student	Form 1			Form 2			Form 3		
	Items 1-10	Items 11-20	Items 21-30	Items 1-10	Items 11-20	Items 21-30	Items 1-10	Items 11-20	Items 21-30
Grade 6	x	x	x	x					
Grade 7				x	x	x	x		
Grade 8			x				x	x	x

another form to provide a linkage between test forms. Thus, each test form will actually have 40 points.

Once a test specification with values such as that in Table 6.2 is developed, the number of items may then be decided. Multiple-choice items are typically scored as right (1) or wrong (0), and constructed and performance items are typically scored using a scoring rubric by awarding scores from 0 to a maximal score (e.g., 5). Once the total number of items is decided for each of the forms of the instrument, a linking scheme among the different forms of the instrument must be created. A sample linking design is represented graphically in Table 6.3.

In the test specification in Table 6.3, cells with x indicate that students respond to the corresponding questions in the specified forms, and blank cells indicate that students do not respond to the corresponding questions in the specified forms. Form 1 is indented for Grade 6, Form 2 for Grade 7, and Form 3 for Grade 8. Based on the design, students from each grade will respond to a total of 40 items, with 30 from the intended form and 10 additional from another form. This common item linking enables measures from Forms 1-3 to be on the same scale and will be directly comparable. Although there are no absolute rules available for deciding the required number of common items, a rule of thumb is that linking items should be about 20 items, or 20% of the total items in each form (Wolfe, 2004).

In addition to using items from different forms to be linked, which is called internal anchoring, items may also be from external sources. This latter design is called external anchoring (Wolfe, 2004). The external anchoring uses a common set of items from other sources not to be part of the two forms as linking items. When using external anchoring, it is important to make sure that the external anchoring items measure the same construct of the learning progression.

If assessment of learning progression is for formative uses, that is, informing teachers and students on students' learning trajectories during

Table 6.4.   A Sample Scoring for Items on Using Evidence

Score	Outcome
4	Response accomplishes Level 3 AND goes beyond in some significant way, such as questioning or justifying the source, validity, and/or quantity of evidence.
3	Response provides major objective reasons AND supports each with relevant and accurate evidence.
2	Response provides *some* objectives reasons AND some supporting evidence, BUT at least one reason is missing and/or part of the evidence is incomplete.
1	Response provides only subjective reasons (opinions) for choice and/or uses inaccurate or irrelevant evidence from the activity.
0	No response; illegible response; response offers no reasons AND no evidence to support choice made.
X	Student had no opportunity to respond.

a course, a test specification will involve scheduling the time points at which repeated tests will be given to students. A general consideration is to give tests repeatedly throughout the course plus giving a pretest at the beginning and a posttest at the end of the course. Although the number of questions for each of the tests may vary according to specific content, all the tests must be linked by a common scoring rubric along the defined dimension of progression on the construct, although specific indicators for different levels in the scoring rubric will be specific to the assessment questions. Table 6.4 shows a sample scoring rubric that is used for all formative tests during the course.

When using a common scoring rubric for all formative assessment tests, it is possible to graph students' learning trajectories both individually and as a whole group. Figure 6.1 shows sample learning trajectories.

Figure 6.1 shows that there are 10 formative assessment tests, F1 to F10, during the course, and there are five different levels of students' performance on the measurement construct (e.g., understanding matter). Changes in their performance from F1 to F10 are represented by growth curves for both individual students (e.g., Debbie Franks) and the entire class. These types of trajectories should be very informative for teachers in planning their ongoing instruction during the course.

One issue in designing a learning progression assessment for formative uses is the changing state of students' abilities. It should be expected that students' abilities on the defined construct will increase as learning progresses. As students' abilities increase, each time a new formative assessment test is given, we have a new group of students, which creates a potential problem for later Rasch modeling because of the lack

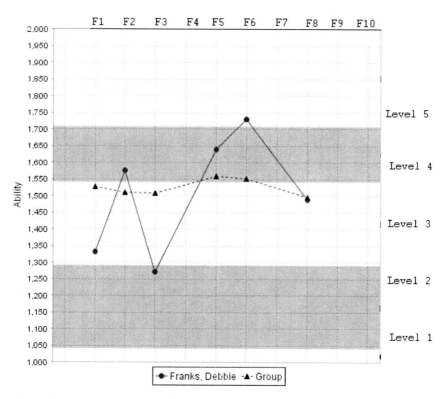

Figure 6.1. Learning trajectories during a course (adapted from Kennedy, 2005). A student's (Debbie Franks) learning trajectory is compared to that of the class.

of linkage in both items and students. Internal and external anchoring designs described earlier specifically address this problem. For example, in the BEAR assessment system applied to the EYE curriculum, in addition to the assessment tasks that are part of the teaching and learning activities, a series of link tests that are not specific to the teaching and learning activities and use conventional item types (e.g., multiple-choice) were also given at major junctures (e.g., end of a unit) along with formative assessment tests. In this way, the formative assessment tests are linked by common linking tests—external anchoring. In fact, the BEAR assessment system for EYE includes pretest, linking tests, and posttest, in addition to the formative assessment tests during various curriculum units.

Construct an Initial Pool of Items

Items for assessment of learning progression vary in format depending on the purpose of the assessment. If assessment of learning progression is for summative purposes, items are typically in selected response (e.g., multiple-choice) and short constructed response question formats. If assessment of learning progression is for formative purpose, items are typically in short or extended-constructed response format. The following item is from the BEAR assessment system:

> You run the shipping department of a company that makes glass kitchenware. You must decide what material to use for packing the glass so that it does not break when shipped to stores. You have narrowed the field to three materials: Shredded newspaper, Styrofoam pellets, and cornstarch foam pellets. Styrofoam springs back to its original shape when squeezed, but newspaper and cornstarch foam do not. Both Styrofoam and cornstarch foam float in water. Although Styrofoam can be reused as a packing material, it will not break down in land fills. Newspaper can be recycled easily, and cornstarch easily dissolves in water. Which material would you use? Discuss the advantages and disadvantages of each material. Be sure to describe the trade-offs made in your decision. (Wilson & Sloan, 2000, p. 190)

Items Review

Items for assessment of learning progression should be reviewed by a panel of experts. In addition to the common expectation that the panel should possess expertise in the content domain, psychometrics, and pedagogy, special efforts should be made to include intended users of the learning progression assessment on the expert panel. If the learning progression assessment is for formative uses during a course, then instructors of the course should be represented on the item review panel. Similarly, if the learning progression assessment is for summative uses across multiple grades, then teachers who are knowledgeable about the students and curriculums across multiple grades should be part of the expert panel.

Item Tryouts

After items are reviewed and revised, sample items may be tried out with a limited number of students. During this try-out process, primarily qualitative data, such as interview, think-aloud, and observations, will be collected. The purpose of item try-out is to obtain perspectives on how students will respond to the measurement instrument.

Field-Testing of Items

Considerations for field-testing suggested in previous chapters apply when assessment of learning progression is for summative uses. For formative assessment of learning progression, the field-testing sample should also represent the diversity of teachers. This is because formative assessment of learning progression is integrated into the curriculum units to inform ongoing teaching and learning; how teachers interpret assessment results to plan subsequent teaching and learning activities is an essential component of learning progression formative assessment. Similarly, if formative assessment of learning progression is not specific to a particular sequence of the science curriculum, that is, there is no fixed order among the formative assessment activities, then field-testing should also consider sampling different orders of the formative assessment activities. The ultimate goal for these steps is to collect enough information relevant to the intended assessment contexts of student population, teacher population, and curriculums.

Conduct Rasch Modeling

After data have been collected from field-testing, analysis of item and test properties through Rasch modeling will begin. Simultaneous calibration of data from all administrations of assessment should be used whenever possible. Data files for simultaneous calibration can be prepared by creating separate files for each administration first, and then merging them by adding both items and examinees with blanks (i.e., not administered) coded as missing. A typical data structure for a simultaneous calibration of data from different samples of subjects in the situation of summative assessment is shown in Table 6.5.

Table 6.5.   A Typical Data Structure for Simultaneous Rasch Calibration of Data From Different Samples of Subjects

Subjects	Form 1 Items		Form 2 Items		Form 3 Items
Sample 1	x	x	missing		missing
Sample 2	missing		x	x	missing
Sample 3	missing	x	missing		x

Note: x denotes responses to items.

Table 6.6.   A Typical Data Structure for Simultaneous Calibration of Data from a Same Sample of Repeated Assessment

Students	Formative Assessment 1 Items	Linking Test 1 Items	Formative Assessment 2 Items	Linking Test 2 Items	Formative Assessment 3 Items
S11	x	x			
S21	x	x		missing	
...	x	x			
S12		x	x	x	
S22	missing	x	x	x	missing
..		x	x	x	
S13				x	x
S23		missing		x	x
..				x	x

Note: S11 denotes Student 1 at time 1, S12 Student 1 at time 2, S13 Student 1 at time 3, S21 denotes Student 2 at time 1, S22 Student 2 at time 2, S23 Student 2 at time 3; x denotes responses to items.

Similarly, Table 6.6 shows a sample data file structure for a simultaneous calibration of data for formative assessment of learning progression based on a same sample of students during a course.

In the assessment design represented in Table 6.6, three formative assessment tests of a construct took place at three time points. In addition, two linking tests were also administered. For students at time 1, the linking test was administered at the same time as formative test 1. For the same group of students at time 2, linking test 1 and linking test 2 were administered at the same time as formative test 2. Similarly, for the same group of students at time 3, linking test 2 was administered at the same time as formative test 3. In the student column, a same student is coded with three different codes corresponding to the three time points. Thus, a same student will have three ability estimates forming a learning trajectory.

As described in previous chapters, a variety of fit statistics should be reviewed. Particular attention should be paid to the linking items. Linking item evaluation includes evaluation of these items individually and as a set for measurement of the construct. Evaluating linking items individually follows the same rules as evaluation of fit for any items, which is based on MNSQ, ZSTD, standard errors of measurement, point-measure correlation, category structure, item characteristic curve, and DIF. Evaluating link items as a set can be based on two overall link fit statistics: Item-

Within-Link fit statistics and the Item-Between-Link fit statistics (Wright & Bell, 1984). In order to compute the above two statistics, each linking item needs to be coded as two different items within the two linked forms. After submitting all items to a simultaneous Rasch calibration, we will have two difficulty estimates and two sets of fit statistics for each linking item.

Item-Within-Link fit statistics is defined as follows:

$$IWL = \frac{\sum_{i=1}^{L} (INFIT_{ij} + INFIT_{ik})}{2L}$$

where IWL is the Item-Within-Link fit statistics, i represents a link item, L is the total number of linking items, $INFIT_{ij}$ is the weighted mean-square residual fit statistics ($INFIT\ MNSQ$) for item i within Form J, and $INFIT_{ik}$ is the weighted mean-square residual fit statistics ($INFIT\ MNSQ$) for item i within Form K. IWL has an expected value of 1.

Item-Between-Link fit statistics is defined as follows:

$$X^2_{IBL} = \sum_{i=1}^{L} \left(\frac{(d_{ik} - d_{ij})}{\sqrt{SE^2_{dik} + SE^2_{dij}}} \right)^2$$

where X^2_{IBL} is a chi-square statistics for Item-Between-Link fit, L is the total number of linking items, d_{ik} is the item difficulty estimate of linking item i on Form K, and d_{ij} is the item difficulty estimate of linking item i on Form J, and SE_{dik} is the standard error of measurement for the difficulty estimate of linking item i on Form K, and SE_{dij} is the standard error of measurement for the difficulty estimate of linking item i on Form J. X^2_{IBL} has a chi-square distribution with L-1 degrees of freedom. A value greater than the critical chi-square value indicates inadequate performance of linking items as a whole. A scatterplot graph between d_{ik} and d_{ij} may also be made to visually demonstrate the overall stability of the estimates of linking items between the two forms.

Table 6.7 presents a hypothetical scenario for an illustration purpose, assuming that there are five linking items Q1 to Q5.

From INFIT statistics, we see that most of the linking items had a good model-data-fit except that Q1 may not be fitting well because the INFIT value is beyond the range of 0.7 to 1.3. In order to evaluate the adequacy of linking items as a whole, we can calculate the Item-Within-Link (IWL) and Item-Between-Link (IBL) statistics as follows:

Table 6.7.   Hypothetical Data for Item-Within-Link and Item-Between-Fit Analysis

Item	Form 1			Form 2		
	Difficulty	SE	INFIT MNSQ	Difficulty	SE	INFIT MNSQ
Q1	1.25	0.34	1.35	0.80	0.33	1.41
Q2	0.55	0.12	1.20	0.07	0.23	1.19
Q3	-0.14	0.19	1.13	-0.51	0.16	1.09
Q4	-0.34	0.23	0.98	-0.89	0.25	0.89
Q5	-0.68	0.45	0.85	-1.15	0.41	0.90

$$IWL = \frac{\sum_{i=1}^{L}(INFIT_{ij} + INFIT_{ik})}{2L}$$

$$= \frac{(1.35 + 1.41 + 1.20 + 1.19 + 1.13 + 1.09 + 0.98 + 0.89 + 0.85 + 0.90)}{2 \times 5} = 1.10$$

$$X^2_{IBL} = \sum_{i=1}^{L}\left(\frac{(d_{ik} - d_{ij})}{\sqrt{SE^2_{dik} + SE^2_{dij}}}\right)^2 = \left(\frac{1.25 - 0.80}{\sqrt{0.34 x 0.34 + 0.33 x 0.33}}\right)^2 + \left(\frac{0.55 - 0.07}{\sqrt{0.12 x 0.12 + 0.23 x 0.23}}\right)^2$$

$$+\left(\frac{0.51 - 0.14}{\sqrt{0.19 x 0.19 + 0.16 x 0.16}}\right)^2 + \left(\frac{0.89 - 0.34}{\sqrt{0.23 x 0.23 + 0.25 x 0.25}}\right)^2 + \left(\frac{1.15 - 0.38}{\sqrt{0.45 x 0.45 + 0.41 x 0.41}}\right)^2 = 9.76$$

The expected *IWL* value is 1.0 when linking items function perfectly. Because the obtained *IWL* is 1.10, which is only 10% deviates from the perfect fit, the linking items overall performed well. In terms of *IBL*, the critical chi-square value when the degree of freedom is 4 is 9.49, and the obtained chi-square value is 9.76, which is greater than the 9.49, overall the linking items do not seem to function well. When the Item-Within-Link and Item-Between-Link statistics suggest different conclusions like the case in this example, a visual display of the scatterplot between the two sets of difficulty estimates may be helpful (see Figure 6.2).

Figure 6.2 shows that the two sets of difficulty estimates are more or less linear, with most observations situated along the straight trend line. Thus, overall we can conclude that the linking items have functioned well.

Because learning progression is multidimensional, multidimensional Rasch modeling is typically needed. Chapter 2 reviewed multidimensional Rasch models and popular computer programs. If multidimensional Rasch modeling is impossible for various reasons, then unidimensional Rasch modeling on one dimension or construct of the

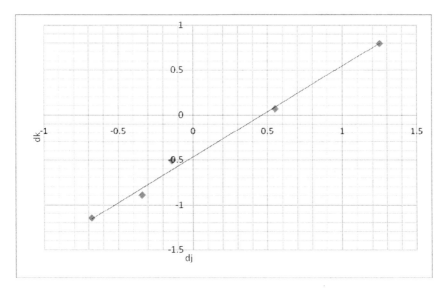

Figure 6.2.   Scatterplots for item invariance between linking forms. Overall, item measures from different forms correlate highly, suggesting good invariance.

learning progression at a time is still acceptable, as long as item and person measures on different dimensions are calibrated on a same scale using anchors of item or person measures.

Design and Conduct Reliability and Validity Studies

Validity Study

Construct validation, which includes establishing evidence related to test content, response processes, internal structure, external structure, and consequences, begins with examination of the construct definition for developing the learning progression measurement instrument. An adequately defined construct of learning progression must be grounded in the research literature, and must present a clear linear, progression from one grade to another or from one time point to another. Related to defining constructs of learning progression, the defined test specifications and scoring schemes should also be consistent with the identified behaviors that define the construct of learning progression.

Because learning progression measurement is derived from the defined learning progression, it is necessary to ensure that item and student parameter estimates agree with the intended or hypothesized

```
               PERSONS        ITEMS
           <more able>|<more difficult>


63                        +   cm4
62                     .  +   ch4
61                     .  +T  cm5
60                     #  T+  ph4
59              .##        +
58               .#        +   cm3     cm3     cn5     ph5
57              .###       +
56             ####       +S  cm5     cn2
55             .####      S+  cm4
54     .########        +   ch3     cm4     ph2
53        ######         +   ch5     cm4     cm4     cn2
52   .###########        +   ch3     ph3
51   .###########        +   cm5     ph2     ph3     ph3     ph4     ph5
50    .##########     M+M  cm3
49     .#######        +   ch3
48    .########        +   ch3     ph2     ph2     ph3
47      .######         +   cm3     cm4     cm4     ph2     ph4     ph4
46      .######         +   ch2     ch3     cm4     ph4
45       .####         S+  cn2
44        .###        +S  cm3     ph2     ph2     ph3
43       .#####         +   ch2     ph4
42         .#          +   cm4     ph3     ph4
41         .#          +
40         .#         T+  ch2     cm3
39         .#         +T
38         .#          +
37          .          +
36         .#          +
           <less able>|<less difficult>
```

EACH '#' IS 8.

Figure 6.3.   Wright map for measurement of understanding of matter. Overall, the distribution of student abilities matches the distribution of items well.

learning progression. In addition to examining item and person fit statistics, dimensionality, item separation and person separation indices, and adequacy of link items, the Wright map is particularly important for theory-based validity interpretation. If the distribution of both items and examinees is consistent with the defined learning progression, then there is evidence to claim construct validity in terms of internal structure. For example, the Wright map for the measurement of student learning progression on matter through PUM (Liu, 2007) is shown in Figure 6.3.

In Figure 6.3, cm, ph, cn, and ch represent four components of matter understanding (composition and structure of matters, physics properties and change, conservation of matter, and chemical properties and changes), and the numerical number after each matter component represents the level of matter understanding (e.g., ch2 meaning level 2 of chemical properties and change). The defined learning progression of matter understanding suggests that students from elementary school to high school develop knowledge and understanding of matter through five levels with each level being the result of integrated understanding, like an "over-lapping wave," of the four components. The Wright map demonstrates the interrelations of the four components through "mixing" of items of different components along the vertical line, and the overall progression from level 2 to level 5 (level 1 was not measured by the instrument). Also, students from elementary to high school distributed well on the left hand side of the Wright map. A one-way analysis of variance on student Rasch scale scores using grades as the independent variable showed that there was a statistically significant difference among students of different grades in their knowledge and understanding of matter. All of the above help support the validity of theory-based interpretation of the instrument.

Learning progression assessment can inform various instructional decisions. An important component of validation of learning progression assessment is to collect data on how assessment results have been used to make various decisions. For example, if a learning progression assessment is used for a summative purpose (e.g., awarding student course grades), data on students' future performances (e.g., later course grades) may be collected to see how learning progression assessment may predict student future performances. Similarly, if a learning progression assessment is used for formative purposes (e.g., embedded in an instructional sequence), data may be collected on teachers to understand how learning progression assessment results have informed their planning for ongoing instruction. Both qualitative and quantitative data are useful for this component of validation.

While it is important that a variety of validity evidence is collected about a learning progression measurement as described above, it is also important to examine the consistency in that evidence. Important questions to ask when evaluating the consistency of the various validity evidences are: (a) clarity, (b) coherence, and (c) plausibility of both inferences and assumptions. A claim about the validity of a learning progression measurement is sound when all types of evidence are clearly stated, coherent, and plausible and the assumptions underlying the arguments are sound.

Reliability Study

Reliability evidence of learning progression assessment instrument may be established through the following aspects: (a) reliability of scoring, (b) reliability of item and examinee estimates, and (c) reliability of the instrument. If some of measurement items are performance or constructed-response type, scoring is typically done following a scoring rubric. Interrater reliability of scoring by independent raters must be empirically established. After item and person parameters are calibrated, standard errors of measurements for each item and person should also be reviewed. In Rasch modeling, there are also two indices produced to indicate the overall test and person reliability. Person separation index and its equivalent Cronbach's alpha should be reviewed for their adequacy of reliability for person measures as a whole. Similarly, item separation index and its equivalent Cronbach's alpha should be reviewed for the adequacy of reliability for item measures as a whole.

Develop Guidelines for Administration, Scoring, and Interpretation of the Test Scores

A final step in developing a learning progression measurement instrument is documentation. Documentation is to facilitate others to use the measurement instrument appropriately and efficiently. In addition to adequate explanation of the purpose of the measurement and constructs assessed as well as instructions to use the instrument, one important purpose of documentation is to facilitate users in interpreting assessment results. Although Rasch modeling plays an important role in developing the measurement instrument, we should not expect users to conduct Rasch modeling to estimate item and person parameters, and also we may not expect users to use logits as their chosen measurement scale because logits are not intuitively meaningful. Thus, one consideration in documentation is to develop a conversion chart between raw scores and Rasch scale scores. In this way, users will only need to score a student's responses to items to obtain a total raw score, and then obtain its equivalent Rasch scale score by checking the conversion chart. Table 6.8 shows the conversion chart for the PUM measurement instrument (Liu, 2007).

CHAPTER SUMMARY

Learning progression refers to gradual and systematic development in knowledge and understanding by students over time. It has three characteristics. Learning progression must pertain to science content as com-

**Table 6.8.   Conversion Table Between
Raw Scores and Rasch Scale Scores**

	Rasch Scale Score		
Raw Score	*Elementary School Form*	*Middle School Form*	*High School Form*
0	31.94	34.31	35.84
1	34.72	35.67	37.64
2	37.13	36.94	39.30
3	39.21	38.13	40.83
4	41.00	39.23	42.26
5	42.53	40.26	43.58
6	43.85	41.22	44.82
7	44.98	42.12	45.98
8	45.96	42.97	47.08
9	46.83	43.76	48.12
10	47.62	44.51	49.13
11	48.38	45.22	50.11
12	49.13	45.90	51.07
13	49.91	46.56	52.02
14	50.76	47.19	52.99
15	51.71	47.81	53.97
16	52.81	48.42	54.99
17	54.08	49.03	56.05
18	55.56	49.65	57.17
19	57.29	50.27	58.35
20	59.30	50.91	59.62
21	61.64	51.57	60.98
22	64.33	52.26	62.44
23	N/A	52.99	64.01
24	N/A	53.75	65.72
25	N/A	54.56	67.56
26	N/A	55.42	69.56
27	N/A	56.34	71.72
28	N/A	57.33	74.06
29	N/A	58.38	76.58
30	N/A	59.51	79.31
31	N/A	60.72	82.25
32	N/A	N/A	85.41
33	N/A	N/A	N/A

pared to general reasoning or performance skills. Second, it is interdisciplinary—learning progression involves topics of more than one science discipline. Third, it also describes different levels of competence, that is, learning progression should map out a hierarchy of student learning outcomes from least competent to most competent. This hierarchy is also called a learning trajectory. There are many ways to realize learning progression in curriculum and instruction. One way is to use a spiral curriculum to organize content. Learning progression may be represented visually as a hierarchical web of learning outcomes.

Only a few learning progression measurement instruments are currently available. There is a need to develop more. Developing measurement instruments for learning progression starts with defining the primary purposes for which the test scores will be used. Assessment of learning progression can be for either formative or summative, or both purposes. A formative use of test scores of learning progression assessment is to inform teachers to plan for ongoing instruction and for students to reflect on the ongoing progress toward learning goals; and a summative use of learning progression is to identify levels of student achievement along a defined learning progression at different times. Next, the construct to be measured must be defined according to research on learning progression. Based on the defined construct, subject behaviors or performances that represent the construct are then identified. Test specification for learning progression measurement should consider the linkage between and among different assessment forms. After items are reviewed and revised, sample items may be tried out with a limited number of students before the measurement instrument is field-tested with a larger sample or samples. When conducting Rasch modeling based on field-testing data, simultaneous calibration of data from all administrations of the measurement instrument should be used whenever possible. Review for model-data-fit should pay particular attention to the linking items. Linking item evaluation includes evaluation of these items individually and as a set for measurement of the construct. Evaluating link items as a set can be based on two overall link fit statistics: Item-Within-Link (IWL) fit statistics and the Item-Between-Link (IBL) fit statistics. Based on Rasch modeling as well as additional sources of data to be collected, the validity and reliability of the learning progression assessment can be claimed through trait interpretation, theory-based interpretation, decision procedures, and qualitative interpretation. Documentation for the learning progression measurement instrument should include adequate explanation of the purpose of the measurement and the assessed construct, instructions to use the instrument, and score reporting.

EXERCISES

1. Compare and contrast the CTT approach and the Rasch modeling approach to developing measurement instruments of learning progression.

2. Identify a science concept that is typically taught continuously from elementary through high school. Use the major understandings specified in the *National Science Education Standards* (NRC, 1996) and the Benchmarks of Science Literacy (AAAS, 1993) to develop a tentative learning progression of students' understanding from elementary through high school. Develop a plan to empirically validate and further refine the proposed learning progression.

3. Mohan, Chen, and Anderson (2009) reported a learning progression of students' understanding of carbon cycling in socioecological systems from upper elementary through high school (*Journal of Research in Science Teaching, 46*[6], 675-698). Based on the learning progression, complete the following steps of developing an instrument for measuring learning progression of carbon-cycling for students from upper elementary through high school: (a) identify student behaviors that represent different levels of the learning progressions, (b) create a table of test specification for three forms (i.e., elementary, junior high school and high school) of the measurement instrument, and (c) write three sample items for each of the progression levels.

REFERENCES

American Association for the Advancement of Science. (1993). *Benchmarks for science literacy.* New York, NY: Oxford University Press.

American Association for the Advancement of Science. (2001a). *Designs for science literacy.* New York, NY: Oxford University Press.

American Association for the Advancement of Science. (2001b). *Atlas of science literacy* (Vol. 1). Washington, DC: the author.

American Association for the Advancement of Science. (2007). *Atlas of science literacy (Vol. 2).* Washington, DC: Author.

Bruner, J. (1960). *Process of education.* Cambridge, MA: Harvard University Press.

Catley, K., Lehrer, R., & Reiser, B. (2005). *Tracing a prospective learning progression for developing understanding of evolution.* Paper commissioned by the National Academies Committee on Test Design for K-12 Science Achievement. Washington, DC: National Academy of Sciences.

Claesgens, J., Scalise, K., Wilson, M., & Stacy, A. (2009). Mapping student understanding in chemistry: The perspectives of chemists. *Science Education, 93*(1), 56-85.

Kennedy, C. A. (2005). *ConstructMap V4.2.* Berkely, CA: Berkeley Evaluation and Assessment Research (BEAR) Center, University of California, Berkeley.

Liu, X. (2007). Growth in students' understanding of matter during an academic year and from elementary through high school. *Journal of Chemical Education, 84*(11), 1853-1856.

Mohan, L., Chen, J., & Anderson, C. W. (2009). Developing a multi-year progression for carbon cycling in socio-ecological systems. *Journal of Research in Science Teaching, 46*(6), 675-698.

National Research Council. (1996). *National science education standards.* Washington, DC: The National Academies Press.

National Research Council. (2007). *Taking science to school: Learning and teaching science in grades K-8.* Washington, DC: The National Academies Press.

Wiggins, G. P., & McTighe, J. (2001). *Understanding by design.* Upper Saddle River, NJ: Prentice Hall.

Wilson, M., & Sloane, K. (2000). From principles to practice: An embedded assessment system. *Applied Measurement in Education, 13*(2), 181-208

Wolfe, E. W. (2004). Equating and item banking with the Rasch model. In E. V. Smith, Jr., & R. M. Smith (Eds.), *Introduction to Rasch measurement* (pp. 366-390). Maple Grove, MN: JAP Press.

Wright, B. D., & Bell, S. R. (1984). Item banks: What, why, how. *Journal of Educational Measurement, 21*, 331-345.

CHAPTER 7

USING AND DEVELOPING INSTRUMENTS FOR MEASURING SCIENCE LEARNING ENVIRONMENTS

This chapter is concerned with learning environments in science. A learning environment is both an outcome and a predictor variable. Various theoretical frameworks about learning environments are available. This chapter will first review these theoretical frameworks. It will then introduce standardized instruments for measuring various learning environments. Finally, this chapter will describe the process of developing new instruments for measuring learning environments using the Rasch modeling approach.

WHAT ARE SCIENCE LEARNING ENVIRONMENTS?

Learning environment research in science education is a relatively young field with only about 30 years of history. Despite this short history, the field has advanced tremendously, particularly in the development of measurement instruments. In fact, "few fields of educational research can boast the existence of such a rich array of validated and robust instruments" (Fraser, 2007, p. 105). This large number of measurement instru-

Using and Developing Measurement Instruments in Science Education:
A Rasch Modeling Approach, pp. 235–266
Copyright © 2010 by Information Age Publishing
235

ments have not only contributed to the development of learning environment research as a field of study in science education, but also increased our understanding of the nature and characteristics of learning environments in science.

Fraser (1994) defines *learning environments* as "the social-psychological contexts or determinants of learning" (p. 493). This definition is rooted in an early view of classroom environments as the shared perceptions of the people, that is, students and the teacher, in that environment (Moos, 1979). It distinguishes learning environments as perceptions from that as physical settings such as arrangement of classroom and lab furniture, positioning of teacher desks, availability of computers in the classroom, etc. Learning environments can be considered as both independent variables and dependent variables. In the former, learning environments are expected to promote or hinder student learning; in the latter, learning environments are considered as outcomes of other factors.

According to Fraser (1994, 1998a, 2007), learning environment research originated from the work by Walberg and Moos during the 1960s and 1970s. The basic premise for learning environment research is that personal goals may be supported or constrained by environmental factors. When personal needs and environmental factors are aligned, student learning outcomes are enhanced. For example, Moos (1979), adopting a social-ecological perspective on educational development, conceptualizes that there is interaction between environmental and personal systems; they influence each other through selection of factors into each system and also through mediating factors. The *environmental system* consists of physical setting, organizational factors, humane aggregate and social climate; the *personal system* consists of sociodemographic variables, expectations, personality factors, and coping skills. *Mediating factors* include cognitive appraisal, activation or arousal, and efforts at adaption and coping. According to Moos, *determinants of classroom environments* may include aggregate student characteristics (e.g., socioeconomic status), teacher characteristics (e.g., teacher's gender), organization factors (e.g., small classes), physical and architectural features (e.g., physical arrangement of classrooms), and school and classroom contexts (e.g., type of school).

Specifically related to social climates, Moos (1979) developed a three-dimensional construct of social climates based on data from various social settings (e.g., student living groups, high school classes, families, working groups, hospitals, correctional institutions, military basic training companies, and so on). The three dimensions, which are also called domains, are relationship, personal growth, and system maintenance and change. The *relationship dimension* is concerned with the extent to which people are involved in the setting, the extent to which they support and help one another, and the extent to which they express themselves freely and openly. For example, relationships in the classroom learning environment may pertain to the attentiveness of students to class activities, and their participation in discussion. It may also pertain to the perceptions of affiliation with the class and supports from the teacher. The *personal growth dimension* pertains to the goals of the setting related to personal development and self-enhancement. For example, in the classroom learning environment, personal growth dimension may involve the task orientation, speed and difficulty of tasks, and competition among students. The *system maintenance and change dimension* pertains to the extent to which the environment is orderly and clear in its expectations, and maintains control and responds to change. For example, in the classroom learning environment, system maintenance and change may relate to the order and organization of the classroom activities, clarification of expectations for achievement, and control and innovation of learning processes.

Walberg (1968a) conceptualizes a *classroom climate* to consist of two dimensions: the structural dimension and the affective dimension. The *structural dimension* refers to student roles within the class, such as goal direction and democratic policy. It applies to shared and group-sanctioned classroom behaviors. The *affective dimension* pertains to idiosyncratic personal dispositions to act in a given way to satisfy individual personality needs, such as satisfaction, intimacy and friction in the class. In an evaluation study of the Harvard Project Physics curriculum, Walberg (1968b) found that students gained the most on the physics achievement test when they perceived their classes as being socially homogeneous and intimate groups working on one goal. Students who grew more in science understanding saw classes as being well-organized with little friction between their fellow students, equalitarian and unstratified, and encouraging a greater variety of student interests. In terms of the affective dimension, Walberg found that students who reported greater enjoyment of laboratory work perceived their classes as unstratified, democratic in policy setting, having clear class goals, and satisfying. Students who gained the most interest in physics saw their classes as being well-organized and unstratified.

There are two most common orientations to learning environment research: the outcome-environment interaction orientation and the person-environment fit orientation (Lesniak, 2007). The *outcome-environment orientation* focuses on the association between learning environment variables and student cognitive and affective learning outcomes. That is, learning environments are considered determinants of student learning outcomes. Research over the past three decades has clearly demonstrated that student perceptions of their learning environments are associated with both their achievements in science and their attitudes towards science, and can account for substantial amounts of the variability in student learning. The *person-environment fit* orientation differentiates the *"actual"* perceived environment from the *"preferred"* environment. The actual perceived environment is what is happening now, while the preferred learning environment is what students would like to see to happen in an ideal situation. Research has shown that student learning is enhanced when students' actual learning environment is closer to the preferred environment. Research has further demonstrated that teachers' perceived learning environment tends to be more favorable than students'. Thus, student learning outcomes will improve by increasing the match between students' preferred learning environment and the actual learning environment, and between teacher perceived learning environment and student perceived learning environment.

While both outcome-environment and person-environment fit orientations consider learning environment variables as predictors or determinants of learning outcomes, learning environments may also be considered as outcomes. This orientation is particularly pertinent in the context of science education reforms. Educational reforms typically entail certain aspects of learning environments to change. Valid and reliable instruments for measuring these aspects of learning environments can help differentiate innovative science teaching and learning from conventional science teaching and learning.

Research by Fraser, his collaborators and others have also found that it is helpful to differentiate learning environments at the collective level and at the personal level (Fraser, 1994, 1998b; Fraser & Tobin, 1991). The *collective learning environment* is what students perceive the class as a whole; while the *personal learning environment* is what students perceive from their own perspectives. The collective and personal learning environments may not necessarily be the same. Differentiating these two versions of a learning environment can help identity individual differences among students within the same class. Similarly, learning environments may also be differentiated based on units of physical learning settings in which learning takes place. These units can be class, school, family, and so on.

Some researchers have pointed out that using and developing measurement instruments on learning environments is based on a reductionist philosophy of the world and assumes that individuals can be separated from their external environments (Roth, 1999). Roth proposes a *"lifeworld" approach* that designates the individual-environment as a unity structured in terms of customary activities and perceptions, conventional uses of tools, materials, language, invariants maintained in it by conventional activities, and so on. From this lifeworld perspective, "world (the Other) and individual Self presuppose each other" (Roth, 1999, p. 235). Studying learning environments based on the above lifeworld perspective calls for a different approach, that is, qualitative approach. In fact, Fraser

(1994, 1998b, 2007) has consistently pointed out values for combining qualitative and quantitative methods to study science classroom learning environments. This mixed research method approach can produce a much richer understanding of the science classroom learning environments than any one approach alone. For example, Fraser (1994), based on a series of qualitative and quantitative studies of various classroom learning environments, made the following conclusions about science classroom learning environments:

1. In whole-class settings, a small group of target students, typically ranging from three to seven are usually higher ability and/or more active and assertive to volunteer, dominate verbal interactions;

2. Teachers tended to direct higher-level cognitive questions to target students;

3. Target students held more favorable perceptions of the learning environment than nonparticipants;

4. Exemplary teachers used management strategies that facilitate sustained student engagement;

5. Exemplary teachers use strategies designed to increase student understanding of science;

6. Exemplary teachers utilized strategies that encouraged students to participate actively in learning activities;

7. Exemplary teachers maintained favorable classroom learning environments;

8. Teachers conceptualized their roles in terms of metaphors that influenced the way in which they taught;

9. Teacher beliefs had a major impact on the way in which the curriculum was implemented;

10. Knowledge limitations of teachers resulted in an emphasis on students learning facts and completing workbook exercises rather than learning with understanding;

11. The student-perceived learning environment of the classes was related to teachers' knowledge and beliefs; and

12. Teacher expectations of and attitudes toward individuals were reflected in individual students' perceptions of the learning environment.

Teacher-student interaction is an important aspect of the science teaching and learning lifeworld. Adopting a communication approach to learning environments, Wubbels and Brekelmans (1998) point out that teacher communication behaviors influence science classroom environments. They specifically recommend that teachers should strive to establish teacher-student relationships characterized by high degrees of leadership, helpfulness/friendliness and understanding behaviors. The also recommend that teachers experiencing undesirable classroom situations should focus on their own behaviors as a means for improvement and should introduce changes in their communication patterns.

Besides the above social-psychological and lifeworld perspectives of learning environments, a *semiotic perspective of learning environments* considers physical settings to be important aspects of learning environment (Shapiro, 1998). In fact, this notion of learning environments is reflected in a later definition given by Fraser (1998b). Fraser defines "learning environment" to encompass "social, physical, psychological, and pedagogical contexts in which learning occurs and which affects student achievement and attitudes" (Fraser, 1998b, p. 1). This expanded notion of learning environment clearly differs from the social-psychological perspective discussed earlier. "When viewed semiotically, the science classroom can be seen as interweaving sets of sign, symbol and signification systems that students learn as texts of science learning" (Shapiro, 1998, p. 611). For example, the furniture arrangement as part of the physical environment is a part of an elaborate system of signification. A row and column arrangement of student desks and chairs may suggest to students that they are expected to follow rules and listen to instructions; a circular arrangement of student desks and chairs may suggest to students that they are expected to contribute to the class and to respect others' views; and an island arrangement of student desks and chairs may suggest to students that they are expected to take collective initiatives and make collaborative decisions. A semiotic approach to studying learning environments thus first attempts to identify the systems of signs, symbols and other significations; it then attempts to understand how those systems have been created and are being interpreted by those involved (i.e., students, the teacher). "Viewing classroom semiotically helps us to see that entire systems of signification within school settings serve as a resource for learners and a means by which they access knowledge. When teachers master the signs and symbols of our culture and become aware of those of others, they know when to break the unspoken rules to become inventive in using new approaches in interaction" (Shapiro, 1998, p. 618). Specifically in terms of laboratory physical settings, Arzi (1998) suggests that science laboratories should be flexible, multifunctional, and practical.

Learning environments research in science education has benefited from multiple theoretical perspectives and research methodology orientations. As Tobin and Fraser (1998) pointed out that "learning environments can be described through multiple windows to highlight different issues that are pertinent to the stakeholder goals and extant classroom practices. Any methodology used to explore learning environments will produce a landscape that is incomplete and represents only one of the possible portraits which is likely to be appealing and relevant to different stakeholders" (p. 627). Thus, researchers need to be aware of limitations of using and developing a particular measurement instrument on science learning environments, and recommend possible ways to address them.

INSTRUMENTS FOR MEASURING
SCIENCE LEARNING ENVIRONMENTS

A variety of standardized measurement instruments related to learning environments are available; the majority of them have been developed based on CTT. These instruments are for various intended uses and based on primarily the social-psychological framework of learning environments. The following descriptions of the instruments are for readers' information only; whether or not a science education researcher will choose an instrument for a particular research question requires a critical review of the instrument by the researcher, which is beyond the scope of this book.

The Learning Environment Inventory (LEI)
(Anderson & Walberg, 1974; Fraser, Anderson, & Walberg, 1982)

LEI measures secondary school classroom environments. It contains 15 scales; they are: cohesiveness, friction, favoritism, cliqueness, satisfaction, apathy, speed, difficulty, competitiveness, diversity, formality, material environment, goal direction, disorganization, and democracy. Each scale has seven statements about typical school classes; respondents are asked to indicate their degree of agreement to each of the statements by selecting *strongly disagree, disagree, agree,* and *strongly agree.* LEI originated from the Classroom Climate Questionnaire used in the evaluation of the Harvard Project Physics in the 1960s. Scales contained in the final version relate to concepts previously identified as good predictors of learning outcomes, or being relevant to social-psychological theories. Reported alpha reliability coefficients for the 15 scales ranged from 0.54 to 0.85 (Fraser, 1994).

The Classroom Environment Scale (CES)
(Moos & Trickett, 1974, 1987; Trickett & Moos, 1973)

CES focuses on the social-psychological environment of junior and high school classrooms. It has three parallel forms: the R Form—Real form to assess the actual classroom environment, the I Form—Ideal form to assess the ideal classroom environment, and the E Form—Expectation form to assess expectations about a new classroom. All the forms have 90 items. Students and teachers answer the same items. A complete R form is available as an appendix in Moos (1979).

CES conceptualizes a classroom environment as a dynamic social system that includes not only teacher behaviors and teacher-student interactions, but also student-student interactions. The conceptual framework for CES comes from relevant literature on educational and organizational psychology. CES contains three dimensions: relation, system maintenance, and personal growth. The relation dimension involves affective aspects of student-student and teacher-student interactions. System maintenance and change dimension involves aspects of rules and regulations of the classroom and teaching innovations. Personal growth or goal orientation dimension pertains to specific functions of the classroom environment. There are nine sub-scales related to the above three dimensions.

KR-20 internal consistency indices for the subscales ranged from 0.67 to 0.86. Intercorrelations among the subscales averaged about 0.25, suggesting good discrimant validity. Factor analysis also conformed to the expected subscales. CES scores were also found to differ statistically significantly among classrooms with distinct teacher teaching styles. Specifically, based on different CES scores on various dimensions, classroom environments could be classified into the following six types: innovation oriented, structured relationship oriented, supportive task oriented, supportive competition oriented, unstructured competition oriented, and control oriented. There were also statistically significant differences in CES scores on some subscales between teachers and students. Perceptions of real and ideal classroom learning environments were also found to be statistically significant on most sub-scales.

An updated version of CES measures has 10 scales, each with 10 items. The one additional scale is related to differentiation (Moos & Trickett, 1987). A 24-item short form of CES, with only six scales, each having 4 items, has also been developed (Fraser, 1982; Fraser & Fisher, 1983).

My Classroom Inventory (MCI) (Fisher & Fraser, 1981)

MCI is a simplified version of LEI for elementary and lower junior high school classrooms. It contains only five of LEI's 15 scales, which are cohesiveness, friction, satisfaction, difficulty, and competiveness. Numbers of items per scale range from 6-9; the total items are 38. Other modifications made on LEI to form MCI include a lower level of reading comprehension, reducing the four-point responses to two point-responses (i.e., yes/no), and presenting both questions and responses on the same sheet of paper. Reported alpha reliability coefficients for the MCI scales ranged from 0.62 to 0.78 (Fraser, 1994). A short form of MCI was created based on statistical analysis of selected items (Fraser, 1982; Fraser & Fisher, 1983). It has five scales, each with five items. A copy of the short form MCI is available as appendix in Fraser (1994).

College and University Classroom Environment Inventory (CUCEI)
(Fraser & Treagust, 1986; Fraser, Treagust, & Dennis, 1986)

CUCEI measures learning environments of small university classes or seminars with up to 30 students. It is not appropriate for university lectures or labs. CUCEI contains seven scales—personalization, involvement, student cohesiveness, satisfaction, task orientation, innovation, and individualization. Each scale has 7 items, and each item has four choices of responses (*strongly agree, agree, disagree, and strongly disagree*). Items for CUCEI were selected and adapted from LEI, CES, and ICEQ according to their relevance to higher education settings. Validation involved expert review and field-testing. Reported alpha reliability coefficients for the seven scales ranged from 0.70 to 0.90 (Fraser, 1994). The complete instrument of CUCEI is available as an appendix in Fraser (1994).

Individualized Classroom Environment Questionnaire (ICEQ) (Fraser, 1990)

ICEQ is a 50-item instrument measuring secondary school classrooms in terms of the degree of individualized learning and teaching. It has five dimensions/scales, each containing 10 items. The five dimensions relate to personalization, participation, independence, investigation, and differentiation. Items are presented in a five-point rating scale ranging from *almost never, seldom, sometimes, often,* and *very often*. ICEQ originated from the initial long version of the ICEQ instrument (Rentoul & Fraser, 1979). The dimensions included in the instrument met the following criteria: (a) addressing open and inquiry-based classrooms, (b) being considered salient by interviewed teachers and students, (c) meeting expectations of experts, teachers, and students, and (d) meeting item and scale statistical expectations. Reported alpha reliability coefficients for the five scales ranged from 0.68 to 0.79 (Fraser, 1994). Validation for the different forms of ICEQ, that is, student perceived actual learning environment, student preferred learning environment, teacher perceived actual learning environment, and teacher preferred learning environment, was conducted using both individual and class means as units of analysis (Fraser, 1994). A short form of ICEQ was later created based on statistical analysis of selected items (Fraser, 1982; Fraser & Fisher, 1983). This short form has five scales with each scale having five items.

Science Laboratory Environment Inventory (SLEI)
(Fraser, McRobbie, & Giddings, 1993)

SLEI measures high school and university science laboratory class environments. It has five scales, that is, student cohesiveness, open-endedness, integration, rule clarify, and material environment. Each scale has 6-7 items; each item has five responses to choose from (*almost never, seldom, sometimes, often, and very often*). Validation involved 5,447 students in 269 classes in six different countries (United States, Canada, England, Israel, Australia, and Nigeria). Reported alpha reliability coefficients for the five scales ranged from 0.70 to 0.83 (Fraser, 1994). Alpha reliability coefficients for different forms of SLEI, that is, student perceived actual laboratory environment, student preferred laboratory environment, and for different countries were also reported (Fraser, 1994). A personal form (i.e., students' perceptions of themselves as individuals in the class), as compared to the class form (i.e., students' perceptions of the class as a whole) as originally developed, was also created (McRobbie, Fisher, & Wong, 1998).

Questionnaire on Teacher Interaction (QTI)
(Wubbles, Breklmans, & Hooymayers, 1991; Wubbels & Levy, 1993).

QTI measures students' perceptions of the teacher-student interactions in elementary and secondary school classrooms. It has eight scales—helpful/friendly, understanding, dissatisfied, admonishing, leadership, student responsibility and freedom, uncertain, and strict. Each scale has 8-10 items, and each item has five-point responses ranging from *Never* to *Always*. QTI is based on the theoretical model of proximity (cooperation-opposition) and influence (dominance-submission). Validation was conducted in USA, Australia, Singapore, and Brunei. A shorter 48-item version of QTI for elementary grades has also been created (Goh & Fraser, 1996).

Constructivist Learning Environment Survey (CLES)
(Taylor, Fraser & Fisher, 1997)

CLES measures the degree to which a particular secondary classroom learning environment is consistent with a constructivist epistemology. It has five scales—personal relevance, uncertainty, critical voice, shared control, and student negotiation. Each scale has seven items. A complete version of CLES is available in the appendix of Fraser (1998a).

Cultural Learning Environment Questionnaire (CLEQ)
(Fisher & Waldrip, 1997).

CLEQ measures secondary school students' perceptions of culturally sensitive factors of learning environment. It assumes that at the classroom level, there are distinctions in the preferred learning styles among different high school students. Culture is based on Hofstede's (1984) four dimensions of culture, namely power distance, uncertainty avoidance, individualism, and masculinity/femininity. Initial items for CLEQ were identified from various existing learning environment instruments that were aligned with the above four dimensions. The final CLEQ has 40 items defining eight scales; each scale has 5 items. The eight scales are role differentiation, collaboration, risk involvement, threat of competition, teacher authority, modeling, congruence, and communication. Role differentiation measures the extent to which gender roles are differentiated or overlapped by students; collaboration measures the extent to which students are part of a strong cohesive group; risk involvement measures the extent to which students feel threatened by involvement in class discussion; threat of competition measures the extent to which the students feel threatened by competition from other students; teacher authority measures the extent to which students expect and accept that power is distributed unequally in a school; modeling measures the extent to which the students prefer to learn by a process of modeling; congruence measures the extent to which the students feel threatened by learning in ways that are different from their own cultural pattern; and finally communication measures the extent to which students have more direct forms of communication with the person they are interacting with. All questions are presented in a five-point scale between two extreme alternatives of *disagree* and *agree*.

Validation of CLEQ was based on 1,834 students in 95 classrooms of 34 schools. Principal component factor analysis revealed structures of the expected eight scales. Cronbach's alpha internal consistency reliability coefficients for the eight scales ranged from 0.67 to 0.85. Mean correlation coefficients among the scales ranged from 0.08 to 0.22, suggesting the discriminant validity of CLEQ. Further, students' scores on CLEQ were found significantly correlated with students' attitudes and enquiry skills. That is, more favorable student attitudes and greater enquire skills were found to be associated with those who perceived classroom environments with less role differentiation, more collaboration, less teacher authority, less threat of competition, less risk involvement, less modeling, more congruence and more communication.

What Is Happening in This Class (WIHIC) Questionnaire
(Aldridge & Fraser, 2000)

WIHIC is a combination of modified versions of a number of previously published learning environment scales and additional scales on equity and constructivism. It has seven scales; they are student cohesiveness, teacher support, involvement, investigation, task orientation, cooperation, and equity. Each scale has eight items. Items are in a five-point format with choices of *almost never, seldom, sometimes, often, and very often*. Both the personal and class forms of WIHIC are available. WIHIC has been translated into a few languages and validated in such countries as Australia, Canada, South Korea, Singapore and Taiwan. Confirmatory factor analysis with a sample of 3,980 high school students from Australia, Britain, and Canada supported the seven-scale a priori structure of the WIHIC (Dorman, 2003). The items of WIHIC are available in Aldridge, Fraser, and Huang (1999).

Learning Environment Scales (LES) (Nolen, 2003)

LES is a 20-item Likert-scale instrument measuring student perceptions of classroom learning environments in terms of teacher goals in mastery, independent thinking and performance, and the classroom competitive and cooperative climate. Validation involved 463 high school students attending one U.S. high school. Principal component factor analysis with varimax rotation resulted in a three-factor solution. The three factors form three scales; they are the science-learning focus scale consisting of items related to teacher goals of mastery and independent thinking, the ability-meritocracy scale consisting of items related to the teacher performance goal as well as competitive climate, and the cooperative climate scale consisting of items related to competitive and cooperative climate. Correlation among the three scales ranged from −0.11 to 0.42. Cronbach's alpha reliability coefficients for the three scales were 0.86, 0.70, and 0.77.

The Outcome-Based Learning Environment Questionnaire (OBLEQ)
(Aldridge, Laugksch, Seopa, & Fraser, 2006)

OBLEQ measures students' perceptions of their actual and preferred classroom learning environments in outcome-based learning settings. The development and validation of the questionnaire involved review of literature on outcome-based education, interviews with science curriculum advisors and with Grade 8 science teachers, references to Moos's (1979) three dimensions of social environments (i.e., relation, personal development, and system maintenance) and other relevant learning environment instruments. OBLEQ consists of seven scales with eight items per scale. The seven scales are:

1. *Involvement*—the extent to which students have attentive interest, participate in discussions, do additional work and enjoy the class.

2. *Investigation*—the extent to which emphasis is placed on the skills and processes of inquiry and their use in problem-solving and investigation.

3. *Cooperation*—the extent to which students cooperate rather than compete with one another on learning tasks.

4. *Equity*—the extent to which students are treated equally and fairly by the teacher.

5. *Differentiation*—the extent to which teachers cater to students differently on the basis of ability, rates of learning, and interests.

6. *Personal Relevance*—the extent to which teachers relate science to students' out-of school experiences.

7. *Responsibility for Own Learning*—the extent to which students perceive themselves as being in charge of their learning process, motivated by constant feedback and affirmation.

Items are in a five-point rating scale consisting of *always, often, sometimes, seldom,* and *never*. The actual and preferred response scales of the OBLEQ items are placed side-by-side on a single form of the questionnaire to provide a more economical format. Validation data were collected from 2,638 students in 50 schools. Principal component factor analysis using oblique rotation suggested that some items did not conform to the expected dimensions. The Cronbach alpha reliability coefficients for the scales ranged from 0.66 to 0.84 when the individual was the unit of analysis, and ranged from 0.67 to 0.98 when the class mean was the unit of analysis. For the actual version of the OBLEQ, the discriminant validity (mean correlation of a scale with other scales) ranged from 0.12 to 0.31 when the individual was the unit of analysis, and ranged from 0.13 to 0.42 when the class mean was the unit of analysis. For the preferred version of the OBLEQ, the discriminant validity ranged from 0.18 to 0.43 when the individual was the unit of analysis, and ranged from 0.01 to 0.63 when the class mean was the unit of analysis. OBLEQ scales also differentiated significantly ($p < 0.01$) between classes.

The Science Teacher School Environment Questionnaire (STSEQ)
(Huang, 2006)

STSEQ measures secondary school science teachers' perceptions of the school environment. School environment is defined broadly; it involves science teachers' relationships with students, other teachers, and principals and other administrators. In addition, school environment also involves science teachers' professional development, and their thoughts about resources, work pressure, gender equity, innovation, and staff freedom.

Items for STSEQ were based on themes identified from interviews of 34 science and mathematics teachers, and reference to two other related instruments. It contains 45 items distributed equally over nine scales—teacher-student relation, collegiality, principal leadership, professional interest, gender equity, innovation, staff freedom, resources and equipment, and work pressure. Each item is presented in a five-point rating scale with choices of *almost always, often, sometimes, seldom,* and *almost never.*

Validation of STSEQ took place in Taiwan involving 900 secondary science teachers from 52 secondary schools. An exploratory factor analysis with promax rotation resulted in a nine-factor structure, with five items in each factor. The factor loadings of the 45 items ranged from 0.35 to 0.87, and the eigenvalues of the nine factors ranged from 1.22 to 10.01. The interscale correlation among the nine scales ranged from 0.12 to 0.36 with an overall mean correlation coefficient of 0.28, suggesting that the instrument had adequate discriminant validity. The Cronbach's alpha reliability coefficients of the nine scales, using the individual science teacher as the unit of analysis, ranged from 0.63 to 0.87.

Students' Perception of Assessment Questionnaire (SPAQ)
(Dhindsa, Omar, & Waldrip, 2007; Fisher, Waldrip, & Dorman, 2005)

SPAQ measures secondary school students' perceptions of the assessment process. Assessment refers mainly to tests and homework. It has five scales: Congruence with planned learning; assessment of applied learning, student consultation on assessment types, transparency in assessment, and accommodation of students' diversity in assessment procedures. Congruence with planned learning measures the extent to which assessment covers the students' learning experience; assessment of applied learning measures the extent to which assessment evaluates the application of students' learning to daily life; student consultation on assessment measures the extent to which students are consulted in deciding the assessment tasks; transparency in assessment measures the extent to which students are informed about the assessment procedures; and diversity in assessment measures the extent to which assessment accounts for individual differences. Each scale has six items presented in a four-point rating scale: *almost always* (4), *often* (3), *sometimes* (2), and *almost never* (1).

Validation of the instrument took place in Brunei. The questionnaire was administered to 1,028 upper secondary science students 15-16 years.

The three university lecturers who read the original instrument judged that the language of the content and construct of the instrument was valid for upper secondary students but less appropriate for the lower secondary students who were less familiar with the English language. For the original 30-item instrument, the Flesh Reading Ease (FRE) and Flesh–Kincard Grade Level (FKGL) coefficients were 56.7 and 7.5 respectively. Principal component factor analysis using varimax rotation found that 24 of the original 30 items loaded highly on the five expected dimensions; the five factors reported in this study accounted for 50.6% variance. For the 24-item version, the FRE and FKGL coefficients were 68.6 and 6.4. The mean correlation among the five scales ranged from 0.15 to 0.20, indicating that the SPAQ measures distinct, although somewhat overlapping aspects of dimensions of assessment. Statistical significance was also found among different classes, suggesting discriminant validity. Cronbach's alpha reliability coefficients for the five scales of the 30-item instrument ranged from 0.64 to 0.77. Qualitative data from interviews and classroom observations were also used to cross-validate the instrument.

DEVELOPING INSTRUMENTS FOR MEASURING SCIENCE LEARNING ENVIRONMENTS

Identify the Primary Purpose(s) for Which the Measurement Result Will Be Used

Although there is a dynamic interaction between individuals and their environments, it is necessary to conceptually differentiate individuals from their environments. Specifically, we could conceptualize learning environments to be both determinants of student learning outcomes and outcomes of student learning. Therefore, there can be two main purposes for measuring learning environments; one is to study how a particular learning environment is related to or can predict a certain student learning outcome, and the other is to study how a learning environment changes as the result of an intervention or differs from other learning environments due to different types of learning and teaching. For the first purpose, units of analysis can be either individual students or classes; but for the second purpose, units of analysis should be classes. For example, measurement of students' perceptions of the learning environment can help in understanding how different perceptions of a learning environment may be related to different levels of science achievement. In this case, units of analysis are individual student scores on a learning environment scale. As another example involving program evaluation of a science curriculum innovation, the measurement of learning environments will help in understanding if the intended learning environment has been created by implementation of a science curriculum innovation. In this case, units of analysis can be both individual student scores and class means on the learning environment scale.

Besides the above two main purposes, one other historical purpose of measuring learning environments is to study the fit between the actual learning environment and the preferred or ideal learning environment, the so-called person-environment fit study (Fraser, 1996, 1998a; Moos, 1979). The basic premise for this approach is that personal goals may be supported or constrained by environmental interactions. When personal needs and environmental factors are aligned, student learning outcomes will be enhanced. Measurement of learning environments for this purpose typically involves developing parallel forms of a learning environment scale and administering them simultaneously to students. Units of analysis are typically the different scores between two forms. Person-environment fit studies have played and will continue to play an important role in understanding the context of science teaching and learning.

Define the construct to be measured

Learning environments have been commonly considered as the social-psychological contexts in which learning takes place. This social-psychological approach naturally focuses on individuals' perceptions instead of external observations of a learning environment. Because different perceptions of the environment are results of different interactions between individuals and the environment, learning environments can be defined based on different components and patterns of the human-environment interactions. Moos (1979), based on studies of various social settings such as student living groups, hospitals, correctional institutions, military training camps, and school classrooms, identified three fundamental dimensions of a learning environment: relationship, personal growth, and system maintenance and change. The relationship dimension is concerned with the extent to which people are involved in the setting, the extent to which they support and help one another, and the extent to which they express themselves freely and openly. Personal growth dimension pertains to the goals of the setting related to personal development and self-enhancement. Finally, the system maintenance and change dimension pertains to the extent to which the environment is orderly and clear in its expectations, maintains control and responds to change. Majority of learning environment instruments described earlier are based on this conceptualization of learning environments.

Adopting a different social-psychological conception of learning environments, Walberg (1968a) conceptualizes learning environments to consist of two dimensions: the structural dimension and the affective dimension. The structural dimension refers to student roles within the class such as goal direction and democratic policy. It applies to shared, group-sanctioned classroom behaviors. The "affective" dimension pertains to idiosyncratic personal dispositions to act in a given way to satisfy individual personality needs, such as satisfaction, intimacy, and friction in the class.

Although physical settings have not been typically conceptualized as part of learning environments in the past four decades, the semiotic approach to learning environments distinguishes itself by explicitly focusing on signs in the environment (Shapiro, 1998). If a "learning environment" is defined broadly to encompass "social, physical, psychological, and pedagogical contexts in which learning occurs and which affects student achievement and attitudes" (Fraser, 1998a), then, separation between the social-psychological aspects from the physical settings of a learning environment is difficult. No matter what theoretical approach is to be adopted to define learning environments, one thing is clear: learning environment is not a unidimensional construct, but it is multidimensional. Different theories may focus on different dimensions of a learning environment, and some dimensions may pertain to physical settings. Further, learning environment is not a generic construct; it is specific to settings. For example, an elementary science classroom learning environment may be defined differently from that of a secondary school science classroom. Similarly, an online learning environment may be defined differently from that of a classroom learning environment. Defining the construct of learning environments to be measured must take into consideration not only the theoretical framework in which learning environments are conceptualized, but also the nature of the learning setting and characteristics of the students.

Identify Behaviors That Represent the Construct

Once the construct to be measured is defined, specific behaviors, that is, the domain of a learning environment, must be identified. Depending on the purpose of the measurement of the learning environment, the identified behaviors should reflect the hypothesized or inferred differences in measured learning environment. That is, if the purpose of measuring a learning environment is to study the relationship between the learning environment and student learning outcomes, then what perceptions of the learning environment are associated with higher student learning outcomes and what perceptions are associated with lower student learning outcomes should be derived from the defined construct so that a variation or a range of student perceptions of the learning environment may be anticipated. For example, if the purpose of measuring a learning environment is to study the relationship between student conceptual understanding and the inquiry learning environment, then it is necessary to identify desirable student perceptions of the inquiry learning environment, such as students being encouraged to change their research questions during the inquiry, that may lead to higher student conceptual understanding; it is also possible to identify less desirable student perceptions of the inquiry learning environment, such as students only studying the problems given by the teacher, that may lead to a lower level of conceptual understanding.

Similarly, if the purpose of measuring a learning environment is to study how different learning environments are created by different curriculum innovations, then different student perceptions of the learning environment at different levels of implementation of the curriculum innovation should be derived. For example, if our interest is to study the difference between an inquiry science learning environment and an didactic science learning environment, what student perceptions of the learning environment are associated with inquiry learning and what student perceptions are associated with didactic learning should be inferred from the theory.

The above rationale for identifying student behaviors is also applicable to person-environment fit studies. In these situations, no external references are available to guide the inferences of student perceptions corresponding to different degrees of learning environments. No matter what purpose measurement of a learning environment serves, the learning environment must be considered as a continuum that can be quantified by a continuous variable based on a measurement instrument. Based on this continuous variable, the learning environment measured can be differentiated into various degrees that are thought to be associated with different student perceptions of the learning environment. This process must rely on a valid theory. Without a valid theory, it is difficult to conceptualize various degrees of a learning environment, and in turn it is difficult to identify different student behaviors or perceptions.

Prepare a Test Specification and Construct an Initial Pool of Items

Test specification for a learning environment measurement instrument involves deciding how many items are needed for each construct. Although the exact number of items necessary for the construct can only be known later based on statistical analysis and Rasch modeling, basic consideration is that there should be enough items of sufficient variation to cover the anticipated range in student perceptions of the measured learning environment. Thus, a more heterogeneous student population will require more items to measure the construct. It is always a good practice to develop more items than what may be needed in the final instrument allowing for more flexibility in the revision stage.

Once the number of items needed is tentatively decided, the next step is to create a pool of preliminary items. Because measurement of learning environments is primarily based on students' and teachers' perceptions, types of items appropriate for measurement of learning environments are the same as that for measurement of affective variables. Likert scale and rating scale are commonly used; other formats, such as semantic differential, inventory, and checklist, may also be used.

The following are sample items from the Constructivist Learning Environment Survey (CLES) (Taylor, Fraser, & Fisher, 1997):

In this class …

1. It is OK for me to ask the teacher "Why do I have to learn this?"

    Almost never (1)   Sometimes (3)   Seldom (2)   Often (4)   Almost always (5)

2. 2. It's OK for me to question the way I'm being taught.

    Almost never (1)   Sometimes (3)   Seldom (2)   Often (4)   Almost always (5)

3. It's OK for me to complain about teaching activities that are confusing.

    Almost never (1)   Sometimes (3)   Seldom (2)   Often (4)   Almost always (5)

The above items are in a rating scale format. Students are asked to rate how often each of the described teaching practices actually takes place in the classroom. The above items are for the actual form of CLES. If they are for the preferred form, then the instruction should be that students are asked to rate how often they PREFER each of the described teaching practices to take place in the classroom. Thus, although the statements and choices may be the same, students will be asked to rate based on different perspectives, actual or preferred.

Item Review and Try-Out

After a pool of items has been created, it is necessary to have items reviewed by a panel of experts consisting of both content experts and methodologists. After items have been reviewed by a panel and necessary revisions made to the items, the items should then be tried out by a small number of respondents. The respondents will not only respond to the items, but also state their impressions or comment on the clarity of the items. Interviews with a few respondents may also be helpful.

Field-Test

The resulted items from the previous development steps will then go for a field-testing. The sample chosen for the field testing should represent the intended population in terms of the range along the construct to be measured. Depending on the item format, a minimum of 25 observations per category are preferred. For example, if items are written in a checklist format, thus each item has two categories (yes/no), the preferred sample size for field-testing should be minimally 50. The selected sample should also possess sufficient variation in student perceptions of the measured learning environment construct similar to that of the intended population.

Conduct Rasch Modeling

Data collected from field-testing are used for Rasch modeling. In the situation of learning environment measurement, item difficulty and person ability parameters have different meanings. Item difficulty may be interpreted as the difficulty for an individual to endorse a category of an item (e.g., selecting *agree*, *always*, or *yes* to a positively phrased statement). Consider the following example:

1. It is OK for me to ask the teacher "Why do I have to learn this?"

    Almost never (1)   Sometimes (3)   Seldom (2)   Often (4)   Almost always (5)

The difficulty for the above item reflects the tendency for an individual to select *almost always*. Because item difficulty is on the interval scale without absolute zero, an item with a difficulty of 0.5 is more likely for individuals to endorse as *almost always* than an item with a difficulty of 0.2, but less likely for individuals to endorse as *almost always* than an item with a difficulty of 1.0. Similarly, an individual's ability may be interpreted as the individual's overall level of positive perception of the learning environment. Thus, a person with an ability level of 0.5 is overall more positive about the learning environment than a person with an ability level of 0.2, but less positive than a person with an ability level of 1.0

The following items are extracted from the 2006 PISA Student Survey Questionnaire (Organization for Economic Cooperation and Development, 2006); they may be conceptualized as measuring students' perceptions of inquiry science learning environment:

When learning school science topics at school, how often do the following activities occur? (Please tick only one box in each row)

	In all lessons (4)	In most lessons (3)	In some lessons (2)	Never or hardly ever (1)
Q1. Students are given opportunities to explain				
Q2. Students spend time in the laboratory doing practical experiments				
Q3. Students are required to design how a school science question could be investigated in the laboratory				
Q4. The students are asked to apply a school science concept to an everyday problem				
Q5. The lessons involve students' opinions about the topics				
Q6. Students are asked to draw conclusions from an experiment they have conducted				
Q7. The teacher explains how a school science idea can be applied to a number of different phenomena (e.g., the movement of objects, substances with similar properties)				
Q8. Students are allowed to design their own experiments				
Q9. There is a class debate or discussion				
Q10. Experiments are done by the teacher as demonstrations				
Q11. Students are given the chance to choose their own investigations				
Q12. The teacher uses school science to help students understand the world outside school				
Q13. Students have discussions about the topics				
Q14. Students do experiments by following the instructions of the teacher				
Q15. The teacher clearly explains the relevance of broad science concepts to our lives				
Q16. Students are asked to do an investigation to test out their own ideas				
Q17. The teacher uses examples of technological application to show how school science is relevant to society				

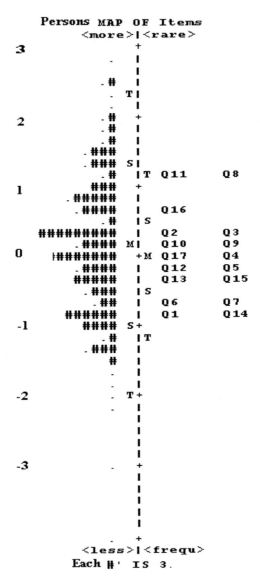

Figure 7.1.   Wright map of PISA inquiry science learning environment scale.
there are noticeable gaps in the distribution of items.

Figure 7.1 presents the Wright map for the above set of items based on
a 5% random subsample ($n = 278$) of the U.S. sample.

From Figure 7.1, we can see that Q8 and Q11 are the most difficult for
students to endorse, while Q1 and Q14 are the easiest for students to

endorse. Q8 is "Students are allowed to design their own experiments" and Q11 is "Students are given the chance to choose their own investigations." These two practices are characteristics of open-ended inquiry. Although they are essential for authentic science inquiry, they are not common in science classrooms, which is why they are the most difficult for students to endorse. On the other hand, Q1 is "Students are given opportunities to explain," and Q14 is "Students do experiments by following the instructions of the teacher." These two practices are not essential characteristics of science inquiry, and they are common in science teaching, which is why they are the easiest for students to endorse. Figure 7.1 also shows that the 17 items do not have a sufficient difficulty range to match the range of students' perceptions of the inquiry science teaching environment, thus more items on both ends, that is, more easy to endorse and more difficult to endorse, are needed. In terms of the continuum among the items, there are three noticeable gaps, one between Q11/Q8 and Q16, another between Q16 and Q2/Q3, and the last between Q13/Q15 and Q6/Q7. More items are needed at the gaps. The person separation index is 2.54, and person reliability coefficient is 0.87. Although both indices are acceptable, there is room for further improvement, and adding more items on both ends to fill the gaps should help achieve this.

An examination of item fit statistics shows that, overall, items have a good fit with the rating scale Rasch model. Examination of dimensionality also indicates that, overall, the 17 items are unidimensional. In terms of the rating scale structure, Figure 7.2 shows that the progression from category 1 to category 4 is quite orderly, indicating that the four-step structure of the rating scale is appropriate.

When conducting Rasch modeling for learning environment measurement, one common issue is to equate measures between parallel forms. Consider two parallel forms of a learning environment instrument, the actual form and the preferred form. It is necessary to directly compare students' perceptions on the two forms by calculating the difference between the two scores. Because student' responses to individual items as well as their sums are ordinal raw scores, computing differences between ordinal scores is not appropriate. It is necessary to convert the raw scores into interval scale scores, which is exactly what Rasch modeling accomplishes. We need to obtain two sets of scale scores based on Rasch modeling: one for the actual form and another for the preferred form. Given that two parallel forms measure two different constructs, in order to make the scales of the two constructs directly comparable, we need to equate them so that they have the same measurement units, that is, means and standard deviations. The ideal way to accomplish this is to conduct multi-dimensional Rasch modeling using such computer programs as ConQuest (Wu, Adams, & Wilson, 1997). In multidimensional

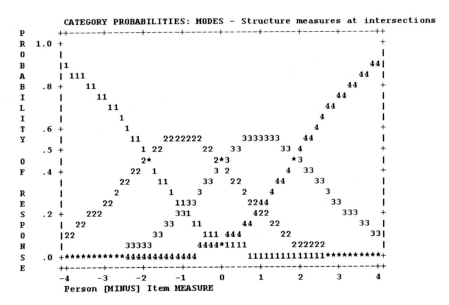

Figure 7.2.   Rating scale structure for PISA inquiry science learning environment scale. all categories have distinct characteristic curves, suggesting a good item category structure.

Rasch modeling, items for the actual form measure one construct, and items for the preferred form measure another construct. Using a simultaneous calibration, we will obtain two scale scores for each student, one for each construct. We will also know the correlation between the two constructs.

If multidimensional scaling is not feasible for various reasons, we may still use unidimensional Rasch modeling. Because simultaneous calibration is not appropriate due to lack of linkage between the two forms and more importantly, violation of the unidimensionality requirement, we have to conduct two separate Rasch modeling sessions, one for the actual form and another for the preferred form. In order to place scale scores from the two separate calibrations on the same scale, we can use a set of scaling commands, such as UMEAN and USCALE in Winsteps, to force one scale onto another. That is, after Rasch modeling for one form (e.g., actual form), the mean and standard deviation of the item measures for this form are noted. When conducting Rasch modeling for the second form, we will then use commands UMEAN and USCALE to force the mean and standard deviation of item measures of the second form to be equal to that obtained from the previous form. For example, if the mean and standard deviation of item difficulties on the actual form are 0.0, and

1.1, then the commands for Rasch modeling for the preferred form should be UMEAN = 0.0 and USCALE = 1.1.

After examination of model-data-fit of items, the Wright map, and dimensionality as well as invariance properties, some items may be revised or deleted, and a new set of items may be created. This new set of items will form a revised version of the measurement instrument. The revised measurement instrument will then go through another cycle of field-testing and Rasch modeling until all items and the measurement instrument as a whole meet the quality expectations. The final measurement instrument consisting of the finalized items are now ready for validity and reliability studies.

DESIGN AND CONDUCT VALIDITY AND RELIABILITY STUDIES

Validity Study

Construct validation includes establishing evidence related to test content, response processes, internal structure, external structure and consequences. Construct validation may begin with examination of the definition of the learning environment construct measured. Important questions to ask about the construct definition may include: (a) Is the definition based on commonly accepted theories? (b) Does the defined construct have an underlying linear progression for the construct? (c) Are the specific behaviors described by the items clearly related to the construct? Answers to the above questions should all be positive; a negative then requires review of test content.

Because Rasch modeling is a theory-based approach, when there is good model-data-fit of items and model-data-fit of persons, the measurement instrument which produces the data can be considered valid in terms of internal structure. The Wright map and dimensionality also provide important evidence for the validity related to the internal structure of the instrument. That is, when the Wright map shows that items are evenly distributed and target the population well, and items measure one single construct with minimal randomly distributed residuals, then the measurement instrument possesses an adequate internal structure.

Also, the agreement between the actual order of items and the predicted order of items based on valid theories can also provide evidence for validity related to external structure. For example, the order of items for the PISA inquiry learning environment scale described earlier according to the obtained Rasch difficulties is presented in Figure 7.3. Items are presented from the most difficult item (on the top) to the easiest item (on the bottom). Is the order reasonable? For example, is Q11 more indicative

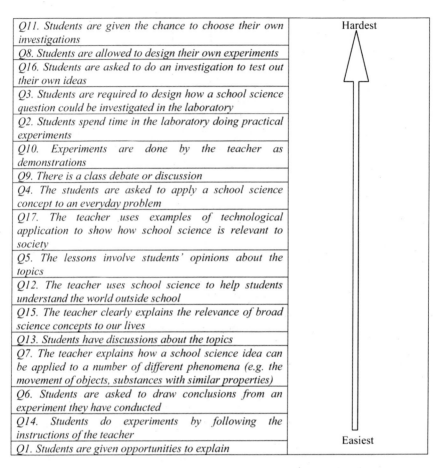

Q11. Students are given the chance to choose their own investigations	Hardest
Q8. Students are allowed to design their own experiments	
Q16. Students are asked to do an investigation to test out their own ideas	
Q3. Students are required to design how a school science question could be investigated in the laboratory	
Q2. Students spend time in the laboratory doing practical experiments	
Q10. Experiments are done by the teacher as demonstrations	
Q9. There is a class debate or discussion	
Q4. The students are asked to apply a school science concept to an everyday problem	
Q17. The teacher uses examples of technological application to show how school science is relevant to society	
Q5. The lessons involve students' opinions about the topics	
Q12. The teacher uses school science to help students understand the world outside school	
Q15. The teacher clearly explains the relevance of broad science concepts to our lives	
Q13. Students have discussions about the topics	
Q7. The teacher explains how a school science idea can be applied to a number of different phenomena (e.g. the movement of objects, substances with similar properties)	
Q6. Students are asked to draw conclusions from an experiment they have conducted	
Q14. Students do experiments by following the instructions of the teacher	
Q1. Students are given opportunities to explain	Easiest

Figure 7.3.   Item Order of the PISA Inquiry Learning Environment Items. teaching practices noted on the top are harder to implement than that noted at the bottom.

of inquiry science teaching than Q8? Is Q1 easiest to implement in inquiry science teaching? Besides comparing the orders of items between the theoretical prediction and the actual one, we may also ask experts to predict the order of items and compare it to the obtained one.

Results from learning environment measurement are typically used for developing instructional interventions. Validation related to consequences is thus about the effectiveness of such interventions for improving student learning. Results from program evaluation of instructional improvement efforts should provide evidence on the validity related to consequences. Of course, insignificant results of an instructional improvement effort are possible. In this case, the validity of the measurement instrument in terms of consequences may not necessarily be lacking, because the insignificant instruction improvement may be due to ineffectiveness of the intervention. However, a reexamination of the measurement instrument should nevertheless be necessary.

Finally, qualitative studies should also be helpful in measurement validation in terms of response processes. In addition to qualitative studies of item functioning during item try-out, qualitative evidence collected from respondents through observation, interview, and artifacts can enhance claims about the validity of the measurement instrument related to response processes, which in turn add to the credibility of the use and interpretation of measurement results.

Reliability Study

Reliability evidence of learning environment measurement may be established through review of reliability of item and subject measures, and review of the reliability of the instrument as a whole. After item and person parameters are calibrated, standard errors of measurement for each item and person should be reviewed. Person separation index and its equivalent Cronbach's alpha should be reviewed for their adequacy of reliability for person measures as a whole. Item separation index and its equivalent Cronbach's alpha coefficient can also provide an indication of overall item distribution and measurement accuracy.

Develop Guidelines for Use of the Instrument

Appropriate documentation should be available to facilitate users to appropriately use the measurement instrument. Documentation should include the construct definition, test specification, scoring, validity and reliability evidence, and score reporting and interpretation. In order to help users convert raw scores into Rasch scale scores, a raw score to Rasch scale score conversion table should be included. When possible, a learning environment baseline may be provided so that users can compare their measured learning environments to the baseline.

CHAPTER SUMMARY

Learning environments are social, physical, psychological, and pedagogical contexts in which learning occurs and that affect student learning outcomes in science. The basic premise for learning environment research is that personal goals may be supported or constrained by environmental factors. When personal needs and environmental factors are aligned, student learning outcomes are enhanced. Learning environments include three dimensions or domains; they are relationship, personal growth, and system maintenance and change. The relationship dimension is concerned with the extent to which people are involved in the setting, the extent to which they support and help one another, and the extent to which they express themselves freely and openly; the personal growth dimension pertains to the goals of the setting related to personal development and self-enhancement; and the system maintenance and change dimension pertains to the extent to which the environment is orderly and clear in its expectations, maintains control and responds to change.

There can be three orientations to learning environment research: the outcome-environment orientation, the person-environment fit orientation and the environment-outcome orientation. The outcome-environment orientation focuses on the association between learning environment variables and student cognitive and affective learning outcomes; the person-environment fit orientation differentiates various forms of the learning environment, such as the *"actual"* perceived environment and the *"preferred"* environment; and the environment-outcome orientation is concerned with how a learning environment may change as the result of changes in other factors of a science teaching and learning system. A wide variety of measurement instruments are currently available; they possess various degrees of validity and reliability.

Developing instruments for measuring learning environments begins with stating the purposes of the measurement in terms of the three orientations and clearly defining the construct of learning environment to be measured. Items to be constructed for the measurement instrument should define a domain to provide adequate coverage of the anticipated variation in the measured learning environment of a particular population. Rasch modeling facilitates development of the measurement instrument by providing various statistics and measures related to model-data-fit, the person-item match, dimensionality, person and item separation and reliability, and scale equating. Measurement instruments developed through Rasch modeling produce interval scale scores that are directly comparable between parallel forms.

EXERCISES

1. CLES, Constructivist Learning Environment Survey (CLES) (Taylor, Fraser & Fisher, 1997), is one of popular science learning environment scales of science education research. A complete version

of CLES is available in the appendix of Fraser (1998a). Apply the validity and reliability standards described in Chapter 1 to critique this instrument. What are strengths and weakness of the instrument? What do you recommend on how to use the instrument?

2. Almost all the measurement instruments introduced in this chapter have been developed using the CTT approach. From the perspectives of Rasch modeling, what are common limitations of these measurement instruments? What do we need to consider when using these measurement instruments? How may Rasch modeling help address the limitations?

3. Identify one specific science learning environment for which a measurement instrument is currently not available, complete the following initial steps of developing a measurement instrument for this science learning environment: (a) define the science learning environment construct and support the definition with pertinent theories, (b) identify student or teacher behaviors that represent the defined construct, and (c) write five sample items for each of the levels of the defined construct.

REFERENCES

Aldridge, J. M., & Fraser, B. J. (2000). A cross-cultural study of classroom learning environments in Australia and Taiwan. *Learning Environment Research: An International Journal, 3*, 101-134.

Aldridge, J. M., & Fraser, B. J., & Huang, T. -C. I. (1999). Investigating classroom environments in Taiwan and Australia with multiple research methods. *Journal of Educational Research, 93*, 48-62.

Aldridge, J. M., Laugksch, R. C., Seopa, M. A., & Fraser, B. J.(2006). Development and validation of an instrument to monitor the implementation of outcomes-based learning environments in science classrooms in South Africa. *International Journal of Science Education, 28*(1), 45-70.

Anderson, G. J., & Walberg, H. J. (1974). Learning environments. In H. J. Walberg (Ed.), *Evaluating educational performance: A sourcebook of methods, instruments, and examples* (pp. 81-98). Berkeley, CA: McCutchan.

Arzi, H. J. (1998). Enhancing science education through laboratory environment: More than walks, benches and widgets. In B. J. Fraser & K. G. Tobin (Eds.), *International handbook of science education* (pp. 595-608). Dordrecht, The Netherlands: Kluwer.

Dhindsa, H. S., Omar, K., & Waldrip, B. (2007). Upper secondary Bruneian science students' perceptions of assessment. *International Journal of Science Education, 29*(10), 1261-1280.

Dorman, J. P. (2003). Cross-national validation of the *What Is Happening In this Class?* (WIHIC) questionnaire using confirmatory factor analysis. *Learning Environments Research: An International Journal, 6*, 231-245.

Fisher, D. L., & Fraser, B. J. (1981). Validity and use of my class inventory. *Science Education, 65*, 145-156.

Fisher, D. L., & Waldrip, B. G. (1997). Assessing culturally sensitive factors in the learning environment of science classrooms. *Research in Science Education, 27*, 41-49.

Fisher, D. L., Waldrip, B. G., & Dorman, J. (2005, April). *Student perceptions of assessment: Development and validation of a questionnaire.* Paper presented at the Annual Meeting of the American Educational Research Association, Montreal, Canada.

Fraser, B. J. (1982). Development of short-forms of several classroom environment scale. *Journal of Educational Measurement, 19*, 221-227.

Fraser, B. J. (1990). *Individualized classroom environment questionnaire.* Melbourne: Australian Council for Educational Research.

Fraser, B. J. (1994). Research on classroom and school climate. In D. Gable (Ed.), *Handbook of research on science teaching and learning* (pp. 493-541). New York, NY: Macmillan.

Fraser, B. J. (1998a). Science learning environments: Assessment, effects and determiants. In B. J. Fraser & K. G. Tobin (Eds.), *International handbook of science education* (pp. 527-564). Dordrecht, The Netherlands: Kluwer Academic.

Fraser, B. J. (1998b). The birth of a new journal: Editor's introduction. *Learning Environment Research: An International Journal, 1*, 1-5.

Fraser, B. J. (2007). Classroom learning environments. In S. K. Abell & N. G. Lederman (Eds.), *Handbook of research on science education* (pp. 103-124). New York: Routledge.

Fraser, B. J., Anderson, G. J., & Walberg, H. J. (1982). *Assessment of learning environments: Manuals for learning environment inventory (LEI) and My class inventory (MCI) (third version).* Perth: Western Australian Institute of Technology.

Fraser, B. J., & Fisher, D. L. (1983). Development and validation of short forms of some instruments measuring student perceptions of actual and preferred classroom learning environment. *Science Education, 67*, 115-131.

Fraser, B. J., McRobbie, C. J., & Giddings, G. J. (1993). Development and cross-national validation of a laboratory classroom environment instrument for senior high school science. *Science Education, 77*, 1-24.

Fraser, B. J., & Tobin, K. (1991). Combining qualitative and quantitative methods in classroom environment research. In B. J. Fraser & H. J. Walberg (Eds.), *Educational environments: Evaluation, antecedents, consequences* (pp. 271-292). London: Pergamon.

Fraser, B. J., & Treagust, D. F., (1986). Validity and use of an instrument for assessing classroom psychosocial environment in higher education. *Higher Education, 15*, 37-57.

Fraser, B. J., Treagust, D. F., & Dennis, N. C. (1986). Development of an instrument for assessing classroom psychosocial environment at universities and colleges. *Studies in Higher Education, 11*, 43-54,

Goh, S. C., & Fraser, B. J. (1996). Validation of an elementary school version of the questionnaire on teacher interaction. *Psychological Reports, 79*, 512-522.

Hofstede, G. (1984). *Culture's consequences.* Newbury Park, CA: Sage.

Huang, S. L. (2006). An assessment of science teachers' perceptions of secondary school environments in Taiwan. *International Journal of Science Education, 8*(1), 25-44.

Lesniak, K. (2007). Positive classroom and laboratory environments for science learning: Barry J. Fraser's contributions to science education. In X. Liu (Eds.), *Great ideas in science education* (pp. 15-30). Rotterdam, The Netherlands: Sense.

McRobbie, C. J., Fisher, D. L, & Wong, A. F. L. (1998). Personal and class forms of classroom environment instruments. In B. J. Fraser & K. G. Tobin (Eds.), *International handbook of science education* (pp. 581-594). Dordrecht, The Netherlands: Kluwer Academic.

Moos, R. H. (1979). *Evaluating educational environments.* San Francisco, CA: Jossey-Bass.

Moos, R. H., & Trickett, E. J. (1974). *Classroom environment scale manual* (1st ed.). Palo Alto, CA: Consulting Psychologists Press.

Moos, R. H., & Trickett, E. J. (1987). *Classroom environment scale manual* (2nd ed.). Palo Alto, CA: Consulting Psychologists Press.

Nolen, S. B. (2003). Learning environment, motivation, and achievement in high school science. *Journal of Research in Science Teaching, 40*(4), 347-368.

Organization for Economic Cooperation and Development. (2006). *Assessing scientific, reading and mathematical literacy: A framework for PISA 2006.* Paris: Author.

Rentoul, A. J., & Fraser, B. J. (1979). Conceptualization of enquiry-based or open classrooms learning environments. *Journal of Curriculum Studies, 11*, 233-245.

Roth, W. -M. (1999). Learning environment research, life world analysis, and solidarity in practice. *Learning Environment Research: An International Journal, 3*, 225-247.

Shapiro, B. (1998). Reading the furniture: The semiotic interpretation of science learning environments. In B. J. Fraser & K. G. Tobin (eds.), *International handbook of science education* (pp. 609-621). Dordrecht, The Netherlands: Kluwer Academic.

Taylor, P. C., Fraser, B. J., & Fisher, D. L. (1997). Monitoring constructivist classroom learning environments. *International Journal of Educational Research, 27*, 293-302.

Trickett, E. J., & Moos, R. H. (1973). The social environment of junior high and high school classrooms. *Journal of Educational Psychology, 65*, 93-102.

Tobin, K. G., & Fraser, B. J. (1998). Qualitative and quantitative landscapes of classroom learning environment. In B. J. Fraser & K. G. Tobin (Eds.), *International handbook of science education* (pp. 623-640). Dordrecht, The Netherlands: Kluwer.

Walberg, H. J. (1968a). Structural and affective aspects of classroom climate. *Psychology in schools, 5*, 247-253.

Walberg, H. J. (1968b). Classroom climate and individual learning. *Journal of Educational Psychology, 59*(6), 414-419.

Wu, M. L., Adams, R. J., & Wilson, M. (1997). *Conquest: Generalized item response modeling software—Manual.* Melbourne: Australian Council for Educational Research.

Wubbels, T., & Brekelmans, M. (1998). The teacher factor in the social climate of the classroom. In B. J. Fraser & K. G. Tobin (Eds.), *International handbook of science education* (pp. 565-580). Dordrecht, The Netherlands: Kluwer.

Wubbles, T., Breklmans, M., & Hooymayers, H. (1991). Interpersonal teacher behavior in the classroom. In B. J. Fraser & H. J. Walberg (Eds.), *Educational environments: Evaluation, antecedents and consequences* (pp. 141-160). London: Pergamon.

Wubbles, T., & Levy, J. (Eds.). (1993). *Do you know what you look like: Interpersonal relationships in education*. London: Falmer Press.

CPSIA information can be obtained at www.ICGtesting.com
Printed in the USA
LVOW011850141011

250591LV00002B/3/P